From Earth to the Moon

&

Around the Moon

Jules Verne

First published 2021 by
C.L. Wriggs Publishing House
Sydney, Australia

Copyright 2021 S.D. Metcalfe

All rights reserved.
No part or whole of this publication may be
reproduced, stored in a retrieval system,
or transmitted, in any form or by any means,
electronic, mechanical, photocopying,
recording, or otherwise, without the prior
written permission of the publisher.

Contents:

Introduction...........4

From Earth to the Moon........7

Interlude...............153

Around the Moon...........155

Introduction

When first-conceiving of this work, the only expected valuable addition to the extant translations of Jules Verne's novels had been through the provision of an abridged version of the works '*From Earth to the Moon*' and '*Around the Moon*' in one volume. However, becoming aware there were no versions of the sequel '*Around the Moon*' available by any major publishing houses, it was decided to publish both books in full.

In older times, there was an innocent simplicity of ideas regarding the exploration of our near and profound natural satellite which abounded. This alluring vision of adventure and the imagination which the moon and other planetary fantasies once offered held a potential that is reflected even in our culture today. As shown across a diverse range of periods- for example, from Voltaire's '*Micromegas*' to Antoine de Saint-Exupéry's book '*le Petite Prince*', the human psyche encounters the true unknown- and ultimately perceives beauty.

The lunar ideals of Victorian perception remain relevant today. That depiction of space in past eras is demonstrated admirably by the cover art from the Smashing Pumpkins music album '*Melancholy and the Infinite Sadness*' released in 1998. This conveys a level of charm and naivety which has continued to our present understanding- so much so that for modern readers '*From Earth to the Moon*' and '*Around the Moon*' could easily be viewed within the framework of 'steampunk' and historical fantasy genres as classical French literature.

It seems an incredulous idea to have expected a relative simplicity of Jules Verne's style, based on an understanding of his translated works. When working on the original French, it was quite a shock to discover within the first paragraphs of '*From Earth to the Moon*' a richly-vibrant, amazingly-tenacious and ornate literature which Verne employed in his technique.

English readers of Verne have an expectation that his genius tends to rest more upon his astounding scientific imagination. The phrase 'visionary' is often propounded, often synonymously in the context of any non-literary discussion. It is now due to the completion of these works can one feel with certainty the greater appreciation towards Verne, which those who learned of Verne's words in his original language are already aware of; Jules Verne was as much a 19th century literary genius and masterful story-teller as the pioneer of early science fiction, and as sociologically concise as Zola.

Many previous translated versions sought to arrive at a simplification of Verne's approach in order to appeal to a younger reading audience or our modern syntax. This seemed be an injustice and greatly motivated this work to present a preservation of its original style, steeped and deeply embedded within the dramatic excitement of scientific discovery in that period.

In certain cases there are terms and phrases out of place within the context of our modern society- for example, his use of the word '*tradesman*' versus our preference today to say '*tradesperson*'. It is with deliberation that a more precise vision of Verne's own vocabulary and societal norms should be presented.*

Likewise, modern readers understand how the France's perception of America and her incredibly diverse and inspiring people was affected by the vision which her sister democracy shaped independently. During a time when the other side of the globe was indeed a vast distance- when movies and modern communications media did not exist. Before these replacements there were levels of fantasy and, perhaps at times in very subtle ways, misconceptions and generalizations.

These imprecisions are outweighed by Verne's clear and profound admiration of the United States and their incredibly powerful forces of innovation and achievements- indeed, it was this fascination of Jules Verne and of the French in general at this time which led him to choose to set the entire work in Florida, America; a decision that was ultimately prophetic.

If the translator may humbly beseech anything from the reader, it is simply to be forgiven for having retaining the antiquated style in order to provide a more-complete homage and to explore the possibility from new approaches in the translation of 19th century French literature. And to if at all be possible from meager abilities, showcase the fact that indeed Jules Verne was a literary genius.

With humility and respect then these two works are presented in a complete and unabridged form, translated from 19th century classical French, having minimal inversions committed and seeking to retain as completely as possible Verne's own style.

S.D. Metcalfe.

* In 1864-70 when the original story was written, it was a century when many misconceptions and racially-unjust idioms were culturally accepted across parts of the world- ultimately a detrimental force to all. This work offers an explanation of the incorporation of historical ideology towards comparison with 21st century ideals, including gender culture.

From Earth to the Moon
[1864]

Jules Verne

Chapters

I. The Gun Club..10

II. The Announcement of President Barbicane...................16

III. The Effect of Barbicane's Communication....................22

IV. Response from the Cambridge Observatory..................25

V. The Romance of the Moon..29

VI. What it is Impossible Not to Know.................................33

VII. The Hymn of the Cannon Ball..37

VIII. The History of the Cannon..45

IX. The Question of Powder...50

X. One Enemy amongst Twenty-Five Million Friends........56

XI. Florida and Texas..61

XII. Urbi et Orbi..66

XIII. Stone Hill..69

XIV. Pick and Trowel..76

XV. The Festival of Casting..81

XVI. The Columbiad..83

XVII. A Telegraphic Dispatch...85

XVIII. The Passenger on the Altlanta……………...………….91
XIX. A Meeting…………...………………..……..…...….….99
XX. Thrust and Counterthrust………..……………....……106
XXI. How a Frenchman Settles a Matter.………...…..…..….114
XXII. The New Citizen of the United States…….....……...….121
XXIII. The Projectile Carriage…………..…..………...….….126
XXIV. The Telescope on the Rocky Mountains……..…....…..132
XXV. Final Details..……………………..………...…..….136
XXVI. Fire!.………………..………………….…...….….142
XXVII. Cloudy Weather.……………………....………...….….146
XXVIII. A New Star.………...…………………….......…..….150

1. The Gun Club

During the civil war in the United States a very influential club was established in the city of Baltimore, Maryland. An energetic military instinct had developed amongst a people of ship-owners, shop-keepers, tradesmen and mechanics. These simple merchants changed into improvised captains, colonels and generals without ever qualifying for schooling at West Point Military Academy; soon equaling their colleagues on the continent in the '*Art of War*', and like them delivering victories with a prodigal force of bullets, millions of dollars and men.

However the Americans uniquely surpassed the Europeans in the science of ballistics. It was not that their guns had attained a higher degree of perfection, rather by offering larger and more-unusual dimensions the distances they attained were unequalled. In fact in close-range shooting, from above or firing completely indiscriminately; in an offensive attack or retreat; the English, the French and the Russians had nothing to learn. It was that their cannons, shells and mortars were nothing but pistols against the formidable engines of American artillery.

This should surprise no person. The Yankees, premier mechanics of the world, are as ingenious to their art as the Italians are to music and the Germans to metaphysics; that is to say, from birth. There is nothing more natural, it is true, than to apply their audacious ingenuity to the science of ballistics. With their gigantic cannons, as numerous as sewing machines, they are astonishing and admirable. In this field the marvels of Parrott, Dahlgren and Rodman are well-known. Armstrong, Paliser and Treuille de Beaulieu may only nod their heads in appreciation towards their transatlantic rivals.

Therefore, regarding the terrible struggle between Northern and Southern Americans, it was the artillery which reigned supreme; the newspapers of the Union celebrated their inventions with enthusiasm and there was no craftsman so humble, no fool so naive, who did not calculate those insensitive trajectories.

Now when an American has an idea, he searches for a second American who is party to this pursuit. If there are three, he elects a president and two secretariats. Four, he nominates an archivist and there will now be a functioning bureau. Five, he will convene a general assembly and the club is constituted. This is how it began in Baltimore. The premier inventor of the new cannon associated with the one who cast the cannon and the person who bored it. They were the nucleus of the Gun Club. Within one month of its formation there were 1,833 resident members and 30,575 members by way of correspondence.

One condition strictly imposed on all persons who wished to enter the association was they must have invented or at least improved upon the perfection of the cannon; if not the cannon, then some other kind of firearm. However to tell the truth candidly, the inventors of 15-shot revolvers, pivoting rifles and saber pistols were not held in as-high esteem as the artillerists; who maintained their precedence throughout all circumstances.

"The esteem one obtains," said one of the most knowledgeable orators of the Gun Club, "is proportionate to the mass of their cannons and in direct ratio to the distance attained by their projectiles!"

Indeed, Newton's laws of universal gravity had been transposed into an order of morality.

The Gun Club formed, one can only imagine the kind of results produced in the field of ballistics by the inventive genius of the Americans. The engines of war attained colossal proportions and their projectiles went beyond surmisable limits to cut harmless pedestrians into two. All these inventions left far behind the timid instruments of European artillery. One may judge for themselves from the following figures.

In the olden days, '*the good times*', a 36-pound cannon ball at a distance of one hundred yards could traverse through 36 horses and at their flanks 68 men. This was the infancy of the art. Since then the science of projectiles has come a long way. The Rodman cannon, shooting a projectile that approached the weight of half a ton up to a distance of seven miles, could have easily knocked down 150 horses and 300 men. It was a question which the Gun Club wished to solemnly prove. However whilst the horses, being inexperienced, may have consented to such an experiment the men who were to be fired upon vehemently refused.

Be that as it may, the effect of these cannons was extremely murderous- at every discharge combatants fell thickly as though having been swept by a scythe. Where was the significance, when comparing the projectiles of the famous cannon balls which in action at Coutras in 1597 cut down 25 men in combat, or those used in Zorndoff in 1758 that killed 40 infantrymen, or, in 1742, the Austrian cannons of Kesseldorf that with every ejection laid 70 enemies into the earth? Where was the supreme fire of Jena or Austerlitz which decided the fate of the battle? Things were very different in the Civil War! In the combat at Gettysburg, a conical projectile thrown from a rifle-bored cannon hit 173 Confederates; and, during the passage at the Potomac, a Rodman cannon ball sent 215 Southerners to a world that was evidentially better.

We should also mention that formidable mortar invented by J.T. Maston, distinguished member and perpetual secretary of the Gun Club, since, during its testing the resultant explosion from bursting murdered 337 people- which was brilliant, it is true!

Of what more can be said of these elegant numbers? Nothing. We must therefore admit without contest the following calculations, obtained from the statistician Pittcairn: who divided the number of victims killed by cannon balls due to the designs of the Gun Club members, and found that on average every member was responsible for the death of 2,375 persons plus a fractional remainder.

In consideration of these figures, it is evident that the unique preoccupation of this society of savants was the destruction of humanity for philanthropic reasons, in the perfection of arms used in war; which were considered the instruments of civilization.

They were a reunion of exterminating angels, as well as the best kind of men in the world.

In addition, these Yankees- brave and entirely dauntless- did not confine themselves to formulas and theories; rather they earned their experiences in person. Amongst the society were officers of all grades and rank, from lieutenants to generals, military men of all ages- from debutants in the carriage of arms to others who had grown old standing watch over their poignant guns. Many members were left on the field of battle, however their names lived-on, inscribed on the Gun Club's honor roll; and most of those who had retained their health bore the marks of its excruciating integrity. Crutches, legs of wood, brass articulations, hands made of hooks, rubber jaws, silver craniums, noses of platinum- nothing was missing from the collection; and the previously mentioned-Pittcairn calculated that, amongst the Gun Club, there was not quite one arm per four persons, and two legs for every six.

However these valiant artillerists did not regard those details too-closely, and were justifiably proud whenever bulletins about battles revealed the number of victims were ten times the quantities of projectiles dispensed.

Yet, one day, one sad and lamentable day, a peace agreement was signed by the survivors of the war. The detonations ceased their sounds of shooting, the mortars turned silent, the musket shooters were muzzled for a long time and the cannons, that main foundation, were retired from the arsenal, and their bullets piled-up in parks as unassuming souvenirs of blood; cotton farms surged with magnificent fields of fertilized abundance, the clothing worn by mourners completed this sorrowful sense of sadness and the residents of the Gun Club were plunged into profound idleness.

Certain arcane axe-men of the club, persistent workers, still continued to deliver ballistic calculations; they dreamed of gigantic bombs and incomparable shells. However, without practical application, what use were vain theories? And so the rooms of the Gun Club became deserted; its domestic servants slumbered in the antechambers, the newspapers left on tables went moldy, obscure corners resounded with sad snoring and the members of the Gun Club, once so buoyant and noisy, were steadily reduced into silence by the disastrous peace- lethargic in their reverie of platonic artillery!

"It is inconsolable," said one evening the brave Tom Hunter, as his legs slowly charred and turned to carbon before the hearth fire of the smoking room. "Nothing to do! Nothing to hope for! What a fastidious existence! Where are those times when the cannon reverberated every day with joyous detonations?"

"Those days are no longer here," responded the dashing Bilsby, as he tried stretching his mannequin arms. "Certainly they were pleasurable! One invented a rapid-fire rife, and once cast, immediately faced it towards the enemy; and on retiring to camp receive the encouragement of Sherman or a solidly-hearty handshake from McClelland! But now today, the generals have returned to their shop counters and in lieu of projectiles they dispatch harmless balls of cotton! Ah, my saintly Barbe! The future of artillery has perished in America!"

"Yes, Bilsby," cried Colonel Bloomsberry. "There it is- a cruel disappointment! One day you quit your tranquil habitude to exercise the management of arms, you abandon Baltimore for the fields of battle, you conduct yourself as a hero, and, in two years, three years if you are tardy, the fruits of your efforts perish; and you sleep in the deplorable leisure of your hands thrust into your pockets."

Put this way, the valiant colonel could not himself demonstrate the same mark of indolence; however this was not due to any lack of pockets.

"And no war in sight!" said the famous J.T. Maston, as he scratched at his rubber skull with the iron hook extending from the end of his arm. "There is no cloud at the horizon, and yet there is so much to be done in the science of artillery! If I may say so, why this morning I have completed plans for a mortar, which with the correct elevation, is destined to change the laws of war!"

"Really?" replied Tom Hunter, involuntarily shuddering at the recollection of the honorable J.T. Maston's previous test-firing.

"Really," responded Maston firmly. "But what does it serve undertaking so much intriguingly-fine study, so much difficulty in vain? The work has been done in pure futility! The people of the new world seem to be entirely given to a life of peace, and our belligerent *New York Tribune* has prognosticated the next catastrophes will be due to the scandalous increase of the populations!"

"It depends, Maston" replied Colonel Bloomsbury, "There is always fighting in Europe for the principles of nationality!"

"Eh? What do you mean to say?"

"Oh yes! There will always be something happening there to tempt us, if they would accept our services..."

"What are you saying?" cried Bilsby. "Offering our ballistics to the profit of strangers!"

"Better that than wallowing here with nothing to do," responded the colonel.

"Without a doubt," said J.T. Maston, "it is better than wallowing; but I think it would not be expedient."

"And what is that?" demanded the colonel.

"Because in the old world, their ideas of promotion and advancement are quite contrary to the habits of us Americans. They imagine that one cannot be a general in charge unless he has already served as a second-lieutenant, which is the same as saying one cannot be a good gunner unless they have cast the mold for the barrel themselves! Why, it is simply..."

"Absurd!" completed Tom Hunter, tearing at the armrests of his chair with his bowie knife. "However, since there is nothing else remaining for us to do, other than plant tobacco or distill oil from whale carcasses!"

"You mean to say," cried J.T. Maston in a resounding voice, "that for the remaining years of our existence, we shall not employ them in perfecting arms of fire!? That there will be no further occasions to test the distance of our projectiles! That the atmosphere will never again be illuminated by the bright glare of destruction from our cannons! That the world shall be without the international difficulties which will permit us to declare war on some transatlantic country! That the French will not sink a single one of our steamers, or the English will not hang just one of our citizens, in direct violation of international law?"

"No, Maston," responded Colonel Bloomsbury. "We shall never be so lucky- oh no! None of these incidents would produce anything; and if they did, it would not be to the profit of us! The susceptibility of Americans for war fades day by day, soon our nation will be but a tomb fit for old women!"

"Yes, that's right. Oh, the humility!" replied the dashing Bilsby.

"And we are being humiliated!" responded brave Tom Hunter.

"It is entirely true," replied J.T. Maston, with new vehemence. "There are a million reasons for battle, but we don't fight once! We economize the arms and legs, to the profit of those who don't even know what such limbs are for! And look, it does not take long to find the motive for war- North America previously belonged to the English, is it not true?"

"Without any doubt," responded Tom Hunter, stabbing the fire in rage with his crutch.

"Well then," replied J.T. Maston, "Why should it not be the Americans turn to own England?"

"That is only justice," reasoned Colonel Bloomsbury.

"Go propose this to the president of the United States," cried J.T. Maston. "You will see the kind of reception he gives you!"

"It would be quite a negative reception," murmured Bilsby through the four teeth he had retained from so many battles.

"I swear," cried J.T. Maston, "that for the approaching elections he shall not have my vote!"

"Nor shall he have ours!" responded the belligerent invalids in communal accord.

"In the meanwhile," J.T. Maston told them, "for conclusion, if I am not provided with an occasion to test my new mortar on a live field of battle, I shall decommission my membership with the Gun Club and enter into the wild savannas of Arkansas!"

"And we will do the same," responded the interlocutors of the audacious J.T. Maston.

Now, these things established, their spirits rising more and more, the club faced the impending menace of dissolution when an unexpected event occurred which served to prevent a regrettable catastrophe.

The day following this conversation, all members of the circle received a memo written in these terms:

Baltimore, October 3

The president of the Gun Club has the honor of informing his colleagues that during the meeting on the 5th he will be making a communication, the nature of which will be of the greatest interest to you. In consequence, therefore, he politely beseeches that you may be able to cease your affairs and accept this invitation for your presence.

Most cordially yours,

Impey Barbicane, President of the Gun Club.

2. **The Announcement of President Barbicane**

The 5th October, at 8 o'clock in the evening, a dense crowd had gathered with urgency in the salons of the Gun Club, 21 Union Square. All members of the resident circle at Baltimore who had received their invitation from the president were present; regarding those who were members by the way of correspondence, hundreds had disembarked the express train into the streets of the village- and around the huge beer barrel in the meeting hall the society of savants had taken their places. Also surging from the neighboring rooms, flowing from the middle to beyond the limits of the rear and spilling into the exterior, gathered the simple population; who pressed at the windows, everyone seeking a front row position, all avidly wanting to receive the important communication from the president Barbicane- and they pushed and they knocked-against one another overwhelmingly, an active protest which those crowded masses of particular liberty, elevated by the ideas of democracy, often display.

On this evening a stranger would be unable to obtain entry into that meeting room in Baltimore for any price, or even be able to physically penetrate that great room; it was exclusively reserved for the resident members and for members by way of correspondence. No other power could take a place; and the notables of the city, the magistrates and elected council members jostled and mixed with their public administrate to take account of any news emerging from the interior.

Meanwhile the immense hall offered a curious spectacle. The vast space offered a marvelously appropriate situation. The high columns formed by the cannons superimposing themselves above the mortars served as a suitable basis for the fine framework about the vault, veritable lace-icing for the central cast iron piece. The display of blunderbusses, muskets, harquebuses and carbines formed a complete array of combustion weapons; both ancient and modern, picturesquely entwined. A magical form was created by gas flames emerging from a thousand revolvers grouped into a bright glowing light; while the barrels of the pistols bundled together in the candelabra were in fact the fusillade, which completed that splendid source of illumination. Models of cannons, those songs of bronze, were the focal-point of this riddle of terror. Piled around them, behind silver and gold-plated plaques, litters of the cannon balls of the Gun Club; assortments of suppression and control, rosaries of bombs, necklaces of projectiles, garlands of shells- in a word, all the tools of artillery amazing the eye with their impressive decorative arrangement which would lead one to think their veritable purpose as being more decorative than murderous.

At the place of honor was a splendid display held in its own gaudy shelter, a piece of breech, broken and tortured by the effort of its gunpowder explosion; the precious debris of the legendary cannon mortar of J.T. Maston.

At the extremity of the meeting room the president, assisted by his four secretaries, occupied a large esplanade. His seat before the ensemble was elevated, sculptured from the powerful form of a 32 pound mortar; it was turned to an angle of 26° and suspended by trunnions to create for the president the powerful impression of a rocking chair, sturdily and agreeably-balanced, useful at warding away times of excessive heat. On the desk was a vast plaque of steel supported by 6 cannonades, where a rudely-distasteful yet exquisite inkwell stood- it was, in fact, a canister shot delightfully carved for the occasion. Beside this also was a bell, which could be rung like the detonation from a revolver. As a counterpoint during vehement discussions, it cracked a sound sufficiently painful to cover the voice of overexcited artillerists.

In front of the desk the seats were arranged in zigzag fashion, like the circumvallation of trenches forming a succession of bastions and short curtains, where there were places for all members of the Gun Club; and on this evening, according great power and status, looking for all the world like ramparts. All were of sufficient acquaintance with the president to know he did not disturb his colleagues without possessing motives of the highest gravity.

Impey Barbicane was a man of 40 years, calm, cold, austere, with a spirit of austere concentration; exact like a chronometer, with an unfailing temperament, of unwavering character; chivalrous, however adventurous, but apporting practical ideas to the limits of recklessness; he was a man of the excellence of New England, the Northern colonizer, the descendant of the Roundheads who were so deadly to the Stuarts, an implacable enemy of Southern gentlemen from the South, those ancient knights of the motherland. In short, he was a dyed-in-the-wool Yankee.

Barbicane possessed a grand fortune from the timber industry. He was nominated to direct the artillery during the war and demonstrated a great fertility of inventive ways; audacious in his ideas, he contributed greatly to the progress of the army, and with great flair gave to it many experimental things.

He was a person of average height, and, in rare exception for the Gun Club, all his limbs were intact. His strong facial features accentuated the resemblance of lines drawn with a set-square, and, if it is true that to determine the instincts of a man one must regard him from his profile Barbicane thus offered the indications of a great certainty of energy, audacious and cold-blooded.

In that instant he was demurely-still in his armchair; speechless, absorbed, regarding his inner-most thoughts, sheltered beneath the form of his high hat, those black cylinders which seem adhesively stuck onto the heads of all Americans.

His colleagues, causing excited stirs of conversation around him, failed to distract him; they interrogated one another, continuing to offer fields of suppositions- they examined their president and searched, but in vain, to extricate what lay beyond his impenetrable physiognomy.

When the clock thunderously rang 8 hours throughout the great hall Barbicane, as though imbued with a spring, suddenly straightened; there was a general silence and the orator, in an emphatic tone, began to speak in these following terms:

"Brave colleagues, there has been for a long time a fecund peace which has plunged the members of the Gun Club into a regrettable disconsolation. After a period of several years without incident, the abandonment of our work has occurred; which has arrested the way of progress. I do not fear proclaim with high voice that any war which would bring back our arms would be welcome..."

"Yes, some war!" cried the impetuous J.T. Maston.

"Hear, hear!" replicated shouts on all sides.

"But war," said Barbicane, "war is impossible in these actual circumstances, and, even with the powerful hopes of my honorable interrupter the long years will pass by before cannons thunder on the field of battle once more. It is fact and therefore we must take a new course of action with the research and ideas of our order, for us to have an activity to consume ourselves with!"

The assembly sensed that their president approached a delicate point. They all redoubled their attention.

"For several months, my brave colleagues," continued Barbicane, "I have demanded of myself, entirely remaining within the realms of our specialty, a powerful undertaking which is befitting to the dignity and grand experience of our 19th Century- and if the progress of our ballistics permits us to bring it to a good finish. I have therefore researched, toiled and calculated and the results of this study have led me to the conviction we must be successful in an enterprise which seems impracticable for other countries. This project, long and elaborate, is the object of my communication; it is dignity for you, a dignity surpassing the Gun Club- and it cannot fail to make a powerful noise throughout the world!"

"A lot of noise?" cried out a passionate artilleryman.

"A lot of noise in the truest sense of the word," assured Barbicane.

"No interruptions!" several voices repeated.

"Therefore I pray of you, brave colleagues" Barbicane continued, "that you provide me with your entire attention."

A quiver passed through the assembly. Barbicane, making rapid gestures to ensure his hat remained atop his head, continued his discourse in a calm voice:

"There is not one of you, brave colleagues, who have not seen the moon; or in the very least, have heard it spoken of. Do not be astonished to know it accompanies the stars in the night sky. It is reserved for us to become the Columbuses of that unknown world! Do you understand me? Provide me with all of your power, that I may lead you in this conquest, and the name of the Moon will join the 36 which form the grand United States!"

"Hurrah for the moon!" cried the Gun Club in one voice.

"'There has been a lot of study regarding the moon," continued Barbicane. "It's mass, density, weight, volume, constitution, distance and role in the solar system have been perfectly determined; selenographic maps have been drawn with perfect equality, or even surpassing, terrestrial maps. Photography has given to our satellite prints of incomparable beauty. In a word, our knowledge of the moon is complete from the perspective of the sciences of mathematics, astronomy, geology and optical observation; however thus far we have been unable to establish direct communication."

Violent murmurs of interest and surprise from the listeners accompanied his words.

"Permit me," he continued, "to recall a few words written by ardent spirits, embarking on imaginary voyages, claiming to penetrate the secrets of our satellite. In the 17th Century, a certain David Fabricius boasted to have seen with his own eyes the inhabitants of the moon. In 1649, a Frenchman, Jean Baudoin, published the facts regarding a voyage from the Earth to the Moon with Dominique Gonzales, a Spanish adventurer. And in the same era Cyrano de Bergerac made publication of that expedition whose success was celebrated throughout France. Then later, another Frenchman- this was regarding the many occupants of the Moon- whose name was Fontenelle wrote *The Plurality of Worlds*, a leading work of the times. However science, marching onwards, crushes even these great works! Around 1835, a translated pamphlet recounted from the New York American Sir John Herschel, correspondent onboard the Bonne-Esperance for astronomical studies, had, with the means of a telescope with perfect clarity from interior lighting, reconnoitered the moon to the distance of 80 yards. Then he had distinctly seen in his general survey caverns where hippopotamus lived, the green mountains fringed with jagged veins of gold, sheep with ivory horns, white goats, the habitants with membranous wings which were similar to bats. In this brochure, the expedition of scientific observation was led by an American named Locke to great success. However soon it was recognized that these '*scientific mysteries*' were a hoax, the French were the first to laugh."

"Laughing at an American!" cried out .T. Maston. "But that is an act of war!"

"Let me reassure you, my dignified friend. The French, before they laughed, were also perfectly duped by our compatriots. For the termination of this rapid history, credence was provided to a certain Hans Pfaal of Rotterdam, who soared upwards in a balloon filled with nitrogen thirty-seven times lighter than hydrogen, reaching the Moon in 19 days of travel. This voyage, like those tentative precedents previously, was simple imagination originating from a popular American writer. A work of strange contemplative genius, by Edgar Allen Poe!"

"Hurrah for Poe!" cried the assembly, electrified by the words of their president.

"And to finish," continued Barbicane. "From the tentative appeals of pure literature, it is perfectly insufficient to establish serious relations with any of the heavenly bodies of the night sky. However, there have been some credulous efforts by practical minds to attempt providing serious communication with the Moon. For example, a few years ago, a German geometer proposed to send a commission of scientists to the steppes of Siberia. There, on the vast plains, they would excise immense geometrical figures designed to reflect the lunar light, between others the square of hypotenuse- vulgarly called the '*Point of Donkeys*' by the French. '*For any intelligent being, upon seeing the geometry, would comprehend the scientific purpose of the figures. Then, the Moon's Selenites, if they exist, with a suitable figure and once communication has been established, this would facilitate the creation of an alphabet which would permit conversation with the inhabitants of the moon*,' the German geometer proposed. But this project has not been executed, and there is no direct link existing between the Earth and its satellite. Hence it is reserved to the practical genius of the Americans to put into place a rapport with this neighboring world. The means to reach the Moon is simple, easy, certain, faultless, and is the core object of my proposition."

A loud series of conversations erupted, tempered with approving exclamations, regarding this speech. There was not a soul amongst them who was not enthralled, entrained or carried away by the words of the orator.

"Listen! Listen! Silence!" were the cries heard from all parts of the hall.

When the agitation had fully-calmed, Barbicane continued with a grave voice from where his discourse had been interrupted.

"You know, as I do, the progress of ballistics has reached during these recent years and the degree of perfection which firing weapons would have achieved if war had continued. You cannot ignore, in a general way, the resistant force of cannons and the powerful, expansive potential of gunpowder is unlimited. Ah yes! Running with this principle, I demanded of myself to figure the means of sufficient apparatus and establish the necessary conditions of resistance in order to determine if it was possible to convey a cannon ball to the Moon!"

At these words, the moaning sound of stupefied "ohs!" escaped from a thousand panting breasts; in the subsequent moment of silence, the semblance of a profound calm preceded a thunderous blow. It was, in effect, a thunderous brilliant explosion; but it was the thunder of applause. The cries, the clamor, caused the meeting hall itself to tremble. The president tried to speak: he lacked the vocal power to do so. It was about ten minutes before he could entreat them any further.

"Allow me to finish," he continued coldly. "I have examined the question from all aspects, with unassailable resolve, and the result of my indisputable calculations are that a projectile with an initial velocity of 12,000 thousand yards per second, aimed towards the Moon, is necessary to reach it. And therefore it is my honor to propose to you, my brave colleagues, to attempt this little experiment!"

3. The Effect of Barbicane's Communication.

It is impossible to depict the effect produced at the end of the honorable president's speech. Such cries! Such vociferations! Such a succession of grumblings, the hurrahs, the "hip, hip, hoorays" and the many other onomatopoeias suitable for times of celebration in the America language! It was a disorderly, excited sound of voices that was indescribable! Mouths cried, hands battered and stomping feet shook the wooden planks of the meeting hall. If all the weapons in that artillery museum had fired at once it could not have provided a more agitated, violent sonorous sound. This should not be surprising. It is the case that the cannoneers themselves are nearly as loud as their cannons.

Barbicane was demure and calm amidst this enthusiastic clamor; perhaps he wished to address a few more words to his colleagues, making gestures to reclaim the silence, and the bell on the desk was sounded espousing violent detonations. His entreaties went in vain. Soon he was besieged, carried aloft triumphantly, and from the hands of his loyal comrades he was passed into the arms of the excited crowd.

Nothing is known to astonish an American. It is often repeated that the word '*impossible*' is not French; yet it is evidently contained in their dictionary. In America, everything is easy, everything is simple, and of mechanical difficulties- they are dead before they are born. From the onset of the project which Barbicane had realized, no veritable Yankee would permit an apprehension of seeing any difficulty. So it is said, so it is done.

The triumphant promenade of the president prolonged into the evening. It was a veritable march of blazing torchlight. Irish, Germans, French, Scotsmen, the entire heterogeneous individuals who composed the population of Maryland, cried in their mother languages and the cheers, the hoorays, the bravos comingled into a melee of inexpressible momentum.

And then with precision, as though it had comprehended the agitation below, the Moon brilliantly appeared with serene magnificence; eclipsing the intense radiation of their flaming environment. Every Yankee turned their eyes towards the sparkling disc. They saluted it with their hands, and some shouted affectionate names, some measured it with their eyes, some shook their fists menacingly; between 8 o'clock and midnight an optician on Jones-Fall Street made a fortune in selling lunar telescopes, as though the stars of the night sky were a famous and beautiful opera singer. The Americans looked upon the Moon in the casual manner of its proprietors. It appeared the blonde Phoebe belonged to those audacious conquerors and was already part of the territory of the United States. And yet they intended only to send a projectile, which was a brutal mannerism to entreat a new relationship, even with our own satellite; however such a strong occasion like this is used by all civilized nations.

Even at midnight, enthusiasm had yet to wane; maintaining itself equally across all classes of the population- the magistrate, the scientist, the merchant, the tradesman, the laborer, men of intelligence and men of simplicity. Their sentiment moved them to their innermost fibers; a national enterprise had presented itself, and from the highest point of the village to the lowest point, to the bathing quays on the water of Patapsco, the maritime ships imprisoned in their docks; all burst and overflowed with joyous crowds filled with joy, gin and whiskey; everyone conversing together, considering, discussing, disputing, approving, applauding, from the nonchalant gentlemen on their sofas in the bar-rooms with their tankards of sherry-cobblers to the boatmen getting drunk on moonshine in the somber taverns of Fells-Point.

However, towards 2 o'clock in the morning, the emotions calmed. The president Barbicane managed to reach his house; bruised, flattened, ground-down. No herculean effort could have resisted such enthusiasm. The crowd abandoned bit-by-bit the parks and the roads. The four railroads from Ohio, Susquehanna, Philadelphia and Washington that converge at Baltimore gathered the excess crowds of visitors and jettisoned them to the four corners of the United States and the village was returned to its relative tranquility and repose.

It would be in error to imagination that, during this memorable evening, Baltimore was the sole prey of this agitation. The great cities of the Union; New York, Boston, Albany, Washington, Richmond, Crescent City,

Charleston, Mobile, from Texas to Massachusetts, from Michigan to Florida, all enjoyed their part in the delirium. In effect, the 30,000 members of the Gun Club by way of correspondence had received their letter from their president, and they had attentively waited with equal impatience for the famous communication due 5th October. So, on that same evening, the words which escaped the lips of our orator were instantly recorded and then transferred into the electric current of the telegraph where they traversed the States of the Union with a velocity of 248,447 miles per second. So, therefore, with absolute certainty it can be said that at the same instant across the United States, a country ten times greater than the size of France, there was uttered one single hurrah; and 25,000,000 hearts, swollen with pride, beat in one pulse.

The following day, fifteen hundred journals- daily, weekly, bi-monthly and monthly- seized upon the question; they examined the various aspects of physics, meteorology, economies and morality which related to it, and from their own points of view pondered the political implications for our civilization. They demanded to understand if the Moon was a world complete, or if it were still subject to transformation. Did it resemble Earth before its own atmosphere had formed? And what spectacle presented itself on the invisible face of that spherical planetoid? Although, yes, it was only planned to send a projectile into the Moon, all viewed this as a point of departure for a series of experiments; all hoped for the day when American penetrated the final secrets of this mysterious disc, and some of them seemed to think this conquest might disrupt the balance of European power.

The project discussed, not one paper doubted its realization; the reviews, the brochures, the bulletins, the magazines published by scientific societies and the religious literatures all firmly reported the advantages; and the Boston Society of Natural History, the Albany American Society of Sciences and Arts, the New York Society of Geography and Statistics, The Philadelphia Society of American Philosophy and the Washington Smithsonian Institute sent thousands of letters of felicitation to the Gun Club, with immediate offers of service and monetary contributions.

So it may be told, that never before had any proposition united such an unparalleled number of supporters; hesitations, doubts and anxieties were totally out of the question. Regarding the jokes, caricatures and songs which would have normally in Europe, particularly in France, accompanied an idea such as sending a projectile to the Moon; it would have been exceedingly dangerous to do so now. All the life-preservers in the world would not protect such impudence from general public indignation. There are some things which one does not joke about in the new world. Impey Barbicane from that day was thereafter seen as one of the greatest citizens of the United States, somewhat like the Washington of science, and this trait was justified amongst themselves to all people, down to a man.

Some days after the famous meeting in the Gun Club, the director of an English theatrical troupe announced they would be presenting in Baltimore Shakespeare's '*Much Ado About Nothing*'. But the population of the city, perceiving the title as an allusion of insult towards the project of president Barbicane; besieged the theatre, broke up its seats, and obliged the unfavorable director to change his bill. So then the spirited director, acquiescing to the will of the public, replaced his ill-chosen comedy with Shakespeare's '*As You Like It*,' and for many weeks received phenomenal receptions.

4. Response from the Cambridge Observatory

However Barbicane, the object of thousands of ovations, was not wasting an instant. His first choice of action was to call together his colleagues to the offices of the Gun Club. There, after discussion, it was decided to consult the astronomers regarding the astronomical considerations of the enterprise. When their response was known, they could then discuss the mechanical means, and nothing could be neglected to assure the success of this grand experiment.

A very precise note with the context of these special questions was drawn and addressed to the Observatory of Cambridge, Massachusetts. This city, where the first University of the United States was founded, is justly celebrated for its bureau of astronomy. There one finds an organization of scientists of the highest merit; the function of its powerful telescope permitted Bond to resolve the Andromeda Nebula and for Clarke to discover the satellite of Sirius. Hence the celebrated establishment had the qualifications to justify the confidence of the Gun Club.

Then two days later, impatiently waited-for, the observatory's response arrived into the hands of the president Barbicane. It contained these following terms:

Cambridge, 7th October.

The Director of the Observatory of Cambridge to the President of the Gun Club, of Baltimore.

On the receipt of your honorable note on 6th October, addressed to the Cambridge Observatory in the name of the members of the Gun Club of Baltimore, our office immediately met and estimated the following remarks in consideration:

The questions that you have posed are these:

1. Is it possible to send a projectile to the Moon?

2. What is the exact distance that separates the Earth from its satellite?

3. What would the duration and trajectory of the projectile be in order to transmit it with sufficient initial velocity, and, as a consequence, at what moment should it be launched to reach the Moon at a determined point?

4. At what is the precise moment the Moon will present itself in a position most favorable for the projectile to attain its target?

5. At what point in the sky should the cannon be aimed to launch the projectile?

6. What place would the Moon occupy in the sky at the moment of departure for the projectile?

On the 1st question:- Is it possible to send a projectile to the Moon?

Yes, it is possible to send a projectile to the moon- for it to reach the projectile must be driven with an initial velocity of 12,000 yards per second. Calculations demonstrate that this velocity is sufficient. When measuring the distance as moving away from the Earth the action of gravity diminishes in an inverse ratio to the square of the distance, that is, for a distance 3 times as great, the action is 9 times less-force. In consequence, the gravity on the cannon ball diminishes rapidly, and finally it will be annulled completely the moment the attraction of the Moon reaches equilibrium with that of the Earth; that is at 4,750'' of the trajectory. At this moment the projectile is weightless, and, crossing this point it falls towards the Moon solely from the effect of the lunar attraction. The theoretical possibility of this experience is absolutely demonstrated; to be successful, it will depend on the unique power employed by its engine.

On the 2nd question:- What is the exact distance separating the Earth from its satellite?

The Moon does not describe a circular circumference around the Earth, but rather an ellipse where our globe occupies the focal point. As a consequence the Moon will sometimes be found approaching the Earth, and at other times moving away, or, in astronomical terms, now at its apogee and then at its perigee. The difference is fairly considerable and in this case, not something negligible. In effect, at its apogee the Moon is 247,552 miles away and at its perigee it is 218,657 miles away, a difference of 28,895 miles, or 1/9th of the total journey. It is therefore the distance at the perigee of the Moon that serves as the basis for these calculations.

On the 3rd question:- What would the duration and trajectory of the projectile be in order to transmit it with sufficient initial velocity, and, as a consequence, at what moment should it be launched to reach the Moon at a determined point?

If the cannon ball indefinitely conserved the initial velocity of 12,000 miles per second at the moment of its departing detonation, in about 9 hours it would reach its destination; but the initial velocity will continually diminish, and all calculations have found the projectiles schedule will take 300,000 seconds, that is 83 hours and 20 minutes, to attain the point where the attraction of the Earth and the Moon are in equilibrium and from this point it will fall towards the moon in 50,000 seconds, or 13 hours, 53 minutes and 20 seconds. You should therefore convene the launch 97 hours, 13 minutes and 20 seconds before arrival of the Moon at its targeted point.

On the 4th question:- At what is the precise moment the Moon will present itself in a position most favorable for the projectile to attain its target?

In view of the discussion above, in order to choose the epoch when the Moon is at its perigee, which should be the same time at which it passes through its zenith, which will reduce the required travel by the distance of the Earth's radius, 3,919 miles; so that the actual trajectory will be 214,973 miles. However, although each month the Moon passes through its perigee, it does not always reach its zenith point at this moment. These conditions are only presented between long intervals. You will therefore need this coincidence for the passage of the perigee and zenith to occur. Due to fortunate circumstances, on the 4th December next year the Moon offers these two conditions: at midnight, when it reaches its perigee, that is when at the shortest distance from Earth, and at the same time it passes through zenith.

On the 5th question:- At what point in the sky should the cannon be aimed to launch the projectile?

The preceding observations being allowed, the cannon must be aimed at the position of the zenith, so that it is fired perpendicular to the horizon's plane, and the projectile can slip most rapidly away from the effects of the Earth's attraction. But, for the Moon to mount its zenith in that particular place, it must not be in a location where the latitude is greater than the declination of the Moon, that is, the areas comprised by the latitudes between 0° and 28° either to the north or south of the equator. At all other places, the firing would have to be by necessity at an oblique angle, and this would be harmful to the success of the experience [as, launched at any greater latitude, a projectile aimed towards the Moon's zenith would be interrupted by the Earth's curvature, and hence only be fired into the ground].

On the 6th question:- What place would the Moon occupy in the sky at the moment of departure for the projectile?

At the moment the projectile is launched into space, for the Moon- which advances each day 13°, 10' and 35"- to travel through its elongated Zenith it needs to be 4 times that number further away; that is 52°, 42' and 20", which is the spacial distance of the durational path the projectile must traverse. But in order to account for the deviation in the cannon ball's trajectory caused by the rotation of the Earth, when it arrives at the Moon it will be seen to have deviated by a distance equal to 16 times the radius of the Earth; and that, calculating the orbit of the Moon is equivalent to 11°, hence these 11° must be included to delay the arrival at the Moon which, as mentioned, which is at 64° in round numbers. So therefore, at the moment of firing, the visual ray of the Moon from the vertical will be 64°.

These are our responses to the questions posed to the Cambridge Observatory by the members of the Gun Club.

In summary:

1. The cannon must be established in a situation between 0° and 28° latitude north or south of the equator.

2. It must be pointed towards the place of zenith.

3. The projectile must be animated with an initial velocity of 12,000 miles per second.

4. It must be launched on 1st December of the approaching year, at 13 minutes and 20 seconds before 11 o'clock.

5. It will rendezvous with the Moon four days after departure, at midnight precisely 4th December, on the moment of passing through zenith.

The members of the Gun Club should therefore commence without delay the necessary work in a concerted enterprise to be ready for that opportune moment which has been determined, that is, when it is the date of 4th December; otherwise one will only reach the Moon when those conditions of the perigee and zenith coincide again 18 years and 11 days later.

The bureau of the Cambridge Observatory are at your disposal for your questions of astronomical theory, and they join in presenting their congratulatory felicitations to you along with the entire United States of America.

From the Office of

J.M. Belfast

Director of the Cambridge Observatory.

5. The Romance of the Moon

An observer endowed with an infinitely-penetrating vision, and placed at the unknown center which the gravity of Earth circles around, would see the myriads of atoms filling outwards into space during the chaotic epochs of the universe.

However, little by little, with the centuries a change was produced; it was one of manifested attraction, obeyed by the errant atoms which until then had been adrift. The atoms combined chemically according to their affinities, these firmed into molecules which formed into masses of nebulae scattered through the profundity of heavenly sky.

Those masses immediately moved together in accordant and animated movement around a central point. At the center formed by vague molecules, they began to move together and progressively condense; and outside this, being subject to the immutable laws of mechanics, as the volume diminished from this condensation, the movement of rotation accelerated and the two effects persisted; resulting in the principle star at the center of the nebulous mass.

In attentive regard, the observer would then have seen these amassing molecules comport themselves around that central star, condensing with their own movement in progressively accelerating rotation, and in the surrounding gravity form innumerable stars. A nebula, of which astronomers actually count 5,000 in existence, is formed.

Amongst these 5,000 nebulas, there is one that men have named the Milky Way which contains 18,000,000 stars- and each of these are the location for the center of solar systems.

If the observer had especially examined within those 18,000,000 stars one of the most-modest and brilliantly-shining, a star of the fourth order, this named proudly the Sun, the entire phenomenon that is due to the formation of the universe would have been successively accomplished before their eyes.

In effect, the Sun, whilst in its gaseous state and composed of loose molecules, moved about on its own axis to achieve this work of concentration. This movement, faithful to the mechanical laws, then caused its acceleration with the reduction in volume the moment arrived when the centrifugal force prevailed over the centripetal force, which tends to reposition the molecules towards the center.

And then as the action of this phenomenon passed before the eyes of the observer, and the molecules situated themselves into a plane along the equator, escaping like a stone from a sling whose cord has abruptly snapped, they formed around the Sun over many years concentric rings resembling those of Saturn's. As these turned, this cosmic material began another rotational movement around their central mass, breaking and disintegrating into secondary nebula; that is to say, planets.

Should the observer have maintained their total attention on these planets, they would have seen the exact action like that of the Sun as it gave birth to those cosmic rings, which became the origin of the plantetoids of inferior order, known as satellites.

So therefore, going from the atom as it assembled to the molecule, the molecule to the nebulous mass, the nebulous mass to the nebula, the nebula into the principle star, the principle star into the sun, the sun to the planet and the planet to the satellite; that is the entire series of transformations undergone by the celestial bodies in the first days of the world.

The sun seems doomed to perdition in an immense stellar world; however it is bound, according to the present theories of science, into the nebula of the Milky Way. The center of a world, although small when compared amidst the ethereal regions, is actually relatively enormous- it is one million, four hundred thousand times larger than the Earth. Around it gravitate 8 planets, assorted from its entrails at the beginning time of Creation. They are, from the nearest to their star moving outwards, Mercury, Venus, the Earth, Mars, Jupiter, Saturn, Uranus and Neptune. As well, between the regulating circular orbits of Mars and Jupiter there are considerable populations of bodies, smaller errant debris from a broken planetary body into thousands of pieces, which the telescope has reconnoitered 97 so far.

These servants of the sun maintain their elliptical orbit according to the grand laws of gravitation and some of them possess their own satellites. Uranus has 8, Saturn 8, Jupiter 4, Neptune perhaps 3, the Earth 1; that latter, one of the most important in the solar system, called the Moon, was the one which those audaciously ingenious Americans intended to lay their claim to and conquer.

The shining body of our night sky, in relative proximity and with a rapid spectacle of its renewing diverse phases, it was accorded completely, along with the Sun, the full attention of the inhabitants of the Earth; but to regard the Sun is fatiguing, and the splendors of its illumination obliges those contemplators to avert their gaze.

Contrarily the blonde, pale Phoebe is very humane; she complacently allows herself to be viewed in all her graceful modesty; she is sweet to our eyes, unambitious, and yet however, she will permit herself on occasion to eclipse her brother, the radiant Apollo, without ever being eclipsed by him. The Mohammadeans, when apprehending with understanding her faithful friendship to the Earth, chose to regulate their calendrical months on her revolutions.

The peoples of early civilizations devoted particular cults to their chaste goddess. The Egyptians named her Isis; the Phoenicians called her Astarte; the Greeks adorned her with the name Phoebe, daughter of Latonia and Jupiter, and explained her eclipses as the mysterious visits of Diane to the handsome Endymion. And in the beliefs of that mythological legend, the lion of Nemee prowled in campaigns upon the Moon before appearing on Earth; and the poet Agesianax, cited by Plutarch, celebrated in his verses her gentle eyes, her charming nose and her amiable mouth, formed by the luminescant parts of the adorable Selene.

But although the ancients comprehended well the character, the temperament, in a word, the moral qualities of the Moon from the point of view of mythology, even their resident savants were entirely ignorant of the science on the Moon.

However, several ancient astronomers of that recumbent epoch discovered certain particularities confirmed in these modern days of science. Whilst the Arcadians pretended to have inhabited the Earth in a time before the Moon existed above; whilst Tatius regarded it as a fragment which had detached itself from the solar disc; whilst Clearchus, the disciple of Aristotle, told that it was a smoothly-polished mirror reflecting the images of the ocean; and others said that it was a mass of vapors exhaled from the Earth, or a globe half of fire, half of ice, which revolved about on itself; some savants, with sage-like observations, without any optical instruments, superstitiously derived most of the laws which regulate our Moon.

Hence Thales of Miletus, 460 years before Christ, emitted the opinion the Moon was illuminated by the Sun. Aristarchus of Samos gave a veritable explanation of its phases. Cleomedes taught that the brilliance of the Moon was due to reflected luminescence. The Chaldean Berosus that the duration of the movement of its rotation was equal to the movement of its revolution, and this explained the fact why the Moon presented always the one face. And finally Hipparchus, 2 centuries before the Christian era, recognized certain inequalities in the apparent movement of Earth's satellite.

These diverse observations were confirmed and continued to the profit of new astronomers. Ptolemy in the 2nd century, and the Arab Abul Wefa in the 10th, completed the remarks of Hipparchus about the inequalities of the orbit of the Moon as it describes an undulating line due to the action of the Sun. Then Copernicus in the 15th century, and Tycho Brahe in the 16th, completely exposed the solar system and the role played by the Moon within the ensemble of heavenly bodies.

At that period it's perceived movements were precisely determined; but of the physical constitution little was known. And then along came Gallileo explaining the phenomena of luminary products during certain phases from the existence of mountains which were about a height of 27,000 feet.

After him, Hevelius, an astronomer of Danzig, reduced these preceding measurements by a remarkable adjustment. He gave an elevation of 15,600 feet, and brought the variation of differences in height to only 400 feet. But Herschel was trumped, and there followed the observations of Shroeter, Louville, Halley, Nasmyth, Bianchini, Pastorf, Lohrman, Gruithuysen, and particularly the patient studies of MM. Beer and Moedeler to definitively resolve this question.

By the thankful favor of these scientists, the elevation of these mountains is perfectly comprehended today. MM. Beer and Moedeler have measured the heights of 1,905 mountains and there are 6 which are over 15,600 feet in height, and 22 are above 14,400 feet. The highest summit dominating the surface of our lunar disk is 22,806 feet.

At the same time, the reconnaissance of the Moon was completed. The planetoid's appraisal revealed that it was riddled with craters that were in nature essentially volcanic as was affirmed by every observation. Due to the absence of refraction upon the rays of light from occulting planets, it was concluded that an atmosphere was almost-completely lacking. This absence of air leads to an absence of water. It therefore manifested that the Selenites, to live upon the Moon in such conditions, must have a specially-organized biology quite different to the inhabitants of the Earth.

And finally, thanks to new methods, the perfected instruments searching the Moon relentlessly, leaving no point upon its face unexplored; and despite the diameter measuring 2,150 miles, with a surface one-thirteenth that of the surface of our globe, in volume one-forty-ninth the volume of our Earthly sphere; none of these secrets had the power to escape the eyes of our astronomers, and these skillful scientists carried on with their prodigious observations.

Thus so, they remarked that during the full Moon, the disk presented in certain parts straight white lines and during its phases, rays of black lines. Studying these with exceptional precision, they rendered in complete their conclusion as to the exact nature of these lines. It was found that they were grooves, long and straight, hollowed into parallel sides, generally arriving at the contours of the craters; in length comprising between 10 and 100 miles in length and one larger being 800 miles up and down. The astronomers called them grooves, but all they could be sure of was their name given.

Regarding the answer to the question if these grooves might have been ancient parched riverbeds, there is no resoundingly-complete opinion although the Americans hoped to successfully determine, one day or another, that geological fact. They equally reserved their intention to explore the series of parallel ramparts discovered on the surface of the Moon by Gruithuysen, scientific professor of Munich; who considered their likeness to a system of fortifications elevated by those ingenious inhabitants of the Moon, the Selenites. To these two points, highly obscure, and without doubt along with many others, we are powerless to definitively settle until there is a direct communication with the Moon.

As to the intensity of the Moon's luminosity, there is nothing further to be known in that regard; our scientists know that it is 300,000 times fainter than the Sun and that it's warmth has no appreciable action upon thermometers. As to the phenomenon known by the name of ashy-luminescence, this is explained by the natural effect of the Sun's rays echoing between the Earth and the Moon and appears to complete the lunar disk when it presents the shape of a crescent during the initial and final phases.

This was the state of the acquired knowledge about the satellite of the Earth; which the Gun Club had proposed to completely encompass from all points of view, cosmographic, geological, political and moral.

6. What it is Impossible Not to Know [and What it is No Longer Permissible to Believe in the United States]

The proposition Barbicane put forth resulted immediately in a remitting order of the day for all astronomical facts relating to the Moon. All gave it assiduous study. It seemed that the Moon appeared for the first time on the horizon and that no person had seen it before meet with the sky. It became fashionable, it was a celebrity- the '*lioness of the day*'- without ever showing a loss of modesty and took its place amongst the '*stars*' without any increase of pride. The journalists revived those old anecdotes where the '*sun of the wolves*' enjoyed a role; they spoke of the influences given to it by the ignorance of earlier ages; they sang praises in all keys and tones, just stopping themselves short of quoting it's '*witty remarks*'; the entirety of America had come down with a case of selenomania, which has also been referred to by physicians as '*moonfever*'.

Alongside, the scientific reviews treated with special attention the questions concerning the enterprise of the Gun Club; they published in full the letter from the Cambridge Observatory, commenting and providing their unreserved approval.

To be brief, it was not permissible for even the most illiterate Yankee to be ignorant of any facts relating to the satellite, or to allow the most narrow-minded of old women to maintain their erroneous superstitious beliefs. Science had arrived in all forms; it penetrated their eyes and ears; it was impossible to be an ignorant dunce... At least, in astronomy.

Before this time, many gentlemen were ignorant that the distance separating the Moon and the Earth had been calculated. Profiting by these circumstances, experts explained that this distance had been obtained by measuring the parallax of the Moon. If the word '*parallax*' caused any surprise, they would explain that this was the angle formed by two straight lines from the extreme edges between the Earth and the Moon. For doubters of the perfection of this method, it was immediately proven to them that not only was this distance 234,347 miles, but that the astronomical variance of this calculation was but 66 miles.

For those unfamiliar with the movements of the Moon, the daily newspapers demonstrated that it has two distinct movements; the first being the rotation on its axis, the second being its revolution around the Earth, both of which are accomplished in an equal length of time, 27 and one-third days.

The movement of rotation is described by a day and a night upon the surface of the Moon; there is but one day and but one night per lunar month, whose duration is 354 hours and one-third. But, fortunately for her, the face turning towards the terrestrial globe is illuminated with an intensity equal to the luminosity of 14 Moons. And for the other face, forever invisible, it is naturally 354 hours and one-third of absolute night; tempered only by the '*pale clarity of the glow of stars*'. This phenomena is unique in that the particular movements of rotation and revolution is accomplished in rigorously equal time, a phenomenon common, surmised Cassini and Herschel, to the satellites of Jupiter, and very probably to all other satellites as well.

Some spirits well-disposed, but slightly-dense, could not comprehend that the Moon maintained invariably the same face towards the Earth for each revolution, that is, the same space of time to make a tour around it. To those it was said: "Go into your dining room, and stride about your table in a manner which always faces to the center; when one full circular promenade has been achieved, your face has turned but once, and your eyes have managed successively to purvey all points within the room. Ah yes! Your room, that is the sky, your table, that is the Earth, and the Moon, that is you!" And always, one was enchanted by this comparison.

Thus the Moon unceasingly has one face towards the Earth; however, to be entirely exact, it must be added, by the continuance of a certain balancing oscillation of the north and south poles which is called '*libration*', from this we are able to see a little-more than half of the disk's surface, about 57% of its environment.

When the ignorant and the learned were as much aware as the director of the Cambridge Observatory of the rotational movement of the Moon, they were disquieted and worried by the movement of the revolution around the Earth. Twenty scientific reviews avidly gave their instruction. They drew attention at first the firmament, with its infinite stars, and to consider it like one vast dial which the Moon promenades along distinct hours to the view of the inhabitants of the Earth. It is this movement with which the Moon presents the different phases; that the Moon is full, when it is in opposition with the Sun, that is when the three bodies are in a direct line, the Earth is in the middle; and the Moon is new when it is in conjunction with the Sun, that is when between the Earth and Sun; and finally, that when the Moon is in its first or in its final quarter, it forms with the Sun and the Earth a right angle, occupying the summit.

Some perspicacious Yankees deduced the consequence of this; that the eclipses seen were produced only at times of conjunction or opposition, and with excellent reasoning. In conjunction, the Moon will eclipse the Sun and when in opposition, it is the Earth which eclipses the Moon; and these eclipses do not arrive at twice per lunar month- this is due to the perceived plane of the Moon being on an elliptical incline, that is to say, the plane which is seen from the perspective of our moving Earth.

As to the height which our lunar body can attain above the horizon, the letter from the Cambridge Observatory had spoken entirely in this regard. Everyone was aware that the height one could survey varied with the latitude of the observer's position. But in certain zones of the globe where the Moon passes zenith, this is when it is placed directly above the heads of those in contemplation, they are by necessity comprised between the area of the 28th parallel and the equator. It was this important recommendation to tender the experiment upon a point somewhere in that section of the globe, so that the projectile might be launched perpendicularly; and thereby most-easily escape the action of gravity. An essential condition for the success of the enterprise and a lively preoccupation for public opinion.

As for the line consistently followed by the Moon in its revolution around the Earth, the Cambridge Observatory had caused sufficient apprehension- even to the most ignorant of locals in all countries- that the curved line it follows is not a circle; but rather an ellipse, with the Earth occupying its focal-point. These elliptical orbits are common for all planets as well as all satellites, and the mechanical rationale of astrophysics rigorously proves it could be in no other way. And so the understanding was well-entertained that the Moon is at apogee when it is at the most-elongated point away from the Earth, and at its closest approach when in the perigee.

And there you have it! This was what every American knew by heart, like it or not; things which no one could have been decently ignorant of. But whilst these principles were disseminated with a vulgar rapidity- a quantity of errors, certain illusory fears, were not as easy to uproot.

Some brave gentlemen, by way of example, maintained the Moon was an ancient comet, which, in pursuit of its elongated orbit around the Sun had passed close to the Earth and became retained in a circle of attraction. The astronomers of the salon purported this explained the brutal aspect of the Moon, an irreparable insult provided by the Sun's radiant astral body. However, whenever those listening to such sorts of dialogue pointed out the observation that comets have an atmosphere, whereas the Moon has none; they were heavily-restrained from responding.

There were others that belonged to the race of tremblers, who manifested certain fears towards the Moon. They had heard of, due to the observations during the times of the Caliphs, that the movement of revolution had been accelerating in a certain proportion and deduced, quite logically, that the acceleration of the movement corresponded in a diminution of the distance between those two astral bodies of the Earth and Moon- and that, if this effect was continued *ad infinum*, the Moon would one day crash into the Earth. However during the reassurances provided in order to cease their fears for future generations, they were provided with the scientific calculations of Laplace, the illustrious French mathematician; which proved that the acceleration of movement is formed within very restrained limits, and that a proportionate diminution will soon afterwards succeed this effect. And thus so, the equilibrium of the solar system will never be deranged in the forthcoming centuries that are yet to occur.

Instating the rear-most place of the class of the superstitious were the ignorants; these are people not only content to be ignorant, they '*know*' things which are untrue, and they proposed a long list of ridiculous facts regarding the Moon. Some of these regarded our disk like a polished mirror with which they could see one another from diverse points upon the Earth and communicate their thoughts. And there were others who pretended that from out of a thousand new Moons observed, 950 had caused notable changes.

These were cataclysms, revolutions, earthquakes, deluges, etc.; and thus they understood a mysterious influence emerging from that luminescent body of our night sky fell upon the destinies of humanity; they regarded it to be a veritable '*counterpoint*' of our existence; and thought that every Selenite inhabitant of the Moon was attached to an inhabitant of the Earth in a sympathetic connection. They were in accordance with Dr. Mead, who maintained that our vital systems are entirely submissively-dependent upon the moon, stubbornly insisting that more boys were born during the new moon and that girls were born in the last quarter etc. etc. Finally they were forced to renounce these vulgar errors and revert to the only truth; which is that the Moon, deprived of its influence, diminished the spirit of certain courtesans of all their powers, to the fury of some but to whom the immense majority pronounced in favor of. As for the Yankees, their only ambition was to take possession of this new continent in the air and plant on its highest summit the star spangled banner of the United States.

7. The Hymn of the Cannon Ball

The Cambridge Observatory had in its memorable letter dated the 7th October treated the experimental question from an astronomical point of view. It waited now to be resolved mechanically. Practical difficulties which were in essence insurmountable for any but the Americans, here it was child's play.

The president Barbicane, without losing time, nominated from within the Gun Club an executive committee. The committee had after three meetings elucidated the three great questions of the cannon, the projectile and the explosive gunpowder. It was composed of four members highly knowledgeable in these matters: Barbicane, with the deciding vote in case of a deadlock, General Morgan, Major Elphiston, and finally the inevitable J.T.

Maston- also entrusted with the function of secretary-reporter i.e. taking minutes of their meetings.

The 8th October, the committee met at the house of president Barbicane, 3 Republican Street. Because it was important that the stomach did not trouble them with its cries during the serious discussion, the four members of the Gun Club had taken places at a table covered in sandwiches and considerably-sized teapots. As J.T. Maston fixed a pen into his iron hook, the meeting commenced.

Barbican began to speak:

"My dear colleagues, I say, together we must resolve the most important problems of ballistics, that excellent science which examines the traits of the movement of projectiles, or bodies launched into space with some kind of implosive force, and then abandoned to themselves."

"Oh! Ballistics! Ballistics!" cried J.T. Maston in an excited voice.

"Perhaps it would have been more logical," Barbicane continued, "to devote this first meeting to the discussion of the engine i.e. the cannon..."

"In effect, yes..." responded General Morgan.

"However," interjected Barbicane, "upon my reflections, it seemed to be the question of the projectile being detonated from the cannon, and it was these dimensions being derived which the dimensions of the other were dependent upon."

"I demand to speak," cried J.T. Maston.

Speech was accorded to him with all the dues earned by the impressive merit of his past magnificence.

"My brave friends," he said in an inspired tone, "it is most-proper our president has reasoned that we should attend to the question of the projectile before all others. The cannon ball we shall launch to the Moon; it is our messenger, our ambassador, and I demand your permission to examine it from a purely moral view."

This new method of envisaging a projectile singularly piqued the curiosity of the members of the committee and thereby they provided a lively sense of attention to the speech of J.T. Maston.

"My dear colleagues," continued the former, "I shall be brief; I discard the physical character of the cannon ball, the cannon ball that kills, so that we may envisage the cannon ball mathematically- the cannon ball's morality. The cannon ball is for me clearly the manifestation of humane power; it is this which summarizes it entirely; it was in this creation that man has most-closely approached the Creator!"

"Very well!" said Major Elphiston.

"In effect", cried the orator, "it was God who formed the stars and the planets, man formed the cannon ball, the criterion of earthly velocities; that reduction into a miniature version of stars moving in space, and which are, to speak truthfully, actually projectiles! To God the speed of electricity, the speed of light, the speed of stars, the speed of comets, the speed of planets, the speed of satellites, the speed of the sun and the speed of wind! But to us is the speed of the cannon ball, a force one hundred times superior and more rapid to the speed of trains and horses!"

J.T. Maston was transported, his voice pronounced lyrical accents as he sang this hymn of the sacred cannon ball.

"Do you want to hear the figures?" he continued, "And you shall have them most-elegantly! Consider simply the modest 24 pound cannon ball; it is short by 800,000 times the speed of electricity, 640,000 times less than the speed of light, 73 times less than the speed of the Earth's movement of translation around the Sun. However, at the outburst of a cannon, the speed of her projectile is faster than sound! Thus, if one has heard the sound of firing a cannon ball, they cannot have been struck by the projectile! It moves at 1,200 feet in a second, 12,000 feet in ten seconds, 14 miles in a minute, 840 miles in an hour, 20,100 miles per day- this is close to the velocity of a point at the equator during its movement of the globe's rotation- and 7,336,500 miles per year. At this speed therefore it would need 11 days to reach the Moon, 12 years to reach the Sun, and 360 years to attain Neptune at the limits of our solar system. And there you have but the modest cannon ball, the product of our hands! Ah, to imagine something with twenty times that velocity, fired with the rapidity of 7 miles per second! Ah! Cannon ball superb! Splendid projectile!- I believe when I consider that you shall be received with the highest honors as an ambassador of the Earth!"

Cheers of approval roared in unison and J.T. Maston, overcome emotionally, sat down amidst the congratulatory felicitations of his colleagues.

"I maintain," said Barbicane, "that now we have given such a large share to poetry, we may attack the question directly."

"We are now prepared," responded the members of the committee, each absorbed in beginning to eat their sixth sandwich.

"You are aware of the problem requiring resolution," replied the president. "That we must detonate a projectile with the velocity of 12,000 yards per second. I hereby believe that we shall succeed. But, for the moment, we should now examine the velocities obtained so far; General Morgan can provide us with an edification to that regard."

"Which I can do with great ease," responded the General, "since, during the war, I was a member of the experimental commission. I can tell you that the hundred pound cannons of Dahlgreen, which had a range of 3 miles, could impart onto a projectile the initial velocity of fifteen-hundred feet a second."

"Good. And the Columbiad Rodman?" demanded the president.

"The Columbiad Rodman, initially tested at Fort Hamilton, near to New York, launched a cannon ball almost half-a-ton to a distance of 6 miles, with a velocity of 800 yards per second; a result which has never been obtained by Armstrong and Paliser in England.

"Oh! The English!" said J.T. Maston, with his free hand brandishing that redoubtable hook of his towards the horizon.

"And so then," replied Barbicane, "this 800 yards was the maximum velocity attained thus far?"

"Yes," answered Morgan.

"I will mention, however," added J.T. Maston, "that if my own mortar had not burst..."

"Yes, but it did burst," responded Barbicane with a kindly gesture. "Let us take as our point of departure this velocity of 800 yards. We need to increase it fifteen-fold. Although, we shall reserve for another meeting the discussion how we will manage to produce this velocity, and I call for your attention, my dear colleagues, on the suitable dimensions we will give to the cannon ball. As you can well imagine, we won't be concerning ourselves with a projectile only weighing half a ton!

"And why is that?" asked the Major.

"That is because our cannon ball," responded the lively J.T. Maston, "must be big enough to attract the attention of the Moon's inhabitants, should there exist any."

"Yes," said Barbicane, "and also for another reason even more important."

"What are you saying, Barbicane?" the major demanded.

"What I mean to say is that it is insufficient to send a projectile and pay it no further attention; we must be able to watch it travel right until the moment when it attains its target."

"Hey!?" exclaimed the general and the major, in surprise at the proposition.

"Without doubt," replied Barbicane confidently, "without doubt, or our experiment will not produce any result."

"But then," reasoned the major, "you must send a projectile of enormous dimension?"

"No. Please listen well. You are aware that optical instruments have acquired a grand perfection; with certain telescopes they have managed already to obtain a magnification 6,000 times and reduce the Moon to 40 miles away. At such a distance, objects which are 60 feet wide are perfectly visible. It comes to pass that with any further penetrating power of telescopes, this additional power exercises a detriment to the clarity, and the Moon, which is a reflecting mirror, does not deliver a luminosity to provide a greater magnification- and that is the limit."

"Very well! And what shall we do?" asked the General. "Will you give the projectile a diameter of 60 feet?"

"Certainly not!"

"Will you, therefore, then attempt to render to Moon brighter?"

"Correct."

"That is a bold suggestion!" cried J.T. Maston.

"Yes, it is quite simple," Barbicane answered. "In effect, if I manage to diminish the density of atmosphere that the Moon's luminosity traverses through, then have I not rendered the luminosity more-intense?"

"Evidently."

"Very well! For us to obtain such a result, I intend to establish a telescope on a mountain's elevation. And that is what we shall do."

"I give up, I give up," surrendered the Major. "You have the facility of simplifying things. And what is the magnification you are expecting to obtain?"

"A magnification of 48,000 times; which will render the Moon a distance of 5 miles, and for objects to be visible they only need be 9 feet in diameter."

"Perfect!" exclaimed J.T. Maston, "So our projectile will therefore be 9 feet in diameter?"

"Precisely."

"Permit me to mention, however," interjected Major Elphiston, "that seems to be so quite a heavy weight, that..."

"Oh! Major," Barbicane responded quickly, "before we discuss the weight, allow me to say that our forefathers accomplished marvels in that area. I am far from suggesting that ballistics has not progressed, but in that era of early development, the Middle Ages, they obtained supreme results. I dare to say, results supreme even to ours."

"Give us an example!" requested Morgan.

"Justify what you have said," cried J.T. Maston in a vivacious manner.

"It is nothing very difficult to ascertain," responded Barbicane. "I give you these examples to support my proposition. For instance, in the siege of Constantinople by Mahomet II, in 1453, stone cannon balls were launched which weighed nineteen hundred pounds, and must have possessed an impressive size."

"Oh! Oh!" exclaimed the Major, "nineteen hundred pounds, that is a huge weight!"

"At Malta, in the days of chivalrous knights, a certain cannon in the Fort of Saint Elmo launched projectiles weighing twenty-five hundred pounds."

"Impossible!"

"And finally, according to a French historian during the period of Louis XI, a mortar launched a bomb that weighed 500 pounds only; but this bomb went from Bastille, where the insane imprisoned the sane, all the way to Charenton, where the sane imprisoned the insane."

"Very good!" said J.T. Maston.

"And since then, what have we done, essentially? The Armstrong cannons launch cannon balls 500 pounds, and the Columbiad Rodman projectiles of half-a-ton! It seems to me that what projectiles have gained in range, they have sacrificed in weight. If we turn our efforts towards the direction of weight we should arrive, with the progress of science, to cannon balls ten times the weight of those of Mahomet II and those knights of Malta."

"That is self-evident," replied the Major. "But what is the metal you intend to employ for the projectile?"

"It would be of cast iron, that much is simple," said General Morgan.

"Peuh! Cast Iron!" cried J.T. Maston in profound disdain. "That is too common for a cannon ball destined to reach the Moon!"

"No exaggerations please, my honorable friend," Morgan implored. "The cast iron will be sufficient."

"That is good! And then," said Major Elphiston, "since the weight is proportionate to the volume, and the cannon ball is iron, measuring 9 feet in diameter, that is an appallingly dreadful weight!"

"Yes, if it is solid; not if it is hollow," said Barbicane.

"Hollow! So it will be a shell?"

"And we can put dispatches in it," reasoned J.T. Maston, "with descriptions of our terrestrial productions!"

"Yes, a shell," responded Barbicane, "it absolutely must be so; a solid cannon ball of 9 feet would weigh 200,000 pounds, and that is evidentially a weight overly-considerable. However, since we must conserve a certain stability to our projectile, I propose that we give it a weight of 20,000 pounds."

"And what will be the thickness of its walls?" demanded the Major.

"If we use the regular proportions," replied Morgan, "a diameter of 9 feet will demand a thickness of the walls of 2 feet."

"That will be too excessive", said Barbicane. "Remember well, our cannon ball here is not destined to pierce armor; it is sufficient that it will be strong enough to resist the power of the gas from the gunpowder detonation. So there you have our problem: what thickness does our shell of cast iron require to weigh 20,000 pounds? Our skillful calculator, the brave Maston, can derive a tentative result for the purposes of this meeting."

"It is nothing at all difficult!" replied the honorable secretary of the committee.

And he began to write, tracing several formulas onto a piece of paper; on which occasionally appeared beneath his pen the symbols for *Pi* and *X* squared. He even gave the air, as a final touch, to extract a certain cube root, and then said:

"The walls would be 2 inches thick."

"You believe that is sufficient?" demanded the major with an air of doubt.

"No," responded Barbicane, "no, evidentially."

"Ah well! What will we do?" asked Elphiston in an embarrassed way.

"Employ a metal other than iron."

"Copper?" said Morgan.

"No, that is also too heavy and clumsy; I have something else to propose."

"And that is?" asked the Major.

"Aluminum," answered Barbicane.

"Aluminum!" exclaimed the three colleagues of the president in unison.

"Without any doubt, my friends. You will know of that illustrious French chemist, Henri Sainte-Claire-Deville, who succeeded in 1854, in obtaining aluminum in a compact mass. It is a precious metal that is as pale as silver, as unalterable as gold, as tenacious as iron, as fusible as copper and as light as glass; it is easily worked, extremely widespread in nature since alumina forms the basis of most rocks and three times less the weight of iron- and it seems to my view completely created to form the material of our projectile!"

"Hurrah for aluminum!" cried the secretary of the committee, always very noisesome during moments of enthusiasm.

"But, my dear president," said the major, "is not the price for extracting aluminum
extremely elevated?"

"It was," responded Barbicane, "at the premier time of its discovery, a pound of aluminum cost somewhere between $260 and $270; then it fell to $27, and now, finally, it is $9."

"But $9 a pound," replied the major, who did not render himself easily, "this is still an enormous price!"

"Without any doubt, my dear major, but it is not insurmountable."

"And then what would be the weight of the projectile?" asked Morgan.

"These are the results of my calculations", answered Barbicane. "A cannon ball of nine feet in diameter and walls of two inches thick, if it were of cast iron, would weigh 67,440 pounds- and cast from aluminum, the weight is expected to be reduced to 19,250 pounds."

"Perfect!" exclaimed Maston. "This will work for our program."

"Perfect! Perfect!" repeated the Major. "But are you aware, that at $9 per pound, the projectile will cost us..."

"$173,250, I am perfectly aware; but do not entertain worrying thoughts, my friends, there will be no shortage of money for our enterprise, rest assured."

"It will rain down in cashboxes," completed J.T. Maston.

"Well then! What are your thoughts about aluminum?" the president asked.

"Adopted," responded the three members of the committee.

"As to the form of the cannon ball," Barbicane continued, "the shape is not important, because, once it has passed the atmosphere, the projectile travels in a vacuum; so I propose the cannon ball to be round. It can turn about on itself, as it pleases, and comport itself according to its own desires."

Thus terminated the first meeting of the committee; the question of the projectile was definitively resolved, and J.T. Maston rejoiced heartily at the thought of sending a shell made from aluminum to the Selenites:

"It will give them an exemplary idea about the inhabitants of the Earth!"

8. The History of the Cannon

The resolutions taken by the committee meeting had a grand effect upon the outside world. Certain timid gentlemen were frightened by the idea of a cannon ball weighing 20,000 pounds launched onto the traverse of space. All demanded to know what cannon could transfer sufficient initial velocity to such a heavy mass. The process as verbally recorded in the minutes of the second meeting of the committee victoriously responded to these questions.

At the subsequent evening, the four members of the Gun Club were seated by the dining room table around new mountains of sandwiches and a veritable ocean of tea. The discussion immediately ran to the heart of the matter and, this time, without preamble.

"My dear colleagues," said Barbicane, "we must now occupy ourselves with the construction of the engine; that is its length, its shape, its composition and the weight. It is probable we will arrive at the position of having given it gigantic dimensions; yet however grand the difficulties will be, the careful genius of our industrial complex will facilitate reason. So therefore listen to me, and assail me with your pertaining objections- I do not fear them!"

Groans of approval ceded to this declaration.

"Do not forget," continued Barbicane, "the point of discussion which was our conduit to this moment. Now the problem presented is for us to decide upon the form and how to impart an initial velocity of 1,200 yards per second into a shell which is nine feet in diameter and weighs 20,000 pounds."

"And there you have our problem, in effect," responded Major Elphiston.

"I continue," replied Barbicane. "When a projectile is launched into space, what occurs? It is solicited by three independent forces; the resistance of its medium, the attraction of the Earth and the impulsive force that has animated it. Examine these three forces. The resistant medium, that is to say the resistance of the air, I imagine will be unimportant. In effect, the atmosphere of the Earth is about forty miles. And with the rapidity of 1,200 yards in a second, the projectile will traverse the firmament in 5 seconds- the time taken to form resistance in this medium can be regarded as insignificant.

"Next we arrive at the attraction of the Earth, that is to say the force of gravity acting upon the shell. Now we know by reasoning that gravity will diminish in an inverse square to the distance; in effect, that is what our physics apprehends. When a body is abandoned and left to fall towards the Earth, this plunges 15 feet for the first second; although if this body is transported 257,542 miles, on the other hand, and that is the distance to the Moon, this descent is reduced to a twentieth of an inch in the first second. It is nearly immobile. So, therefore, progressively vanquish this action of gravity. How do you say we shall manage this? By the propulsion of its implosive force."

"There is the difficulty," commented the Major.

"And there it is, in effect," agreed the president. "But we will be triumphant; for the force of implosion will by necessity be the result of the length of that engine, that is to say, our cannon, and the quantity of gunpowder employed. And so the extent is limited only by the resistant strength of our cannon. Therefore we may now occupy ourselves with the dimensions that we shall give to the cannon. We may well extend the limits of power to establish the conditions of resistance unto infinity, and that is because it is destined to never be maneuvered from where it is built."

"It is entirely evident," responded the general.

"As it is," continued Barbicane, "the longest of cannons, the enormous Columbiads, do not surpass twenty-five feet in length; we will then greatly astonish a good many people by the dimensions I imagine we shall be forced to adopt."

"Eh! Without any doubt," J.T. Maston cried aloud. "For my reckoning, I demand a cannon half a mile in length!"

"A half mile!" exclaimed the Major and the General.

"Yes! A half mile, and even that will be half-ways too short."

"Come along, Maston," chided Morgan. "You exaggerate."

"No I do not!" retorted the heatedly-ebullient secretary. "And I do not really know why you tax me with these claims of exaggeration."

"I make these claims because you are going too far!"

"Now see here, sir," responded J.T. Maston, assuming a grand air of deportment. "See that an artilleryman is like a cannon ball, he cannot go too far!"

The discussion had turned personal, but the president intervened.

"Be calm, my friends, and reasonable. It is factually evident our cannon will make a grand volley, and the piece must be long enough to detain the gas accumulated in order to power the projectile, but it is intuitive that it cannot pass beyond certain limits."

"Perfect," said the Major.

"And what are the regulations used in parallel cases? Ordinarily the length of a cannon is twenty to twenty-five times the diameter of the cannon ball, and is as heavy as two hundred and thirty-five or two hundred and forty times its weight."

"That is not sufficient," cried J.T. Maston impetuously.

"I concur, my dignified friend and in effect, in consideration of its proportion- for a projectile 9 feet in diameter weighing 20,000 pounds, the engine naturally would be no longer than 225 feet and only weigh 4,800,000 pounds."

"That is ridiculous," countered J.T. Maston. "As much use as a pistol!"

"I think this also," agreed Barbicane, "which is why I propose we quadruple the length of construction of the cannon to 900 feet."

The General and the Major fired many objections; but nevertheless the proposition, vividly supported by the secretary of the Gun Club, was definitively adopted.

"Now," said Elphiston, "as to the thickness we shall give to the walls."

"A thickness of 6 feet," answered Barbicane.

"You have imagined, no doubt, how to pull such a mass around?" asked the Major.

"It will surely be superb!" exclaimed J.T. Maston.

"But impractical," responded Barbicane. "No, I envisage that we cast the engine in the ground right there, fretted with reinforcing bands of iron, and finally we place around it massive masonry of stone and lime. This will incorporate the Earth's terrain into the overall resistance. When the piece is cast it's going to be carefully aligned and calibrated and in this manner we will prevent both the venting of the cannon ball as well as prevent the dispersion of the gas; thereby all the force of expansion from the powder should be employed towards the implosion."

"Hurrah! Hurrah!" yelled J.T. Maston "Now that is our cannon!"

"Please wait," Barbicane entreated with a calming hand his impatient friend.

"And why?"

"Because we have not discussed its form. Do you think it should be a cannon, a howitzer or a mortar?"

"A cannon," replied the Major.

"A howitzer," responded the General.

"A mortar!" cried J.T. Maston.

A new discussion was about to be engaged, with each predisposed towards his favorite armament, when the president arrested their thoughts.

"I say, my friends, that we shall all meet in accordance; our Columbiad will be all three of these elements in one. It will be a cannon, as the chamber will have the same power as the diameter of its shot. It will be a howitzer, because it will launch a shell. Finally, it will be a mortar, as it will be aimed at an angle of 90° and without as much as possible any recoil, steadfastly unwavering fixed into the soil, it will communicate to the projectile all the power of the implosion accumulated at its flanks."

"Adopted, adopted," replied the members of the committee unanimously.

"One simple reflection," said Elphiston. "Should the cannon-howitzer-mortar have a rifled bore?"

"No," answered Barbicane. "No; we need an enormous initial velocity, and you are aware that a cannon ball is less-rapid from a rifled cannon than from a smooth bore."

"Just so."

"And finally, now we have it- in faith!" said J.T. Maston, repeating his earlier sentiments.

"Although there is still more," replied the president.

"And why?"

"Because we do not know the sort of metal it will be made from."

"Decide now without delay."

"That is what I propose."

And the four members of the committee availed themselves upon a dozen sandwiches, with a correspondingly large bowl of tea, before recommencing the discussion.

"My brave colleagues," said Barbicane, "our cannon must be of great tenacious strength, great durability, infusible to heat, and insoluble and anti-oxidizing to the corrosive action of acids."

"There is no doubt in that regard," agreed the Major. "And when casting such a considerable quantity of metal, we do not have a lot of choice."

"Ah well! There you are," said Morgan. "I propose for the fabrication of the Columbiad the best alloy known thus far; that is one hundred parts copper, twelve parts tin and six parts brass."

"My friends," responded the president, "I avow that this composition gives us excellent results; but, in this situation, it would be very expensive and difficult for us to employ. I think therefore we should adopt an excellent material, but one which has a low price; and that appears to be iron. Do you agree with this, Major?"

"Perfectly," replied Elphiston.

"In effect," continued Barbicane, "cast iron is ten times less than the cost of bronze, it is easily cast in molds of sand, it allows for rapid manipulation; and hence it is as economic for the monetary expense as it is for time. Additionally, the material is excellent; and I recall that during the war, in the siege of Atlanta, there were cast iron pieces that fired a thousand shots 20 minutes after 20 minutes, without suffering.

"However, cast iron is very brittle," Morgan countered.

"Yes, and very resistant also, so that we know it will not burst when it responds."

"A small bursting is no dishonor," pronounced J.T. Maston sententiously.

"Evidentially," agreed Barbicane. "I henceforth pray for our dignified secretary to calculate the weight of a cannon of cast iron 900 feet in length, with an interior diameter of 9 feet, with walls 6 feet thick."

"In an instant," responded J.T. Maston.

And, just as he had done the evening before, aligning formulas with a marvelous facility, he said after one minute:

"The cannon will weigh 68,040 tons."

"And at two cents a pound, it will cost... ?"

"$2,721,600."

J.T. Maston, the Major and the General regarded Barbicane with an air of worry.

"Ah, very well, sirs," said the president. "I shall repeat what I had said yester-evening, remain tranquil, these millions will not be lacking to us!"

On that assurance from the president, the committee separated, with vows to meet again the following evening.

9. The Question of Powder

The question of powders remained to be treated. The public attended with anxiety for the final decision. The size of the projectile and the length of the cannon now established, what would be the quantity of powder necessary to produce the implosion? That terrible agent, of which however man had mastered its effects, would call into play unaccountable proportions of to fulfill its role.

It is generally understood and readily repeated that gunpowder was invented in the 14th Century by the monk Schwartz, who paid with his life for this grand discovery. But it is certainly proven now that this certain history belongs in the realm of medieval legend. Gunpowder was invented by no personality; it was derived directly from Greek fire, composed like it of sulfur and saltpeter. Only that, during our epoch, this mixture, which had been a mixture of deflagration transformed into a mixture of explosive detonation.

But whilst the erudite learned are perfectly familiar with the false history of powder, there are few gentlemen who have rendered complete their understanding of its mechanical power. And this fact must be recognized to comprehend the importance of the question submitted to the committee.

By this fashion a liter of gunpowder weighs 2 pounds; it produces when made flammable 400 liters of gas, and when this gas is rendered liberated the action of this produces a temperature of 2,400°; occupying a space of 4,000 liters. Thus the volume of powder to the gas it produces by deflagration is four thousand to one. And one is able to judge the frightening power that this gas can produce when it is confined in a space four thousand times too small for it.

This was perfectly understood by the members of the committee prior to when they began their third meeting. Barbicane gave the opening speech to Major Elphiston, who had been the director of Gunpowders during the war.

"My dear comrades," said the distinguished chemist, "I will commence with indisputable figures that will serve as our base. The cannon ball of 24 pounds, as mentioned the night before yesterday by the honorable J.T. Maston in such poetic terms, for shooting requires but 16 pounds of powder only."

"Are you entirely certain of that figure?" questioned Barbicane.

"Absolutely certain," replied the Major. "The Armstrong cannon utilizes just 75 pounds of powder for a projectile of 800 pounds, and the Rodman Columbiad dispenses 160 pounds of powder to send 6 miles a cannon ball weighing half-a-ton. These facts are entirely evident and without doubt, for I personally recovered them from the reports of the Artillery Committee.

"Perfect," the general responded.

"Ah, very well!" continued the major. "And that is the consequence of these recorded numerical figures, which is to say the quantity of powder is augmented by the weight of the cannon ball. In effect, 16 pounds of powder for a cannon ball of 24; or in other terms, then, in an ordinary cannon, it employs a quantity of powder two-thirds the weight of the projectile, but these proportions are not constant. Calculating, in this way, for a cannon ball of half-a-ton, this would require 667 pounds of powder, but this quantity is reduced to 160 pounds only."

"What are you trying to infer?" demanded the president.

"If you carry your theory to extremes, my dear Major," said J.T. Maston, "you arrive eventually then to a cannon ball which, if it has a sufficient load, does not require any powder at all."

"My friend Maston, you frolic with playfulness amidst serious things," replied the Major jovially, "but let me reassure you; I shall soon propose quantities of powder to satisfy the true love of an artilleryman. In the maintained certified reports, during the war, it is stated that for the largest cannons the weight per pound was reduced, after experience, to a tenth the weight of the cannon ball."

"Nothing is so exact," said Morgan. "But when we decided the quantity of pounds necessary to give us the implosive detonation, we needed to consider the implicit natures of the different kinds of gunpowder to use."

"We shall employ the coarse-grained gunpowder," declared the Major. "It's deflagration is much faster than fine-grained powder."

"Without doubt," replied Morgan, "but it has a very high brisance and it will eventually deform the cannon's pieces."

"Correct! And this is quite inconvenient for a cannon destined for long service but not for our Columbiad. We run no danger of explosions, and our powder must ignite instantly for its energetic effect to be completely utilized."

"For power," said J.T. Maston "we could penetrate multiple priming holes, and light the different points all at once."

"Without doubt," responded Elphiston, "but this renders the maneuver more difficult. I return, therefore, to coarse-grained gunpowder, which cancels away these difficulties."

"So be it," concluded the general.

"For charging his Columbiad," continued the major, "Rodman employed a powder with grains the size of chestnuts, that used charcoal from a willow tree simply roasted in a foundry. This powder was hard and shiny, no trace of it remained on the hands, included a great proportion of hydrogen and oxygen, ignited instantly and, although very brisant, there was no noticeable deterioration on the gun barrels."

"Very well! It appears to me," responded J.T. Maston, "there is no need to hesitate, our choice is entirely clear."

"Unless that is you prefer powder made from gold," the Major responded, laughing, and this earned him a menacing gesture from the hook of his susceptible friend.

At this stage Barbicane had remained outside the discussion. Refraining from speaking, he had listened. It was evident he had an idea. Then he was content to say simply:

"Now, my friends, what quantity of powder do you propose?"

The three members of the Gun Club regarded one another for a moment.

"200,000 pounds," said Morgan finally.

"500,000," countered the Major.

"800,000!" cried J.T. Maston.

The time, Elphiston could not accuse his colleague of exaggeration. In effect, they were conspiring to send to the Moon a projectile weighing 20,000 pounds and to impart it with an initial force of 12,000 miles per second. A moment of silence followed after the triplicated propositions that had been suggested by the three colleagues.

It was finally intruded upon by the president Barbicane.

"My brave comrades," he said with a tranquil voice, "I begin with the principle that the resistance of our cannon will be constructed under the conditions that its volume is unlimited. I am therefore going to surprise the honorable J.T. Maston when I say that he was timid in his calculations, and I propose we double his 800,000 pounds."

"1,600,000 pounds?" exclaimed J.T. Maston, leaping from his chair.

"Completely."

"But then we return to casting my cannon that is half a mile long."

"That is evident," said the Major.

"1,600,000 pounds of powder," replied the secretary of the committee, "will occupy a surrounding space of 22,000 cubic feet, or, as your cannon has the capacity of 54,000 cubic feet, this implies it will be half-full; and there is no way that is long enough to detain the gas in order to prime the projectile with sufficient implosion."

There was nothing for anyone to respond with to what J.T. Maston had said. They all regarded Barbicane.

"However," said the president, "I maintain that quantity of powder. Consider it, 1,600,000 pounds of powder giving birth to 6,000,000 liters of gas. Six million! Do you understand well-enough?"

"But how can we accomplish this?" asked the general.

"It is very simple; we reduce that enormous quantity of powder whilst conserving the same output of power."

"Yes! But how shall we do that?"

"I shall tell you," Barbicane responded simply.

The interlocutors devoured him with their eyes.

"Nothing is more simple, in effect," he continued. "We considerably reduce the mass of powder in volume by four times. You will know of that curious material constituted by elements of vegetable tissues, which is called cellulose?"

"Ah!" said the Major, "I understand you, my friend Barbicane."

"This material," said the president, "is obtained in a state of perfect purity from diverse sources, and especially cotton, that is the fiber surrounding the seeds of cotton. When the cotton is combined with cold nitric acid it is transformed into a substance entirely insoluble, eminently combustible and eminently explosive. It was some years ago, in 1832, that the French chemist Braconnot discovered this substance, which he called xyloidine. In 1838, another Frenchman, Pelouze, began to study its diverse properties; and finally, in 1846, Shonbein, Professor of Chemistry of Basel, proposed its use as a gunpowder. That powder is known as guncotton..."

"Or proxylin," added the Major.

"Or nitrocellulose," completed the general.

"Wasn't there at least one American involved in this discovery?" questioned J.T. Maston, who was possessed with the sentiment of national pride.

"There was none, unfortunately," replied the Major.

"Howsoever, for the satisfaction of Maston," the president told them, "I'll let you know that it was the work of one of our citizens who discovered an important aspect of cellulose and that is collodion, which is the principle agent in photography. It is simply pyroxylin dissolved in ether and alcohol; and it was discovered by Maynard, who was a student of medicine at Boston.

"That is good! Hurrah for Maynard and for guncotton!" cried the ebullient secretary of the Gun Club.

"I return to guncotton," continued Barbicane. "You all know of its properties which render it precious to us, and it is prepared most easily; the cotton is plunged into nitric acid for a period of fifteen minutes, and then rinsed with water, left to dry. There you have it in its entirety."

"Nothing is more simple, in effect," said Morgan.

"Additionally, guncotton is unaffected by humidity, a precious quality for us, because it will take several days for us to charge the cannon. It is flammable at 160° centigrade instead of 240°, and ignites so suddenly, that if it is set fire to on top of ordinary gunpowder there is no time for the more-irreducible substance to catch on fire."

"Perfect," responded the Major.

"It is only that it is very expensive."

"Is that important?" questioned J.T. Maston.

"Finally it transmits into projectiles a superior velocity that is four times greater than gunpowder. In addition, if it is mixed with 80% of its weight in potassium nitrate, that augments the expansive power to an even greater capacity."

"You imagine that is necessary?" asked the Major.

"I do not think so," said Barbicane. "And so therefore, in lieu of 1,600,000 pounds, we shall have only 400,000 pounds of guncotton; and because there is no danger in compressing 500 pounds of guncotton into 27 cubic feet, the material will only occupy up to 180 feet of our Columbiad. And so in that fashion, the cannon ball will pass through 700 feet of the bore with the effort of 6,000,000 liters of gas; before sending it on towards the Moon, that shining astral body of the night sky!"

At this point in time J.T. Maston could contain his emotions no further; he threw his arms around his friend with the violence of a projectile, and Barbicane would have been without defence, had not he himself been built with the strength to withstand such a bomb.

This incident terminated the third meeting of the Committee. Barbicane and his audacious colleagues, to whom nothing seemed impossible, had effectively resolved the complex questions of the projectile, the cannon and the powder. Their plans were complete and they were now required to execute them.

"A simple detail, a trifle," dismissed J.T. Maston with a wave of that iron hook.

10. One Enemy Amongst Twenty-Five Million Friends

The American public took a powerful interest in the smallest details of the enterprise of the Gun Club. The discussions of the Committee were followed day by day. The most simple preparations for the grand experiment, the questions of the numerical figures which had been solved, the mechanical difficulties to resolve, in a word the entire operation, was attended to with a passion of the highest degree.

More than a year would carefully pass between the commencement of work and its concluding achievement, but that period would not be devoid of the vivid emotions. The place to be chosen for the casting, the construction of the mold, the casting of the Columbiad, the highly-perilous charging of its guncotton; these facts alone were enough to excite the curiosity of the public. The projectile, when launched, would escape from view in a few tenths of a second. Then as it continued, comporting itself into space, would finally attain the Moon and only be a small number of privileged souls would be able to verify this with their own eyes. And so the preparatory experience, the precise details of execution, constituted most of the veritable interest.

However, added to the purely scientific elements of the enterprise was an exciting incident.

We have seen the several numerous legions of admirers and friends that rallied to Barbicane's project. Yet, as honorable and as extraordinary as they were, this majority was not entirely unanimous. There was one man, one man only in all of the United States, who protested the tentative efforts of the Gun Club; he attacked with violence, at every occasion chance offered; and it is the nature of fate that Barbicane was more sensitive to that single opposition than to the applause from all the others.

Regardless, he knew well the motive of antipathy, that source of solitary enmity. Why it was personal and from an ancient date and, finally, the haughty pride of rivalry which had brought about its origin.

Of that persevering enemy, the president of the Gun Club had never set his eyes upon. Fortunately, for such an encounter between the two men would have certainly entailed regrettable consequences. That rival was a scientist like Barbicane; a fiery-natured, audacious, charismatic, violent, pure Yankee. His name was Captain Nicholl. He resided in Philadelphia.

People are not ignorant of that curiously established opposition during the Civil War between the artillery projectile and naval armor; with the former destined to pierce the latter, and the latter deciding to deflect its piercing lances. This led to a radical transformation in the navies of the both states. The cannon ball and the plate armor struggled with exemplary fierce determination. As the projectile grew bigger, the thickness of protecting walls responded in constant proportion. Naval ships, armed with formidable pieces, marched into firing positions with their invulnerable iron plated carapace shells. The *Merrimac*, the *Monitor*, the *Ram-Tennessee*, the *Weehawken* launched enormous projectiles, yet the battleships were protected from the projectiles of the other. They did violence unto the other which they would not have done unto themselves, an immoral principle on which rests entirely the art of war.

You see, Barbicane was a grand founder of projectiles, Nicholl was a grand forger of armor plates. One cast artillery pieces night and day in Baltimore, the other forged protective covers day and night. Each pursued a core idea that was essentially countervailing.

As soon as Barbicane invented a new cannon ball, Nicholl invented new plate armor. The president of the Gun Club pursued a life of penetrating holes, the captain in preventing him. So this rivalry was an instant juxtaposition of the two personalities. Nicholl was an apparition in the reveries of Barbicane taking the form of an impenetrable battleship which he broke against violently; and Barbicane, in the dreams of Nicholl, was a projectile that pierced him into half and half.

Certainly, as they eagerly followed these two divergent lines these scientists were assured to finally encounter one another despite all the axioms of geometry; but it would have occurred as a duel on the field of honor. Quite fortunately for these citizens, so useful to their country, a distance between fifty and sixty miles separated the two; and their friends harassed the route between them with so many obstacles that the one never saw the other.

Now, which of the inventors had apported themselves over the other, no one was quite sure; the results obtained made it difficult to form a just appreciation. It did seem, however, in the final competition that the armored battleship would eventually cede to the cannon ball.

Nevertheless, there was some doubt amongst competent men. In a recent experiment the cylindro-conical projectiles of Barbicane had fired against and been stuck like pins within the armor plates of Nicholl; the forger from Philadelphia had proclaimed victory with merciless contempt towards his rival; but when the conical cannon balls were replaced with standard six hundred pound shells, the captain was rebutted. In effect these projectiles, although animated by a mediocre velocity, exploded and shattered; firing volleys and turning the best of quality metal plates into pieces.

So, things had attained this point where victory seemed to have rested with the cannon ball, when the war finished on the very day Nicholl had completed the forging of a new armored battleship. This was a masterpiece within the genre; it defied all the projectiles in the world. The captain had transported the polygon to Washington, and provoked the president of the Gun Club to fire upon her. Barbicane, now that peace had been established, was uninterested in the experiment.

It followed that Captain Nicholl, furious, offered to expose his plated armor to every kind of cannon ball imaginable; solid, hollow, round or conical. This was refused by the president, who had decided not to jeopardize his most-recent successes.

Nicholl, excited into an even more unqualified rage, intentionally tempting Barbicane with every chance. He proposed to stand the armored plates at two hundred yards from the cannons. Barbicane obstinately refused. A hundred yards? Not even at seventy-five.

"At fifty yards then," cried the captain through the voice of newspapers. "My armor at twenty-five yards, and I will stand behind it!"

Barbicane had replied in answer, that even if Captain Nicholls were standing before it, he would not fire a shot.

Nicholl, when receiving this reply, could not contain himself; things then took a personal air; he insinuated that this cowardice was indivisible, and the man who refused to fire a cannon was scared to do so; that the artillerymen who went to battle at a distance of six miles had prudently replaced individual courage with mathematical formulas, and, furthermore, it took bravery to attend tranquilly behind an armored plate before cannon balls. So much so that this should be regarded as a form of art.

To these insults Barbicane responded with nothing. He may not even have been aware of them, being so carried away by the calculations of the grand enterprise they were undertaking that he was entirely absorbed.

With that famous communication of the Gun Club, the anger of Captain Nicholl evolved into a fit of paroxysm. Within him was a melee of jealousy and the sentiment of absolute impotence! How could anyone have invented something better than the Columbiad of nine hundred feet! What armored battleship could resist the power of twenty thousand pounds! Nicholl, for all that, was appalled, overwhelmed, bristling at this "coup of the cannon" he could not withstand and then later resolved to crush the proposition of by weight of his arguments.

Hence he attacked very violently the work of the Gun Club; he published a number of letters which the newspapers did not refuse to reproduce. He essayed to scientifically demolish the works of Barbicane. And once the war was openly proclaimed, he appealed to reasons of every order and, it must be said, often resorted to arguments that were specious and ill-mannered.

To begin with- Barbicane was violently attacked on his numerical figures. Nicholl attempted to prove that A+B were falsehoods of formulae, and accused him of being ignorant of the rudimentary principles of ballistics. Among other errors, when he saw the calculations were in-place, Nicholl maintained it was impossible to prime an object anywhere near the velocity of twelve hundred yards per second; it withstood that, with algebra on-hand, even with such velocity a projectile so heavy could not escape the Earth's atmosphere! It would return before it had reached twenty miles!

But there was more. In regards to the velocity acquired, for this to hold sufficiently. The shell was unable to resist the pressure of gas which would develop on the combustion of 1,600,000 pounds of powder. And could it even resist that pressure, there was no way to endure such an unparalleled temperature; it would melt as it exited the Columbiad and fall down as molten rain onto the heads of the imprudent spectators.

Barbicane, at these attacks, remained supercilious and continued at his work.

Next, Nicholl approached the question from a different aspect. Without discussing the uselessness of the project from every point of view, he regarded the experiment as extremely dangerous for the citizens who authorized the presence of this condemnable spectacle, and for the towns nearby to that deplorable cannon. He then remarked equally that if the projectile failed to attain its mark, as a successful result which was absolutely impossible, it would evidentially tumble back towards the Earth and plunge with the same mass, multiplied by the square of its velocity, and comporting serious damage onto some point of the globe. Hence, in these circumstances, for the attention and safety of all liberal citizens, the direct intervention of the government was necessary- in order to prevent the dangerous engagement surely being posed against all for the pleasure of one soul.

To such levels of exaggeration Captain Nicholls was driven. There was not another soul who entertained these opinions. No person regarded these prophecies of malcontent. Hence he cried to himself, becoming hoarse of voice, which was convenient. He had attempted to defend a cause which fatally had already been forsaken; for his ideas were entertained, but unheeded, it did not move one single soul away from their admiration towards the president of the Gun Club. So you see, in response, there was no need for Barbicane to offer one retort against the arguments of his rival.

Nicholl, acutely aware of being in the rearmost of his entrenchments, and without the power to offer his own life towards the cause, resolved to risk his own money. He openly proclaimed through the publication known as *The Richmond Enquirer* a serious wager, a proposition according to the following proportions:

1 - That the funds necessary for the Gun Club's enterprise could not be met... $1,000.

2 - That the operation of casting a 900 foot cannon was impracticable and would not succeed... $2,000.

3 - That it was not possible to charge the Columbiad, and the guncotton would be prematurely ignited by the pressure of the projectile... $3,000.

4 - That the Columbiad cannon would burst on its first firing... $4,000.

5 - That the cannon ball could not attain a height of six miles and would tumble back to the Earth within seconds of being fired... $5,000.

This was quite an important sum being risked by the captain in his unyielding fury. It came to an amount of $15,000!

Despite the magnitude of the sum being offered, on 19th May, he received in a folded envelope a superb laconism which concluded the wager in these terms:

Baltimore, 18 October.

Accepted.

BARBICANE.

11. Florida and Texas

However one question still remained to be decided: they must choose a favorable location for the experiment. Considering the recommendation from the Cambridge Observatory, the firing of the projectile had to be perpendicular to the plane of the horizon; that is to say, aimed towards the zenith- and so the Moon would only mount the zenith at places situated between 0° and 28° in latitude. To put this into other terms, its declination is not more than 28°. Hence it was required to determine exactly the point on the globe where to cast the immense Columbiad cannon.

On the 20th October the Gun Club held a general meeting. Barbicane brought along with him a magnificent map of the United States drawn by Z. Belltropp. But before he had time to deploy this cartographic work, J.T. Maston demanded to speak with his habitual vehemence and he spoke in these terms:

"Honorable colleagues, the question put before us is of veritable national importance, and it is the occasion for a grand act of patriotism."

The members of the Gun Club regarded him without comprehending what the orator was intending to say.

"There are none of you," he continued, "who would ever consider transgressing the glory of our country. It is an adroit question for the Union to importantly claim, and it is only right that it receives, the flanks of this formidable cannon of the Gun Club. Now, under these present circumstances..."

"Brave Maston..." said the president, interceding.

"Permit me to develop my thoughts!" silenced the orator. "In these actual circumstances, we are forced to choose a place that approaches near to the equator, for the experiment to have the right conditions..."

"Would you kindly please..." interjected Barbicane forcefully.

"I demand a liberal discussion of these ideas!" replied the ebullient J.T. Maston, "And I maintain the territory from which to launch our glorious projectile must be a part of the Union."

"Without any doubt!" responded several members.

"Ah well! Since our borders aren't sufficiently extended, since the opposing Southern Ocean presents an insuperable barrier, and since we must search beyond the limits of the United States for the 28th parallel it becomes the legitimate cause for an act of war- so I demand we declare was on the Mexicans!"

"But no! But no!" were the cries made from all parts of the hall.

"No!" replied J.T. Maston. "There is a word I never thought would be entertained within these walls!"

"But listen here!...."

"Never! Never!" cried the rogue orator. "Sooner or later that war will be fought, and I demand we declare it on this very day."

"Maston," said Barbicane and a fracas was detonated by the meeting bell. "You are retired from your speech!"

Maston volunteered a reply, but some of his colleagues succeeded in constraining him.

"I convene with the honorable J.T. Maston," said Barbicane, "the experiment must only be attempted on the soil of the Union. However if my impatient friend would allow me to speak, if he had cast his eyes upon this map, he would perfectly understand intuitively there is no need to declare war on our neighboring countries, because certain frontiers of the United States extend beyond the 28th parallel. Look, as you can see from the chart we have at our disposal all the meridional part of Texas and Florida."

The incident was put to rest, but it was not without regret that J.T. Maston allowed himself to be convinced. Hence it was decided that the Columbiad be cast somewhere in the soils of Texas, or in the soils of Florida. But this decision would create a rivalry that was without example between those two grand cities of the United States.

The 28th parallel, when it reconnoiters with the American coast, traverses the peninsula of Florida and divides it into two parts that are almost equal. Then it jettisons into the Gulf of Mexico; tending below an arc formed by the coastlines of Alabama, Mississippi, and Louisiana, adjuncts with Texas, turning at an angle prolongs its traverse into Mexico, reaching Sonora and connecting with the land of California before perishing into the Pacific Ocean. It was, therefore, only those portions of Texas and those of Florida situated below that parallel, which served to fulfill the conditions of latitude recommended by the Cambridge Observatory.

Florida, in its meridian parts, had no cities of importance. There were only forts there which had been erected to control errant Indians. Only one sole city, Tampa Town, possessed any claim in favor of its situation to be able to present itself forward.

In Texas, on the contrary, the cities were more numerous and more important. Corpus Christi, in the Nueces County, and all the cities situated on the Rio Bravo, Laredo, Comalites, San Ignacio in Webb County, Roma and Rio Grande City in Starr County, Edinburgh in Hidalgo County and Santa Rita, El Panda, and Brownsville in Cameron County formed an imposing league countering the pretentions of Florida.

Once the Gun Club's determination had been communicated, Texan and Floridian delegates arrived in Baltimore in great bodies and commencing from that moment onwards, the president Barbicane and influential members of the Gun Club were besieged day and night with their formidable claims. Seven cities of Greece had disputed for the honor of claiming Homer's birthright, now two states of the new world menaced one another and threated to come to blows over a cannon.

So it came to pass that these ferocious brothers armed and promenaded themselves throughout the streets of the town. Every time they saw one another some conflict was feared that would lead to disastrous consequences. Fortunately, the prudence and adroit skill of president Barbicane averted this danger. The personal demonstrations of feelings were given an outlet in the diverse journals and newspapers throughout the United States. As an example, the *New York Herald* and the *Tribune* supported Texas, whereas *The Times* and *The American Review* preferred to fight the cause for the Floridian delegates. The members of the Gun Club were not sure who to listen to.

Texas was proud with its 26 counties, these resembled lines of battery in a battle array; but Florida responded that its 12 counties were more powerful than those 26, since the size of their country was six times smaller.

Texas boasted strongly about their 330,000 indigenous citizens; but Florida, less vast, spoke proudly of their population of 56,000. They further accused Texas of possessing the specialty of malarial fevers which had cost, in one evil year, many thousands of their inhabitants. And this was entirely true.

In retort, Texas replied that when it came to fevers Florida was second to none; and that it was imprudent of them to accuse other places of unhealthy maladies, when it had the honor of possessing a chronic state of fever not long in the past. And that also stood to reason.

"Besides," added the Texans via the organ of the *New York Herald*, "it is in consideration of a state who produces the best cotton in all of America, a state who produces the highest premium quality of oak for naval construction, a state which contains the most superb quantities of coal and iron mines which render their ore at 50% pure mineral."

And *The American Review* responded that the soil of Florida, whilst not as rich, offered the suitable conditions for molding and forging the Columbiad, as it was composed of sand and earthen clay.

"But," replied the Texans, "before you cast in the soil of a country, you need to arrive in that country first. Plus, the communications with Florida are quite difficult, whereas the coast of Texas offers Galveston Bay; which has 35 miles of coastline and the size to hold all the flotillas of the world entirely."

"Good!" retorted the newspapers devoted to Florida, "There will be none of us going to the beautiful Bay of Galveston, as it is situated above the twenty-ninth parallel. Do you know of the Bay of Espiritu-Santo, which opens precisely on the twenty-eighth degree of latitude, and where the ships arrive directly at Tampa Town?"

"A jolly bay!" Texas responded. "It is half silted-up!"

"Silted-up just as you are!" cried Florida. "Are you saying that we are a country of savages?"

[see introductory comments*]

"But it is true, the Seminoles roam across your prairies!"

"Ah well! And your Apaches and Comanche are so civilized!"

The war had maintained itself for several days when Florida attempted to entrain their adversary on another terrain, and one morning the Times insinuated that, as the enterprise was essentially American, it should be performed in a territory that was essentially American!

And in the words of one Texan bandit: "Americans!" they cried. "Are we not just as American as you? Texas and Florida were both incorporated into the Union on the same year: 1845!"

"Without doubt," responded the Times. "But we were apportioned to America in 1820."

"Yes, I believe that is so," replied the Tribune. "After being Spanish or English for two hundred years, when you were then sold to the United States for $5,000,000!"

"Of what importance?" answered the Floridians. "Should that make us blush? Was it not, in 1803, all the land in the Louisiana Purchase was bought from Napoleon for only $15,000,000?"

"It is a shame!" cried loudly the delegates of Texas. "A miserable morsel of land like Florida to dare compare itself to Texas, who instead of acting like a vendor, founded its independence by itself, when it chased away the Mexicans on 2nd March 1836- when it declared itself a federal republic after victory delivered by Samuel Houston on the banks of the San Jacinto over the troops of Santa Anna! A land which voluntarily joined to the United States of America!"

"Which was due to their fear of the Mexicans!" responded Florida.

Fear! On the day that word, really too lively, had been uttered the situation devolved into becoming intolerable. It was expected of the two parties to begin cutting one another's throats on the streets of Baltimore. The authorities were obliged to keep an eye on the delegates at all times.

The president Barbicane was about to lose his mind. The notes, the documents, the letters threatening menace were filling his house. And what would be his decision? From the point of view as the most-appropriate soil, the ease of communications, and the rapidity of transport, the two states were veritably equal. As for the political personalities, this was not relevant to the question.

So, this hesitation, this obstacle continued for a long duration of time. When Barbicane resolved to put it to an end, he called for a reunion meeting with his colleagues and the solution which he proposed was profoundly sage, as shall be seen.

"In good consideration," he said, "of what has been transpiring between Florida and Texas, it is evident that the same difficulties will be reproduced within the towns of whatever state is chosen. The rivalry of this kind descends amongst its species, from states to cities- and there you have it entirely. Texas possesses eleven cities which meet the conditions required, and they will dispute amongst themselves for the honor of the enterprise, and will fight to new endless degrees, whereas Florida has only one. So therefore, for Florida and for Tampa Town!"

This decision, rendered public, appalled and dismayed the delegates from Texas. They entered into an indescribable fury and, in rage, addressed provocations to the many, even nominal, members of the Gun Club. The magistrates of Baltimore had only one course of action, and they took it. A special train was fitted and on it embarked the Texans, whether they liked it or not, and they quit that city in the rapid speed of 30 miles an hour.

But, despite the speed which transported them away, there remained time to hurl one last menacing and sarcastic insult towards their adversaries.

Making an allusion to the narrowness of the Florida peninsula, which was hardly anything between the two seas, they claimed that it could not resist the shock of the blast and would be torn asunder at the first detonation of the cannon.

"Ah well! When that happens!" responded the Floridians with a laconic dignity worthy of ancient times.

12. Urbi et Orbi

The difficulties of astronomy, mechanics, topography having been resolved, next came the inevitable question of money. It remained for them to procure an enormous sum for the execution of the project. No particular person or even country had at their disposal the millions necessary.

The president Barbicane thereby would accept funds from all parties; yes the enterprise was fully-American, but as it was an affair of universal interest it demanded the financial cooperation of all people. It was a right and a duty of the whole Earth to have an influence in the affairs of its satellite. The subscription which had been opened to Baltimore was extended to the entire world, *urbi et orbi*.

And the subscription was successful beyond all hope- even though it was a donation, and not money being lent on terms. It was an operation of pure disinterest from the literal sense of the word, not offering any chance of redeemable benefit.

But the effect of the announcement by Barbicane was not arrested by the frontiers of the United States; it passed beyond the Atlantic and the Pacific, invading the lands of Asia and Europe, Africa and Oceana. The observatories of the Union formed a rapport with the observatories of strange lands; these ones, in Paris, St. Petersburg, Capetown, Berlin, Altona, Stockholm, Warsaw, Hamburg, Buda, Bologna, Malta, Lisbon, Benares, Sydney, Madras, and Peking- they sent their congratulatory compliments to the Gun Club. Others were more guarded with their prudent expectations.

As for the Greenwich Observatory, approved by twenty-two other astronomical observatories in Great Britain, they refused their support; daringly denying the possibility of success, aligning their theories with those of Captain Nicholl. And so whilst the many diverse and prominent scientific societies sent delegates to Tampa Town, the bureau at Greenwich, holding their meeting, brutally passed an order of the day against Barbicane's proposition. This was but a case of the beautiful and good '*jalousie anglaise*'- and nothing else.

In summary, the effect upon the scientific world was excellent and it passed from there onto the masses, who, in general, were passionate towards the question. A fact of high importance, because it was the masses who were availed upon to subscribe to this appeal in order to meet the considerable capital requirements.

The president Barbicane, on the 8th of October, launched an enthusiastic printed manifesto in which he appealed to all the men of goodwill upon the Earth. This document, translated into all languages, was well-received.

The subscriptions were opened in the principle cities of the Union and were centralized in the Bank of Baltimore, 9 Baltimore St; and then subscriptions began in different states across the two continents:

Vienna: *S.M Rothschild*. St. Petersburg: *Stieglitz & Co*. Paris: *Credit Mobilier*. Stockholm: *Tottie & Arfuredson*. London: *N. M. Rothschild & Son*. Turin: *Ardouin & Co*. Geneva: *Lompard, Odier & Co*. Constantinople: *The Ottoman Bank*. Brussels: *S. Lambert*. Madrid: *Daniel Weisweller*. Amsterdam: *The Netherlands Credit Association*. Rome: *Torlonia & Co*. Lisbon: *Lecesne & Co*. Copenhagen: *The Private Bank*. Beunos Aires: *The Maua Bank*. Rio De Janeiro: *same firm as above*. Montevideo: *same firm as above*. Valparaiso: *Thomas La Chambre & Co*. Mexico City: *Matrin Darin & Co*. Lima: *Thomas La Chambre & Co*.

Three days after the manifesto of president Barbicane, $4,000,000 had been deposited in the different cities of the Union. With this unparalleled accomplishment, the Gun Club marched onwards.

But, a few days later, the dispatches advising America that the subscriptions of foreigners had been covered with veritable impressiveness. Certain countries had distinguished themselves in their generosity; others were not so loose with their facility. It was a matter of temperament.

Besides the figures are more elegant than words, so here are the official sums delivered into the assets of the Gun Club after subscriptions had closed:

The Russians for their contingent deposited an enormous sum of 368,733 roubles. For those astonished, they have failed to comprehend the tasteful appreciation with which the sciences of Russia have progressed and published in the fields of astronomy; thanks to their numerous observatories, the largest which cost two million roubles.

The French had commenced by laughing at the pretention of the Americans. The Moon served as a pretext for a thousand caricature memes, puns and a score of distasteful vaudeville musical pieces; whose bad taste equaled their undisputed ignorance. But, just as the French will pay in appreciation after a song they have heard, they now paid, after their rire, in subscriptions to the sum of 1,253,932 francs. At that price, they were allowed a little jest.

The Austrians demonstrated sufficient generosity in the midst of their financial difficulties. For their part they delivered via a public contribution the sum of 216,000 florins; which was warmly welcomed.

52,000 rixdalers were appointed by the Swedes and the Norwegians. The figures were relatively considerable from these countries; but they would certainly have been elevated, if the subscription had taken place in Christiana as well as in Stockholm. For one reason or another, the Norwegians do not enjoy sending their money to Sweden.

The Prussians had sent via envoy 250,000 thalers, a testament of their high approval for the enterprise. Their different observatories contributed with impressiveness for an important sum and their ardor encouraged the president Barbicane.

The Turks conducted themselves with generosity, but they held a personal interest in the affair; the Moon, in effect, is a regent governing their calendar years and the fast of Ramadan. And they gave no less than 1,372,640 piasters, this was donated with a certain ardor that denounced, however, a certain pressure from the Ottoman government.

The Belgians distinguished themselves over all other national states of the second order in size; providing 513,000 francs, amounting to two centimes per citizen.

The interest of Holland and their colonies in the operation ran to the extent of 10,000 florins; demanding only in the interests of goodwill for a 5% discount, since they had paid in cash.

Denmark, although slightly restrained by the size of her territory, gave 9,000 ducats; proving the love of the Danish for scientific expeditions.

The Germanic Confederation was engaged for 34,385 florins, there was nothing more that could have been demanded of them; and besides, to have asked would have been to no advantage.

Although feeling very embarrassed, the Italians dug 200,000 lira from out of the pockets of infants, but they had turned themselves inside-out in doing so. If they had Venetia, there would have been some more; but still they did not have Venetia.

The Papal States had paid no more than 7,040 scudi, and Portugal provided for their devotion to science with just 30,000 crusados.

As for Mexico, now we are reaching towards the end of this list, 326 piastres only; but an empire that is recently founded is always a little short on species.

257 francs was the modest apportion by Switzerland to the undertaking of the Americans. To speak frankly, the Swiss did not see much practical point in the operation; it did not seem that the action of sending a cannon ball to the Moon held the nature of establishing business relations with that shining body of the night sky, and it had been perceived as imprudent to engage their capital in such an uncertain enterprise. After all, the Swiss were listening to reason.

As for Spain, it was impossible to meet more than 110 reals. They gave as their pretext that there were railways that needed finishing. In truth, science is not viewed very-highly in that country. They are still slightly backwards. Plus certain Spaniards, not amongst the least-educated, who did not completely render in their minds the exact mass of the projectile compared to that of the Moon... They feared it could alter the Moon's orbit, troubling its role as a satellite and provoke it into a downward plunge towards the surface of the Earth's globe. Due to that being the case, it seemed valid to abstain. And in fact, this was what they had done precisely.

Remaining was England. We are aware of the contemptible hostility with which they had viewed the proposition of Barbicane. The English are of one single soul and mind for their twenty-five million inhabitants which form Great Britain. They held that the entire enterprise of the Gun Club was contrary to the principle of non-intervention, and they refused to subscribe with even one farthing.

At this news, the Gun Club were content to shrug their shoulders and focus on their grand affair.

When South America; that is to say Peru, Chile, Brazil, the provinces of La Plata and Columbia; had given for their part of personal contribution the sum of 300,000 dollars, the Gun Club found themselves at the head of a considerable sum of capital.

This was broken-down when exchanged into US dollars as follows:

Subscriptions from the United States: $4,000,000.
Subscriptions from foreigners: $1,446,675.

Total: $5,446,675.

$5,446,675 from the public was deposited into the treasury chests of the Gun Club.

A person should not be surprised at the importance of this sum. The work of casting, forging, the masonry framework, the transporting of workers and installing them with living quarters in an uninhabited area, constructing the furnaces for casting and the buildings, equipping the factory machines, the powder, the projectile, the incidental expenses, duties and variances in estimations would absorb bit-by-bit this entire amount. Certain shots of the cannon during the Civil War had required $1,000 per bang; and for the president Barbicane, unique in the splendor of his artillery, it could well have cost five thousand times as much.

On the 20th October, an agreement treaty was signed with the factory of *Goldspring, inc.*, near New York, which, during the war, had cast for Parrott those superlative cannons of cast iron.

This had stipulated, in the contract for both parties, that the factory of *Goldspring, inc.* would be engaged in the transportation to Tampa Town, to the Florida meridian, the necessary material for the casting of the Columbiad. This operation was required to be completed, and no later than, the 15th October of the impending year, and the cannon was to be complete and in good state, under the pain of an indemnity of $100 per day until the moment when the Moon would present the same conditions, that is to say 18 years and 11 days. The engagement of workers, their pay, and any necessary adjustments was incumbent on the company of *Goldspring, inc.*

The treaty, duplicated in good copy, was signed by I. Barbicane, president of the Gun Club, and J. Murchison, director of *Goldspring, inc.*, with the written terms approved by both parties.

13. Stone Hill

    Subsequent to the choice made by the members of the Gun Club, which had been to the detriment of Texas, there were none in America- where the entire population is literate- that did not studiously devour the geography of Florida. Never had the vendor libraries of book merchants sold so many copies of Bartram's *Travel in Florida*, Roman's *Natural History of East and West Florida*, Williams' *The Territory of Florida*, and Cleland's *On the Culture of Sugar Cane in East Florida*. Publishers needed to print new editions. There was furor.

    Barbicane had better occupations than in books; he wished to see with his own eyes the placement marked for the Columbiad. So without losing an instant he disposed the necessary funds to Cambridge Observatory to construct a telescope, and contracted with the house of *Breadwill and Co.* in Albany for the manufacturing of an aluminum projectile. He then quit Baltimore; accompanied by J.T. Maston, Major Elphiston and the Director of the *Goldspring, inc.* factory.

    The following day, the four companions on route arrived in New Orleans. There they immediately embarked on the *Tampico*, a federal marine vessel which the government had provided at their disposal, and, with the fires of the steam engines at full power, the Louisiana rivers disappeared behind them before their eyes.

    The voyage was not long; two days after departure, the *Tampico*, having encompassed 480 miles, reconnoitered the coast of Florida. As they approached Barbicane could see the presence of low-lying terrain, flat, and with a barren aspect. And then in their immediate sight they apprehended continuous rows of coves rich with oysters and lobsters, before the *Tampico* came to the bay of Espiritu-Santo.

    This bay is divided into two long natural harbors; the harbor of Tampa and the harbor of Hillsboro, and the steamer soon crossed into the neck. A short time after Fort Brooke drew near, its low batteries visible above the waves, the city of Tampa appeared- casually nestled within the natural port formed at the mouth of the river Hillsboro.

It was there the *Tampico* anchored, the 22nd October, at 7 hours in the evening, and the four passengers disembarked immediately.

Barbicane sensed his heart fluttering violently when he stepped onto the Floridian soil; he seemed to be tentatively feeling it with his feet, like an architect proving the solidity of a house. J.T. Maston scraped at the earth with his hook.

"Sirs," said Barbicane presently, "we do not have any time to lose. Tomorrow we'll mount horses and reconnoiter this land."

At the moment Barbicane had landed the three million inhabitants of Tampa Town came to meet him, an honor for the president of the Gun Club who had favored them with his choice. They received him with formidable acclamations of praise; but Barbicane slipped away from their widespread ovations, reaching the chambers of his room in the Hotel Franklin refusing to receive any persons. For him, the profession of being a famous celebrity was decidedly unsuitable.

On the next day, the 23rd of October, small horses of the Spanish breed, fiery and full of vigor, pranced about below his window. But instead of four, he saw fifty; all with their riders. Barbicane descended, accompanied by his three companions, and was completely astonished to find himself in the midst of this cavalcade. It was remarkable that each horse rider carried a carbine rifle and a bandelet of pistols at their sides. The reason for the deployment of these forces assembled was explained by a young Floridian, who had said:

"Sir, it is because of the Seminoles."

"What Seminoles?"

"The savages who roam the prairies, and so it is prudent we provide you with a fair escort."

"Peuh!" exclaimed J.T. Maston as climbed onto his mount.

"Still," replied the Floridian, "it is more safe."

"Sirs," responded Barbicane, "I offer you my thanks for your kind attention, and now, *en route*!"

The small troop made off and disappeared into a cloud of dust. It was 5 o'clock in the morning, the sun was resplendent and the thermometer was reaching the mark of 84° Fahrenheit; however the freshness of breeze arising from the sea moderated that excessive temperature.

Barbicane, on leaving Tampa Town, descended towards the south surveying the coast in this manner until reaching Alifia Creek. Here this small river jettisons into the bay of Hillsboro, a dozen miles below Tampa Town. Barbicane and his escort rode along the right-hand bank towards the east. Behind them the waves of the bay soon disappeared past a rise in the terrain, and the Floridian country surrounded their view.

   Florida is divided into two parts. In the north it is more populace with less wilderness. Its capital is Tallahassee, and at Pensacola lies the principle maritime arsenal of the United States Navy. The other part, pressed between the Atlantic and the Gulf of Mexico and embraced by those waters, is a slender peninsula washed by the currents of the Gulf Stream; a small point of earth isolated in the midst of a small archipelago, incessantly interlaced along its waters by the numerous ships travelling via the Old Bahama Channel. It is the sentinel in advance position for the grand tempests and hurricanes from the gulf. The total area is 38,033,267 acres, amongst which they must choose a situation this side of the 28th parallel that was convenient for the enterprise. And so Barbicane, on horseback, attentively examined the soil's configuration for its particular distribution of minerals.

   Florida, discovered by Juan Ponce de Leon in 1512 on the day of Palm Sunday, was first named *Flowery Easter* in Spanish. It little merited such a charming name with its coasts being so arid and the burning hot temperatures. But a few miles along the river, the nature of the terrain changes little by little, and the countryside becomes more dignified for that name; the soil becomes interspersed by creeks, rivers, and bodies of water, ponds and small lakes; and it resembles somewhat the lands of Holland and Guiana. Then the country soon elevates noticeably showing cultivated plains where the thriving produce of vegetables from the north and the south coincide, and immense fields unfold beneath the tropical sun whose water is conserved by clay soils so conducive to cultivation; and which end in prairies of bananas, sweet taro potatoes, tobacco, rice, cotton and sugar cane extending beyond view- an abundance of riches displayed with insouciant prodigality.

   Barbicane appeared very satisfied with the constantly rising elevation of the terrain as they progressed, and when J.T. Maston interrogated him on the subject he said:

   "My dignified friend, it is of the most importance to our interests that we cast our Columbiad cannon on the highest of grounds."

   "For it to be nearest to the Moon?" inquired the secretary of the Gun Club.

   "No!" responded Barbicane with good humor. "What is the importance of a few feet less or more? No, but within elevated terrain the progress of our work will be easier; we will have less struggle with groundwater, so that we will not require as much of its long and expensive tubular-casing. And that is a consideration, when building such a profound length of nine hundred feet into a mineshaft."

"You speak with reason," said the engineer Murchison accordingly; "we should, as much as it is possible, avoid ground-waters during the excavation; but if we do encounter underground springs, it is of no difficulty as we shall either run them clear by pumping the water out with our machines or otherwise we'll divert them. We do not sink an artesian well; where it is narrow and obscure, where the hammers, the drill, the casing walls, the sounding rod and all the other tools of a well-digger must work blindly. No. Our operation is beneath the sky, in broad daylight, with mattocks and picks at hand; and our mine being aided by explosive blasting, the job should progress rapidly."

"Although," replied Barbicane, "if the elevation and nature of the soil empowers us to avoid the struggle with underground water, I expect the work to be done faster and more perfectly; hence we seek to open our trench in terrain which is situated certain hundreds of feet above sea level."

"Spoken with good reason, Mr. Barbicane, and in my opinion we will find shortly a convenient emplacement."

"Ah, I would be most pleased if we had already begun to dig with pickaxes," said the president.

"And I, that we were finished!" cried J.T. Maston.

""We will arrive at that point, sirs," responded the ingenious Murchison, "and believe me, my company of *Goldspring,inc.* will not be paying an indemnity for lateness."

"For your sake I hope so too! Do you realize," cried J.T. Maston, "that at one hundred dollars per day until the Moon once more presents the same conditions, which is a period of eighteen years and eleven days, that well comes to an amount of $658,100?"

"No sir, I did not know that," answered Murdoch, "and it is not something I need be aware of."

It became ten o'clock in the morning. The small troop had covered a dozen miles; and the fertile country was succeeded by a region of forest. They were passing through a wide variety of trees that grew with the very essence of tropical profusion. Here the forest was all but impenetrable and they saw grenadiers, oranges, lemons, figs, olives, apricots, bananas, the grandest of grape vines; whose fruits and flowers rivaled amongst one another in beauty of color and perfumes. In the shady fragrance of these magnificent trees a whole world of brilliantly colored birds sang and flew, frolicking about; and amongst these were the particularly distinguished boatbills, whose nests were surely a treasure box, for the dignity of their jeweled feathers.

J.T. Maston and the major were powerfully-moved, in the presence of such opulent nature, by the admiration of such splendid beauty. However the president Barbicane, insensitive to these marvels, was in a haste for them to advance; this fertile country here displeased him by its fertility; for even without any hydroscope, he sensed water about where they searched, and vainly looked for signs of uncontestable aridity.

Hence they advanced onwards; and as they progressed they had to ford many rivers, and not without certain danger, either- for they were infested with caimans and alligators between 15 to 18 feet long! J.T. Maston menaced them hardily with his redoubtable hook but this only managed to scatter the pelicans, the ducks, the tropical birds and other wild inhabitants of the river whilst the grand red flamingoes regarded him with an air of stupidity.

Finally the hosts of this humid land disappeared from the survey's view. The trees became less closely-scattered and the woods less dense; a few isolated groups detached amidst infinite plains which the troop passed through, frightening away occasional deer.

"And finally!" cried Barbicane as he addressed the others. "This is the region of pines!"

"And also the savages," responded the major.

As though having heard their speech, several Seminoles appeared on the horizon; on their fast horses they moved about agitatedly and courageously, brandishing their long spears and discharging their rifles in the air, producing in the distance muffled sounds of detonation which did not disturb Barbicane or his companions.

They found themselves occupying a rocky plain of vast space, bare, undulating and extending across many acres, where the sunshine inundated with brilliant rays of light. As this area formed a large plateau above the surrounding terrain, its appearance offered to the members of the Gun Club all the conditions they required for the establishment of their Columbiad.

"Halt!" said Barbicane as he arrested his horse's march. "Is there a name for this land?"

"It is called Stone Hill," responded the Floridians.

Barbicane, saying not a word, planted his feet onto the ground, pried forth his instruments from out of their packsaddles and commenced to measure his position with extreme precision. The small troop, arranged around him, examined their leader with profound silence.

And at that moment the sun passed its meridian. Barbicane, after several moments, rapidly figuring the results of his observations then said:

"This emplacement is situated three hundred yards above sea level, 27° and 7' of latitude and 5° and 7' of longitude west. It appears to offer an arid nature and rocky terrain which are all the conditions favorable for our experiment; it is therefore here on this plain that we shall erect our powder magazines, our workshops, our furnaces, the accommodations for our workers- and it is here, right here," he repeated, stamping his foot upon the summit of Stone Hill, "that our projectile will depart for space and onwards to the Moon!"

14. Pick and Trowel

The same evening as having chosen their launch site, Barbicane and his companions returned to Tampa Town and the engineer Murchison embarked aboard the *Tampico* for New Orleans. He was to hire an army of workers and to bring back a large part of the material. The members of the Gun Club would reside in Tampa Town in order to organize the preliminary work, aided by the gentlemen of that land.

8 days after her departure, the *Tampico* returned to the bay Espiritu-Santo with a flotilla of steamers. Murchison had accumulated fifteen hundred workers. In the evil days past perhaps it would not have been possible, however now that America, the land of the free, counted all of the men within its boundaries as free, laborers were acquired from everywhere with the promise of great retribution. By the great stores of money being held by the Gun Club men were offered high pay, with gratification bonuses of considerable proportion. Workers hired for Florida would, on completion of their task, receive their capital which would be deposited in their name in the Baltimore Bank. Murchison had therefore an abundance of choice and he put severe standards of intelligence and skill on his employees. It is authoritatively understood that he enrolled his legion of laborers from the elite ranks of mechanics, drivers, smelters, blacksmiths, miners, brickmakers and manual workers of every kind, blacks and whites, without distinction of

color. Many relocated with their entire families. It was a veritable emigration.

The 31st October at 10 hours in the morning, this army disembarked onto the quays of Tampa Town; we can comprehend the movement and activity reigning throughout that little city whose population had doubled in only one day. In effect, Tampa would gain enormously at this initiative of the Gun Club; not for the workers, who were funneled immediately into transport for Stone Hill, but thanks to the affluence of the curious who converged one by one from all points of the globe onto the Florida peninsula.

During the beginning days everyone was occupied in discharging their tools from the flotilla; the machines, the food provisions and a great number of sheet-iron houses disassembled and numbered. During this time Barbicane planted the first markers in order to build a railway 15 miles long, destined to be the relay between Stone Hill and Tampa Town.

The conditions for the construction of an American railroad, those wonderful paths of iron, are well-known. Capricious in their detours, hardy in their climbs; they represented the highest standards of the art. Escalating the hills, rolling through valleys, the railroad's soul is blind with no concern for a straight line; it is not expensive, nor troublesome to create only that it derails and jumps at great liberty. The train line between Tampa Town and Stone Hill was a simple trick, and it demanded neither a great amount of time nor a great amount of money.

To others, Barbicane was the soul of that insular world who had answered the call of his voice- he animated them, to them he communicated his encouragement, his enthusiasm, his conviction. He appeared everywhere at once, as though endowed with an ubiquity of movement, and was forever accompanied at his side by J.T. Maston who was like a buzzing fly. Barbicane's ingenious and practical mind created thousands of inventions. With him there were no obstacles, no difficulties, never any embarrassing perplexities; he was a miner, a builder, mechanic as well as an artilleryman; he had a response to all demands and a solution to every problem. He corresponded with the Gun Club and the *Goldspring, inc.* factory- and day and night, the fires lit, the steam vapors maintained in precision, the *Tampico* attentively awaited his orders from Hillsboro harbor.

Barbicane, on the 1st of November, left Tampa with a detachment of workers; and the next day a town of mechanical houses constructed with sheet iron grew around Stone Hill. Surrounded with palisades, from movement and ardor it was soon as busy as any of the great cities of the Union. Life here was regulated by discipline and the work commenced with perfect order.

The borer drills painstakingly permitted a practical reconnaissance of the terrain's nature, and the digging of the enterprise began on the 4th November. On that day, Barbicane called a meeting of all the foremen and to them said:

"You all know, my friends, why I have brought you to into the wilderness of Florida. We are about to cast a cannon measuring 9 feet on its interior diameter, 6 feet thick walls and 19 and a half feet of encasing stone; so therefore a total shaft size of 60 feet wide and 900 feet deep. It is a considerable working task to be completed in 8 months; and, you must excavate 2,542,400 cubic feet of ground in 255 days, which, in round figures is 10,000 cubic feet per day. This would offer no acute difficulty for a thousand laborers working together, but in the relatively restrained space there is little elbow room. Nevertheless, this is the work to be done, and it will be, and I count on your courage as much as I count on your skill."

At 8 hours in the morning the first swing of a pickaxe penetrated the Florida soil, and from that moment onwards that valiant tool never rested idly for an instant of a moment in the hands of the miners. They labored in relays of quarter-shifts per day.

Despite the colossal scope of the operation, it never exceeded the point of the limits of human endurance and strength. Far from it. And, for the talk of the similar labors, it is sufficient to cite the Well of Father Joseph, constructed near Cairo by Sultan Saladon, in an epoch when machines were yet to have multiplies the force of a man, which descended beyond the level of the Nile to a profound depth of 300 feet! And there is also the well dug at Coblentz by the Margrave Johann of Baden who sunk it 600 feet into the soil! Ah yes! And what was it they must do, in sum? They needed to triple Saladin's accomplishment, and make it ten times wider, which would render the task of excavation more easier. And thus there was not one foreman, not one workman who doubted the success of the operation.

There was one important decision, performed by the engineer Murchison in accordance with president Barbicane, which allowed for an acceleration to the work's progression. An article of the contract specified the Columbiad was required to be fretted with rings of forged iron whilst still hot from the furnace. The effort required for this precaution was useless, because it was evident the cannon, that Columbiad engine, had the capacity to do without these compression rings. This clause was thereby renounced.

This gave a great economization to forecast time, and it also allowed the employment of a new system of digging to be adopted used in the construction of wells, where the masonry is put into place at the same time as the earth is excavated. Thanks to this very simple procedure, it was not necessary to brace the walls of the shaft; the masonry contains the pressure with unwavering strength and descends under its own weight.

This maneuver would not commence until the moment when the pickaxe attained the solid bedrock part of the ground.

On 4th November 50 workers dug at the center of the encircling palisade, that is to say at the superior and highest part of Stone Hill, a large circular hole with the diameter of 60 feet.

The pickaxes first encountered a sort of black earth, 6 inches thick, which was easily reasoned with. The ground was then succeeded by 2 feet of fine sand which was carefully retired, for it was to serve as the substance for making the interior mold.

After the sand appeared a rather compact white clay, resembling English marl, and this extended in a shoulder of four feet.

Then the iron of the picks rang out upon a durable layer of the soil, a certain kind of rock formed by petrified seashells; very dry, very solid, and the tools did not deviate or give up. At this point, the hole presented a depth of 6 and a half feet, and the work on the supporting masonry was commenced.

At the bottom of the excavation they constructed in the shape of a wheel a wooden disk from oak wood. Strengthened with bolts it was unfailingly solid, pierced in its center with a hole offering a diameter equal to the exterior diameter of the Columbiad cannon. And on this wheel reposed the first sides of the masonry, then hydraulic cement was poured, enchaining the stones with an inflexible tenacity. The laborers, at the center after forming the masonry in a circumference, were contained in a large mine shaft pit of 21 feet across.

With that effort achieved the miners resumed their pickaxes and mattocks, and they opened the rock underneath the oak wheel. As they did this they supported it with extremely solid blocks and when the hole they gouged had reached another 2 feet further in depth, they successively removed the supporting blocks. The wheel sank down bit-by-bit, and with it the massive ring of masonry; above which the masons worked incessantly, always reserving positions for vents, which would permit the gas to escape during the forging operation.

That sort of work demanded on the worker's behalf extreme skill and attention at every instant; in addition, because the hole was round like a wheel, dangerous injuries occurred by the stone bursting and caused mortalities; but their ardor never failed to relent for one single minute, day and night. In the day, the rays of the sun were focused by the sides, but within a few months later, sometimes to the tiring extent of 99° Fahrenheit heat on those burning, calcifying plains. During night, beneath the white layers of electrical illumination, the clanging noises of picks onto the rock, the detonation blasts of mining explosives, the gnashing grinding of the machines, the whirlwinds of escaping fumes in the air traced around Stone Hill terrifying circles that the herds of Bison and the detachments of Seminoles dared to not encounter.

   Meanwhile the work advanced regularly; the steam cranes actively removed the excavated material, obstacles posed little question or attention, and when encountering any foreseen difficulties, these were treated with and overcome by skill.

   The first month flowed by, the pit attained the depth assigned by the time schedule, 112 feet. In December, that depth had doubled, and it tripled in January. Throughout the month of February, the laborers endured against a layer of water which originated from a source within the earth. It followed they employed powerful pumps and compressed air devices to exhaust this leakage, finally blocking the source orifices with concrete; doing so blindly as though repairing a leak onboard a ship. Finally those malcontent currents were reasoned with. However, due to the ground's softness, the wooden disk made from oak had descended partially and became unbalanced, causing the stones behind the masonry to partially fall through; collapsing in places. One may judge for themselves the dreadfully appalling power which that disk of masonry possessed at 75 yards high! This accident cost the lives of several workmen.

   It took a duration of 3 weeks to employ reinforcements onto the stone and to restore the wheel to its previous stability. But, thanks to skill and ingenuity, and to the power of the machines employed, things were edified; some moments of time compromised. Then balance was recovered, and the construction of the earth-forge continued.

   Without any new incidents arresting the operation's onward march of from then on; on the 10th of June, 20 days before the expiration of the deadline date fixed by Barbicane, the pit, entirely reinforced by the encased stone, had attained the depth of 900 feet. At the bottom-most point, the masonry reposed on a massive cube measuring 30 feet at its shoulders, and the highest part was level to the ground's surface.

   The president Barbicane and the members of the Gun Club warmly congratulated the engineer Murchison; whose cyclopean work-task had been accomplished in those conditions with extraordinary speed.

   Throughout those 8 months, Murchison had not left Stone Hill for one minute; he had surveyed with precision the operations of digging and excavation, he incessantly worried for the wellbeing and sanitary conditions of his workers, and due to this he had evaded the unfortunate epidemics which often occur in communes with great agglomerations of humans, that are especially disastrous in those regions of the globe totally exposed by tropical influences.

Several workers, it is true, had paid with their lives for the inherent imprudence in such a dangerous undertaking; but these deplorable tragedies are impossible to avoid, and these are not the sorts of details Americans are particularly preoccupied with. They are more concerned with humanity in general than the individual in particular. However Barbicane possessed principles contrary to these ideas, and they were applied on every occasion. And so, thanks to his attentive care, his intelligence, his relevant and consistent intervention in cases of difficulty, his prodigious and humane sagacity, the rate of catastrophes did not exceed that of countries overseas often cited for the precautions; for example in France, where on average one accident occurs for every 200,000 francs of work.

15. The Festival of Casting

During the eight months those employees worked furiously at the operation of digging and excavating that foundry within the earth, the work in preparation of the castings was simultaneously conducted with extreme rapidity; any stranger arriving at Stone Hill would be overcome by surprise at the spectacle offered before their gaze.

Six hundred yards about the pit, placed in encircling arrangement around the central point, twelve hundred reverberatory furnaces had been erected, each the size of 6 feet wide and separated between one another at intervals of half a yard. A line developed by these twelve hundred furnaces would offer a circumference over 2 miles. They were all constructed according to the same model with high quadrangle chimney, and these produced a most singular effect. J.T. Maston found it to be an array of superb architectural dispositions. It resembled the monuments in Washington. For him, there existed nothing as beautiful, not even in Greece- where of course, he would have admitted if asked, he had never even been.

It will be recalled that in the third meeting the committee had decided to employ cast iron for their Columbiad cannon, a special kind of grey casting-type. That metal is, in effect, extra-tenacious, more ductile, less brittle, more conducive to being bored-out and suitable for all operations of casting into molds; and, treated with coal, it is of superior quality for pieces requiring great resistance such as cannons, steam engines, hydraulic presses, etc.

But melted once, being subjected to only one fusion it rarely homogenizes and requires a second molten fusion to set and cure, and thereby refine, the last annoying deposit that remains from the dirt's impurity.

And so before being expedited to Tampa Town, the iron ore mineral was treated by the huge furnaces of the *Goldspring, inc.* factory and placed into contact with carbon and silica chaff at a high temperature; whereby it carbonized and transformed into iron. After this initial operation, the metal was moved to Stone Hill. But 136,000,000 pounds of iron, a massive weight, was too expensive to send by rail; the price of transport was double the price of the material. It appeared preferable to defray to the New York shipping industry the charge of the iron bars and it required no less than 68 ships each with a capacity of a thousand tons. A veritable fleet that on the 3rd of May, emerging beyond the New York harbors, took an ocean route along the American coast, encountering the Bahama Canal, doubling the Florida point and on the 10th of the same month lay at anchor avariciously ready by the port of Tampa Town, moored in the bay of Espiritu-Santo.

There the boats furiously discharged the iron onto Stone Hill railroad wagons, and in the middle of January the enormous mass of metal had been rendered to its destination.

You will easily comprehend that it took no more than 1,200 furnaces to molten-liquefy those 70,000 tons of iron. Each furnace could contain precisely 114,000 pounds of metal; this had already been established in the models which served to cast the Rodman cannon. These affected a trapezoidal shape and were very low. The apparatus for the heating chimney was at the two extremities of the furnace and this sorted the slag from the useful elements. Those furnaces, composed of heat-resistant firebricks, were composed uniquely with a grill for burning coal, and a sole upon which the bars of iron were deposited; this sole, inclined at an angle of $25°$, permitted the refined metal to be collected into receptacle basins- and then twelve hundred rivulet channels running from the furnaces converged as they bled into the central pit.

At the middle of the day when the work of masonry and the construction of furnaces had been completed, Barbicane then proceeded with the fabrication of the interior mold; this was levered above the center of the pit, and swiveled on its axis- a cylinder 900 feet in length with a diameter of 9 feet exactly filled the space reserved for the bored arm of the Columbiad cannon. The cylinder was composed of a mélange of clay earth and sand, with the addition of straw hay to fortify it. The interval left between the mold and the masonry would be filled with the molten metal, and this would then form a wall 6 feet thick.

The cylinder, for it to maintain its upright equilibrium, was consolidated into place by the framework of iron arms subjoined according to the transverse distance between the sealing stone reinforcements; these blocks of metal would perish during the casting, and offer no inconvenience.

The operation was completed on 8th July, and the casting of the Columbiad was fixed for that following day.

"It will be a beautiful casting ceremony, a festival of forging!" said J.T. Maston to his friend Barbicane.

"Without doubt," responded Barbicane. "But it will not be a festival free to the public!"

"What are you saying? You won't open the gates of the enclosure for viewing?"

"I will guard it well, Maston; the forging of the Columbiad is a delicate operation, not to say perilous, and I prefer it to be done effectively behind closed doors. On the departure of the projectile you may have your festival if you like but until then, no."

The president held to good reason; the action of the operation offered unforeseen dangers, and a grand influx of spectators could prevent the overseeing of the casting. It followed that all involved would need to conserve the freedom of their movements. Persons therefore would not be permitted inside the enclosure, with the exception of delegated members of the Gun Club who had voyaged there from Tampa Town. These included the dashing Bilsby, Tom Hunter, Colonel Bloomsberry, Major Elphiston, General Morgan and not many others- for these men, the casting of the Columbiad was a personal affair. J.T. Maston would be their chaperone and gracefully he did not spare any detail; conducting them throughout, through the magazines, the workshop, the thousands of machines and one at a time he forced upon the visitors the twelve hundred furnaces. At the twelve hundredth inspection, their interest had begun to wane.

The casting was to be at noon precisely; the day earlier, every furnace was loaded with the 114,000 pounds of metal bars layered into crossed piles, so the heated air would freely circulate over them all. During the morning the twelve hundred chimneys vomited a polluting atmosphere in torrents of flames and the ground agitated with dulled tremors. For each pound of metal in the foundry it required a pound of coal to be burned. So there were 70,000 tons of coal which projected their fumes and disfigured the disk of the sun in a black curtain.

The heat was soon untenable inside the circle of furnaces and the roaring resembled the sound of thunder; the powerful ventilators joined to this sound as they continued to saturate the incandescent hearths with oxygen.

For success the operation demanded rapid conduct. At the signal given by the detonation of a blank-loaded cannon, every furnace would deliver its package of molten-liquid iron; emptying itself entirely.

With attitudes of enrapture, the foremen and laborers waited attentively for the moment to begin with an impatience mixed by a certain quality of emotion. There were now no persons within the enclosure, and every head-controller of the foundry-men stood at their posts beside the running-holes where the molten iron would be released.

Barbicane and his colleagues were installed on an eminent position nearby which was slightly raised where they could witness the operation. Before them, a cannon piece was primed, which would be fired upon signal by the ingenious engineer Murchison.

A few minutes before midday, the first globules of metal began to flow. The receptacle basins began to gradually fill bit-by-bit, and when the iron was entirely liquefied, left to rest in that state for a short while to finally facilitate the separation of foreign substances.

Midday chimed. The blow of the cannon's explosion sounded and a jet of fire flared into the air. Twelve hundred running holes were opened by the foundry-men, twelve hundred serpents of fire crawled towards the central pit; unfurling their incandescent rings. There they precipitated with a horrifying fracas to a depth of 900 feet. It was a moving and magnificent spectacle. The ground trembled whilst those cascades of molten iron, launching whirlwinds of fumes towards the sky, volatized the humidity in the mold and ejected through the vents made into the stone reinforcement the forms of impenetrable vapors. These fractured clouds unrolled in thick spirals and mounted towards the zenith at a height of one hundred feet. Any savage, errantly watching by the limits of the horizon, would have thought it the formation of a new volcanic crater of lava being opened in Florida; however this was not an eruption, not an explosion, not a storm, not a struggle of the elements, not any of the terrible phenomena that nature is capable of producing! No!

Man had solely created these red vapors; these gigantic flames which would have dignified a volcano and noises of trepidation resembling the shock of earthquakes, these howling rivers of orange and tempest had been precipitated by the hands of man- and it was an abysmal hole dug to the size of Niagara within which the metal fused.

16. The Columbiad

Had the operation of the casting worked? All had been reduced to simple conjecture. However there was every reason to think it was successful because the mold had absorbed the entire mass of metal, melted by the furnaces.

As to whether it had gone well or not: for a long it would be impossible to assure themselves directly.

In effect when Major Rodman had cast his cannon of 160,000 pounds it had been a matter of fifteen days for the completion of the cooling process. How much time, then, would the monstrous Columbiad, encased in its turbulent vapors and defended by its intense heat, take until it might be unrobed before the gaze of its waiting admirers? It would be very difficult to calculate.

The impatience of the members of the Gun Club as they observed the passage of time was a tough ordeal. But there was nothing to be done. J.T. Maston virtually roasted himself in his devotion. Fifteen days after casting an immense plume of fumes still dressed the plain's sky and the hot soil boiled one's feet within a radius of two hundred yards around the summit of Stone Hill.

The days flowed, the weeks adjoined one another. There were no ways to cool the immense cylinder. It was impossible to approach it. They were forced to wait, and the members of the Gun Club worried as they paced about restraining themselves.

"Now it is August 10th!" said J.T. Maston one day. "Four months of effort separate us from December! And we still must remove the interior core, calibrate the bore, load the Columbiad, and everything else required! We shall not be ready. Currently we can't even approach the cannon! This thing will never cool! It is fooling us so cruelly!"

They essayed to calm the impatient secretary without managing to; Barbicane was saying nothing, but in his silence there hid a secret irritation. Seeing how they were absolutely halted by an obstacle that only time could avail upon- the time which was a redoubtable enemy to their circumstances- being held at the discretion of an enemy was hard for a man of war.

Meanwhile the constant daily observations began to reveal certain changes to the state of the soil. By 15th August the vapors projecting upwards had diminished noticeably in their intensity and density. A few days afterwards the ground exhaled with only a pale mist, the final expirations of the infernal monster in that circle of stone. Bit-by-bit the shuddering from the soil drew inwards upon itself, the heat-energy emanating from the circle restrained itself. The impatient spectators approached; one day gaining ten feet; the next day, twenty; and, on 22nd August, Barbicane, his colleagues, the engineer Murchison, were each able to take their place at the nape of iron touching the summit of Stone Hill, a place fortifying for hygiene, assuredly, as it would not permit cold feet!

"And finally!" the president of the Gun Club cried aloud with an immense sigh of satisfaction.

Work resumed that very day. The extraction of the interior mold proceeded immediately, and at last the bore of the cannon's arm-piece was cleared; the pickaxes, the mattocks, and the tools used for drilling functioned continuously without slackening. The earthen clay and the sand had acquired an extremely hard and durable condition by the action of the extreme heat. However, with the aid of machines, this agglomerated mixture still hot from its contact with the wall of iron was removed. The extracted mixture was rapidly lifted out in carts still steaming with vapor and onwards they went, the ardor of the work telling on the faces of the workers, with the pressing intervention of Barbicane; who presented his arguments with the great force of dollar incentives. On 3rd September, every trace of the inner molding had disappeared.

Immediately the operation of assemblage commenced; the machines were installed without delay and with rapid movements the powerful arms of the trenchants bit into the rough surface of the cast iron. A few weeks after, the interior surface of the immense tube was perfectly cylindrical and the cannon's bore acquired a perfect polish.

And finally, on the 22nd September, less than a year since the communication of Barbicane, that enormous engine the Columbiad cannon, rigorously calibrated and absolutely vertical, carefully checked with delicate instruments, was pronounced functional. They now would wait for the Moon's attendance, and everyone was sure that it would not miss its rendezvous. The joy of J.T. Maston was apparently boundless, for he had almost fallen and plunged into the cannon out of fright when regarding the cliff-face inside a tube of nine hundred feet. If not for the arms of the adroit Bloomsbury, which the dignified colonel had fortunately conserved, the secretary of the Gun Club like a new Errostratus would have met his death at the bottomless depths of the Columbiad.

Hence the cannon was finished: there was no possible doubt that it had been perfectly executed. And so on the 6th October Captain Nicholl, although with reluctance, settled his first wager and president Barbicane made an entry into his personal account books of $2,000. It is known on authority that the choler which the captain possessed reached to the limits of becoming almost a fit of malady. However there were still the bets of $3,000, $4,000 and $5,000- and if he could win two the affair would not be bitter, but rather turn out excellently for him. Yet the money was not the focus of his calculations. It was the success that his rival would obtain, that of casting a cannon which could not be resisted by plates of armor equal to fifty feet in thickness, which was a terrible blow for him.

From the 23rd September the enclosure around Stone Hill had been generously opened to public viewing to show the work accomplished, and the great flow of visitors who came may be imagined easily.

Indeed the innumerable curious, accumulated from every point of the United States, converged on Florida. The town of Tampa had accrued prodigiously over the year, consecrating itself entirely to the work of the Gun Club, and now in complete terms the population was 150,000 souls. After engorging Fort Brook into a tangled network of streets, they now stretched onto the tongue of land which separated the two clades around Espiritu-Santo Bay; the new neighborhoods, the new squares, a complete forest of houses, they had emerged on those formerly deserted shores into the warmth of the American sun. There were companies which had been founded for the erection of churches, schools, personal dwellings; and within a year the town had increased in tenfold proportion.

It is widely-known the Yankees are commercial businessmen; everywhere their kind are thrown, from zones of ice and snow unto zones of torrid tropics, and their instincts for business affairs are exercised with great utility. This is why the simply curious, who had no unique reason to come to Florida other than as purveyors of the Gun Club's operations, allowed themselves to be drawn into commercial interests once installed in Tampa. The freight ships transporting material and laborers onto that port had brought about an unparalled level of activity. Soon other ships, of all shapes and tonnage, loaded with food, provisions, merchandise, crisscrossed the bay to the two clades; and every day the vast counters of ship owners, the offices of brokers established in the town, and the *Shipping Gazette* registered new arrivals onto the port of Tampa.

When the roads multiplied around the town, these being cut in consideration of the prodigious increase in population and business, it was finally connected by steam-train to the other meridional states of the Union. A railway attached to Mobile and Pensacola, the dockyard of the great naval maritime arsenal of the South, and- this point is important, it carried onwards to Tallahassee. There exists a small truncheon of iron rails, 21 miles long, with which Tallahassee communicates with Saint Marks, on the banks of the sea. This section of the railroad was prolonged until reaching Tampa Town, and revived on its passage the relevant portions of dead and sleepy towns of central Florida. And so Tampa, thanks to the marvels of industry due to an idea disclosed on one beautiful day from the mind of a certain man, was able to affect with good reason the airs of a grand city. It had received the nickname Moon City and the capital of Florida subsided in a total eclipse, visible from all points of the world.

Everyone will now comprehend why the rivalry was so great between Texas and Florida, and the irritation of the Texans was so virulent in their protests and pretentions at the choice of the Gun Club. In their sagacious clairvoyance they had well-comprehended the gains which Barbicane's tentative experiment would infer, and what the blast of his cannon would surely accomplish. The Texans had forgone a vast center of commerce, railroads and a considerable increased accumulation of population. Every one of these advantages had been conferred to that miserable Floridian peninsula, jettisoned eastwards amongst the waves of that vague Atlantic ocean. Also, Barbicane was portrayed as sharing with General Santa-Anna an antipathy towards all Texans.

Meanwhile despite the lively and at times furious commercial and industrial ardor, the new population of Tampa Town did not forget to maintain their interest in the Gun Club's operation. On the contraire. The minutest details of the enterprise, every strike of the pickaxe, was passionately followed. There was an incessant travel between the town and Stone Hill; it was a procession, or even more, a pilgrimage.

It was already foreseeable that on the day of the experiment the agglomeration of spectators would number in their millions- they could already be seen arising from all points of the globe to accumulate upon that place. Europe was emigrating to America.

But so far, it must be said, the curiosity of the numerous arrival had received only mediocre satisfaction. Many counted on seeing the spectacle of the casting, yet all they had witnessed was the smoking fumes. This was very little for avid eyes, however Barbicane would not voluntarily allow any person to oversee the operation. So there were murmurs of disagreement and discontent. They blamed the president and they accused him of despotism, and from there proceeded to declare him un-American. In their pressing excitement there was almost a riot around the palisades of Stone Hill. Barbicane, it was seen, rested unwaveringly by his decision.

However now that the Columbiad was entirely completed this closure to the viewing could no longer be maintained; it would have been ungracious, it followed, to shut their doors, and even seemed imprudent and malcontent towards public sentiment. Barbicane therefore opened the enclosure for all to see. Although, possessed as he was by a practical spirit, he resolved to charge an entry fee to the curious public.

It was beautiful to contemplate the immense Columbiad, but to descend into its profound depth was to experience a vision for all Americans of ultra-happiness that could be seen nowhere else in the world. And so there was not one of the curious who did not volunteer joyfully visit the interior of that metal abyss. The planks of viewing platforms, suspended above a trail of vapor, permitted spectators to satisfy their curiosity. This idea was wildly popular. Women, children, elderly, and all the excited looked down to penetrate the mystery of the iron barrel of that colossal cannon. The price to descend was fixed at $5 per person, and in spite of this elevated charge, during the two months preceding the experiment, the affluence of their visitors permitted the Gun Club to pocket into their treasury chests another $500,000.

It goes without saying that the first visitors into the Columbiad's heart were the members of the Gun Club, an advantage justifiably reserved for that illustrious assembly. This ceremony took place with solemn demeanor on the 25th September. A box-cage of honor descended with the president Barbicane, J.T. Maston, Major Elphistan, General Morgan, Colonel Bloomsbury, the ingenious Murchison and other distinguished members of that celebrated club. In total, one dozen. There was still a good degree of heat emanating from the iron of that long metal tube. They were all a little bit stifled! But their joy! What delightful euphoria! A table with ten places set regaled on the massive stone cube which supported the Columbiad and was illuminated by a beam of electric light. Dishes exquisite and numerous, that seemed to descend from the sky, were placed successively for the diners and the finest wines of France gathered in profusion about the splendid repast; served nine hundred feet below the ground.

The festive banquet was very animated and even very noisy; the plentiful toasts raised crisscrossed left and right. To the terrestrial globe, to its satellite, to the Gun Club, to the Union, to the Moon, to the goddess Phoebe, to the goddess Diana, to the Selenites, to that shining body of the night sky, the peaceful courier of the firmament! All the hurrahs, borne aloft on echoing waves of sound acoustically-enhanced by the immense tube, reached the surface and the crowds arranged around Stone Hill, united as one heart, responded with cheerful cries to the convivial sounds of degustation that emerged from the depths of that gigantic Columbiad.

J.T. Maston was possessed by happiness; if he cried out more loudly than he gesticulated, if he drank more wine than he ate, it was a difficult point to establish. In any case, he would not have changed his place for an empire, as he said: "No, not even if the cannon was charged and loaded, set to be fired within an instant," and he was sent "in tiny morsels into planetary space!"

17. A Telegraphic Dispatch

The grand experimental work done by the Gun Club was for all considerations completed; and yet, two months were to come and pass before the day the projectile would be launched towards the Moon. Two months would seem as comparatively long as two years amongst such universal impatience! Thus far along the least details of the operation had been reproduced each day by the journalists and devoured passionately and avidly by their reader's eyes; but it seemed that from now on, this dividend of interest being distributed to the public would diminish in strength, and everybody was afraid to no longer receive that touch of emotional excitement from the daily newspapers.

There was nothing to fear; an incident that gathered much attention, quite extraordinary, quite incredible, which more than resembled fantastically a new spirit of breath that was injected onto the entire world as it entered in an explosion of poignant excitement. One day, the 30th of September at 3:47 p.m. a telegram transmitted by submerged cable running from Valencia, Ireland to Newfoundland and the American coast arrived addressed to president Barbicane.

The president Barbicane tore open the envelope to read the dispatch; and when he had read its contents entirely, his complexion had paled, and his eyes troubled and unfocused themselves at the twenty scant words of the telegram.

Contained in the text of this dispatch, these letters of alphabet maintained in the archives of the Gun Club:

PARIS, FRANCE.
SEPTEMBER 30, 4:00 A.M.
BARBICANE
TAMPA, FLORIDA, U.S.A.

REPLACE SPHERICAL SHELL WITH CYLINDRO-CONICAL ONE. I WILL GO TO MOON IN IT. AM COMING ON STEAMER ATLANTA.

MICHEL ARDAN.

18. The Passenger on the Altlanta

If this stunning news, instead of flying across electrified filaments of wire, had arrived simply through the post in a sealed anonymous envelope- so that the employees in France, Ireland, Newfoundland and America would not necessarily have been confidants in that telegram- Barbicane would not have hesitated for a single instant. He would not, out of a measure of prudence, have even considered its contents. The telegram had likely contained a joke, especially being sent from a Frenchman. What kind of man could, apparently, consider so audaciously such an idea of unparalled voyage? And should that man exist, was he not better suited to an infirmary than being shot from within a cannon ball?

But the dispatch was widely known, for the apparels of transmission via telegraph were not very discrete in nature, and already the proposition of Michel Ardan was being distributed amongst the many diverse states of the Union. And so Barbicane had no plausible reason to stay quiet. He therefore called a meeting of his colleagues who had presented themselves to Tampa Town, and not allowing his voice to become pensive, without discussing the relative credence or merits of the telegram, he coldly read the laconic text.

"Impossible!- It is inconceivable!- Purely a funny hoax!- He is mocking us!- Ridiculous!- Absurd!-" And a series of these expressions serving to express their doubt, incredulity, the tom-foolery of it, the folly, rolled off their tongues for several minutes with the accompanying gestures that are useful in these circumstances. They each smiled, laughed, shrugged their shoulders or exclaimed ridicule according to the disposition of their humor. Only, J.T. Maston had these superb words:

"It is an idea, certainly!" he cried.

"Yes," responded the major, "but seldom is it permissible to avow ideas such as these, unless with the condition one does not consider actually executing them."

"And why is that?" asked the lively secretary of the Gun Club, prepared to make an argument of it. But no one volunteered to press their advantage.

Meanwhile the name of Michel Ardan was already circulating around the town of Tampa. The foreigners and the indigenous regarded, with airs of interrogation and pleasantry, that the certain European was a myth and an individual chimera. But they joked towards J.T. Maston, for believing in this legendary person. When Barbicane proposed to send a projectile to the Moon, everyone had considered this enterprise a natural, practicable affair of ballistics! But whilst it was a reasonable offer to affect the passage of a projectile to the moon; to think of it as an incredible voyage, this was a proposition of fantasy, a humorous prank, a farce, and to employ a word that the French use with precision in the exact tradition of their familiar slang language, '*darn-humbug*!

The mockeries endured throughout the evening without discontinuation, and one could affirm that the entire Union was prized by laughter; and this was hardly usual for a country where impossible enterprises find ready supplies of willing advocates, followers and participants.

However the proposition by Michel Ardan, like all novel ideas, seemed to bother certain minds. It had derailed the course of their accustomed emotions. This was something undreamt of! The incident soon became an obsession due to its very strangeness. People regarded it pensively. Many things are denied one previous evening and then in fact the following day become reality! Why shouldn't such a voyage be accomplished one day? But in any case, it was decided, the man who of his own volition wanted to risk his life in the pursuit of such a project could not be taken seriously, and he would have fared better to have stayed silent than to trouble an entire population with this ridiculous nonsense.

But, at first sight, did this person really exist? A grand question! The name Michel Ardan was not unheard of in America! It belonged to a European often cited for his audacious enterprises. Plus, the telegram had been sent across the depths of the Atlantic, it had designated the name of the ship on which the Frenchman declared his passage, assigned a date of imminent arrival; all these circumstances gave to the proposition a certain character of actuality. They had to get to the heart of the matter. Soon isolated individuals formed into groups, and these groups condensed into one active curious mob in the same way the virtue of atoms attract molecules; and so, finally, the resulting collection being fully compacted, a crowd descended upon Barbicane's temporary residence.

Since the arrival of that dispatch, Barbicane had made no pronouncement; it was left to the opinion of J.T. Maston to perform, without manifesting any approbation or blame. He kept coy, proposing to attend to matters as they developed; but he had not contemplated the impatience of the public, nor expected to the dissatisfaction of his eyes that small contingent of Tampa's population amassed below his window. Soon the murmurs, the vociferations, obliged his response. He had all the appearances of, and in consequence, all the tedium of being a celebrity.

Hence he appeared. A silence fell and then a citizen, presenting himself to speak, posed the question carried on everyone's lips: "The person designated by the telegram under the name Michel Ardan is en-route to America, yes or no?"

"Gentlemen," responded Barbicane, "I do not know any more than you."

"We must know," cried their impatient voices.

"Time will tell us," answered the president coolly.

"Time does not have the right to hold in suspense an entire country," replied the orator. "Have you modified the plans for the projectile, as demanded by the cable telegram?"

"Not yet, gentlemen; but you speak with reason, and we should not restrain ourselves from finding out. It was the telegraph which has been the cause of all this emotion, and it is completely fair for it to have provided more information."

"Send a telegraph! A telegraph," cried the crowd.

Barbicane descended, and preceded by that immense rabble, they diverged upon the bureau of administration for the *Atlanta*.

Several minutes later, a dispatch was launched to the syndicate of ship brokers in Liverpool. It demanded to know the answer of these questions:

"Is there a ship *Atlanta*?- When did it leave Europe?- Is there a Frenchman on board named Michel Ardan?"

Two hours later, Barbicane received precise information which left no place for any doubt.

"'The steamer *Atlanta* of Liverpool left for sea 2nd October, bound for Tampa Town with a Frenchman on board, listed as a passenger under the name of Michel Ardan."

At this confirmation of the initially-dispatched telegram, the eyes of the president flashed brilliantly with subtle flames. His hands clenched violently and he was heard to murmur:

"So it is actually true! It is actually possible! This Frenchman exists! And in 15 days he arrives here! But he is a fool! A certified madman! I shall never consent..."

And yet however, that same evening, he wrote to the house of *Breadwill and Co.* and requested they suspend the casting of the projectile, awaiting a new order.

Now, to recount the emotion that captured all of America entirely- it's effect surpassed Barbicane's announcement by a dozen times- from what was said in the newspapers across the Union, the manner which they had accepted the news and the mode with which they chanted about the arrival of that hero of the old continent; painting a febrile agitation which everyone lived, counting the hours, counting the minutes, counting the seconds; to give one an idea, weakening all, with the fatiguing obsession of all these minds dominated by one single pensive thought; watching the occupations cede to a single preoccupation- their work arrested, their commerce suspended, the boats prepared to leave listlessly resting affixed to their ports awaiting the arrival of the *Atlanta*, the convoys of steam-trains arriving full and leaving devoid of passengers, the bay of Espiritu-Santo incessantly crossed by steamers, packet-boats, pleasure yachts, the fly-boats of all dimensions; to enumerate the thousands of curious that quadrupled in 15 days the population of Tampa Town and had to endure camping in tents like an army on campaign- it was a task of waiting beyond the ordinary forces of humanity, which could not be conceived of without temerity.

On the 20th October at 9 o'clock in the morning, the semaphores along the Bahama Canal signaled a thick cloud stack of smoke-fumes on the horizon. 2 hours later a grand steamer exchanged signals of acknowledgement with them. Immediately the name of *Atlanta* spread in expedited haste throughout Tampa Town. At 4 p.m., the English ship entered the harbor of Espiritu-Santo. At 5 she passed into the harbor of Hillsboro with a head of steam. At 6, they anchored in the port of Tampa.

Before the anchor could found itself in the sand, 500 boat craft surrounded the *Atlanta* and the steamer was taken by assault. Barbicane, the first onboard, even before the ship's rail lines had been connected, spoke in a full voice which he in vain tried to contain emotion from:

"Michel Ardan!" he cried.

"- Present!" responded an individual mounted on the foredeck.

Barbicane, his arms crossed, his eyes interrogating, his lips pursed, fixatedly regarded the passenger of the *Atlanta*.

It was a man of 42 years, grand, but slightly-stooped in posture like those caryatid sculptures who support balconies upon their shoulders. A strong head, veritably as enduring as a lion's, for an instant shaking his hair ardently with the semblance of a veritable mane. A short face, large at the temples, an agreeable moustache that bristled like the whiskers of a cat and petite bouquets of small yellow hairs around his cheeks, and round eyes a little astray as a result of myopia completed that eminently feline physiognomy. But his nose was decidedly hardy, his mouth particularly humane, his forehead high, intelligent and lined like a field that never rests in fallow. And finally his torso was strongly developed and held a pose of aplomb courtesy of long legs, muscular arms, powerful levers well-attached; a decidedly alluring, European countenance that was solidly well-built, '*forged rather than cast*', to borrow an expression of metallurgy.

Disciples of Lavater or Gratiolet would decipher without any effort in the head and the physiognomy of his personage the inscrutable signs of combativeness, that is to say courage in danger and a tendency to smash the obstacles; they would see kindness and marvelous imagination, an instinct towards certain temperaments and a passion for superhuman things; but, in contrast, the lumps of acquisitiveness, the desire to possess and own, were absolutely lacking.

To complete the type of physique of the passenger onboard the *Atlanta*, a convenient signaler was his clothing that was large in shape, comfortably surrounding him, his trousers gave him ample movement and the reason for his nickname '*the dead sheet*', his cravat loosely tied, the collar to his shirt liberally opened, his robust neck emerging and his cuffs invariably unbuttoned allowing his feverish hands to escape and move about. His appearance was of one that, even before the strongest of winters or danger, the man was never cold- except for in his eyes.

There, on the fore dock of the steamer in the midst of the crowd, he paced; his vision wandering, never resting in one place, '*dragging on his anchors*' to use the expression of sailors, gesticulating, addressing everyone in the world around him with familiarity and gnawing at his nails with nervous avidity. Certainly he was one of those originals whom the Creator invents in a moment of fantasy and then afterwards entirely breaks the mold.

In effect, the morale and personality of Michel Ardan offered a large field of observation and analysis. The man was amazingly lively with a perpetual disposition to hyperbole and had not yet passed the age of making superlative expressions; the objects portrayed by the retina of his eyes held unmeasured dimensions and this led to an association with gigantic ideas; he saw everything grandly, except for difficulties and men.

He showed a luxurious nature; an artist by instinct, spiritually still a boy, he would not fire rounds of good words, but rather discriminately deliver his arguments. During discussions he gave little heedfulness to logic, rebelling at syllogism, which he would not have invented. He had his own ways to attack. Veritable destroyer of vitriol, he launched with a plain heart the arguments *ad hominem* to great effect, and he liked to defend tooth and nail the cases of hopeless desperation.

Amongst other manias, he proclaimed of himself '*an ignorance sublime*' like Shakespeare, and professed to despise scientists: "those gentlemen," he said, "who mark the points whilst we enjoy the party." He was, in summary, a bohemian of a country of mountains and marvels; adventurous, but not an adventurer- a daredevil, a Phaeton bridled to the chariot of the Sun, an Icarus with spare wings to change. To the rest of it, he profited as a person and profited well; he would launch head first into enterprises of folly, he burned and destroyed vessels with the enthusiasm of Agathocles, and, ready to break at his reins every hour he invariably fell upon his feet, like the petite wooden puppet acrobats which exist for the amusement of children.

In two words, his motto was: "Even so!" and love of the impossible was his ruling passion, to use that excellent expression by the Pope.

But as well, like any enterprising rogue, he had as many defects as qualities! Nothing risked, nothing gained, said he. Ardan had risked everything he had to disadvantage! He was a borrower of money, who would roll the Danaides.

A man perfectly unselfish, who more often than not followed affairs of the heart before affairs of the head; life-saving, chivalrous, he would not have signed the death warrant of his most cruelest enemy, one who would have rendered himself into slavery to free a slave.

In France, in Europe, the whole world knew of him, his personality brilliant and noisy. Did there ever cease from speaking a different hundred voices that grew hoarse in their service to his renown? He lived in a house of glass, presenting to the entire universe the confidante of his most intimate secrets. But he also possessed an admirable collection of enemies, which he never availed from offending, bruising, tripping without mercy, as he joyously jostled his way through the crowd.

However there was general amiability towards him, and was treated like a spoilt child. He was, according to the popular expression '*a man to take things easily*', and so he was taken. Everyone was interested in his dangerous adventures or they watched with quiet worry. He was so audaciously reckless! Whenever some friend volubly tried to arrest him from an imminent predictable catastrophe approaching he would respond with amiable good humor: '*The forest is only burned by its own trees*' and was no doubt unaware he quoted one of the best Arabic proverbs.

This was to speak of Michel Ardan; the passenger of the *Atlanta*, forever agitated, forever boiling from the action of an interior fire, forever motivated, not in consideration of what he intended to do in America- he was not even thinking of that- but from the effect of his fervent nervous system. If there were ever two individuals who offered such a flippant contrast to one another, this would be the Frenchman Ardan and the Yankee Barbicane- although the two were both totally enterprising, hardy and audacious in their mannerisms.

These contemplations were then abandoned by the president of the Gun Club in the presence of his rival, who had been relegated into second place by the lively interruption of the hurrahs and the cheers of the crowd. It turned into a crisis of frenetic activity, and the enthusiasm formed such personal affections that Michel Ardan, after receiving a thousand handshakes and fearing he might lose his fingers, took refuge in his cabin.

Barbicane had come along beside him without pronouncing a single word.

"You are Barbicane?" demanded Michel Ardan, standing there, and the two fiery souls started to speak together as though after a friendship of 20 years.

"Yes," answered the president of the Gun Club.

"Ah good! Hello, Barbicane. How have you been? Very well? That is better than great! Better than great!"

"And so," said Barbicane, without entering into preliminaries, "you are decided to participate?"

"Absolutely decided."

"Nothing will alter your mind?"

"Nothing. Have you modified your projectile as I indicated in my dispatch?"

"I waited for your arrival. But," asked Barbicane, insisting to know, "have you given it good thought?..."

"Given it good thought! And why waste time doing that? I have come across an occasion for me to tour the Moon, from which I profit- and that is all there is to it. I see no merit in doing any more reflection."

Barbicane stared at the man, intently regarding someone who could speak of this intended voyage to the Moon with such thoughtlessness- an insouciance that was complete in its perfect absence of inquietude.

"But, you must have ready," Barbicane said, "at least some plan, some mode of execution?"

"An excellent one, my friend Barbicane. But permit me to make one request: if I may recount my history all at once, to a good crowd, to the entire world, and that will answer all your questions. This then evades any repetition. Hence, if you would send notice, convey it to your friends, your colleagues, to all of the town, to all of Florida, to all America, if you please; and tomorrow I shall share with you the development of my ideas and you can respond with any questions you feel are sufficient. You may remain calm, I will be ready to answer anyone with firm feet. Is that suitable to you?"

"It suits me well," responded Barbicane.

On this, the president left the cabin and filled the crowd in on the proposition of Michel Ardan. His words were accompanied with trepid groans and acclaims of joy. This arrangement cut short any difficulty. The next day everyone could contemplate at their own ease this European hero. However certain spectators refused to voluntarily leave the decks of the *Atlanta*; and they passed the night on board. Amongst them was J.T. Maston, who had fixed his hook to the railings, it would have required the use of a winch to detach him.

"He is a hero! A hero!" he cried. "We are nothing but a bunch of old women compared to that European!"

As to the president, after attempting to convince the visitors to retire, he returned to the cabin of the passenger and did not leave until the moment the clock of the steamer sounded midnight.

But at that, then, the two rivals in popularity warmly shook hands, and Michel Ardan affectionately addressed the president Barbicane in his farewell.

19. A Meeting

The next day the sun rose too late to be agreeable for the impatient public. It was altogether too lazy for a Sun who was to declare a festival occasion. Barbicane, fearing the questions would be indiscrete for Michel Ardan, would have preferred to reduce the auditors to a small number of experts; his colleagues, for example. But it would have been easier to dam the Niagara. Hence he renounced this idea and let his new friend take his chances with a public conference. The new room of the public stock exchange of Tampa Town, even with its colossal dimensions, was judged insufficient for the ceremony, as the planned discussion approached the proportions of a real meeting.

So the place chosen was a vast plain situated beyond the town. In several hours it was shaded from the rays of the Sun. The ships in the port; rich of sails, rigging, spare masts, and yards; furnished the necessary accessories for the construction of a colossal tent. Soon an immense canvas sky stretched over that sun-hardened prairie and defended it from the ardors of the daylight. 300,000 people travelled to that place and braved for several hours the stifling temperature, waiting attentively for the arrival of the Frenchman. Of that crowd of spectators, the first third could see and hear; the second tier could somewhat see but were unable to entertain the words spoken; and the final third, they could see nothing nor hear anything. This did not prevent, however, everybody's hands from expressing prodigious applause.

At 3 o'clock Michel Ardan appeared, accompanied by the principle members of the Gun Club. On his right arm was the president Barbicane, at his left arm was J.T. Maston, more radiant than the sun at full midday, and nearly as gleaming. Ardan mounted the stage. From his high vantage he saw stretching out before him an ocean of black hats. He seemed without any embarrassment; he was not serious, it was like he was at home- gay, familiar, amiable. To the reception of hurrahs he responded with gracious salute then, with his hands, he asked for their silence, silence, and he spoke in English; and his expressions were quite correct as he presented himself with these terms:

"Gentlemen," said he, "yes it is very hot, and I will take advantage of these moments for you to hear some explanation of this project of which you are all very interested. I am neither an accomplished orator nor a scientist, and I had not contemplated to speak in public- but my friend Barbicane told me this would give you pleasure, and so I am devoted to do so. Hence, afford me your 600,000 ears, and please excuse any faults in my speech."

This debut was not necessarily to the taste of his assistants, but his expressions were to the contentment of the crowd who made an immense murmur of satisfaction.

"Gentlemen," said he, "feel free to mark your approbation or probation as you wish to intercede. If it is convenient, I shall now commence. Firstly, if you would oblige me; of your affair I am ignorant. But this is not an ignorance which can very well ignore the difficulties. Here I was thinking it something quite simple, natural and easy to take a passage on the projectile as it undertakes its journey for the Moon. It is a voyage which must occur sooner or later; and as to what mode of locomotion adopted, that is entirely simply subject to the laws of progress. Man commenced to voyage on all fours, then on two feet, then in a cart, then a coach, then a carriage, and a stage coach, and then in steam-trains; ah yes! The projectile is the transportation of the future; and to speak truly, the planets are merely a kind of projectile, simple cannon balls launched from a cannon by the hands of our Creator.

"But may I return to our vehicle, the projectile? Some of you, gentlemen, will believe that the velocity being transmitted is excessive; this is nothing; all the planetary bodies have a velocity more rapid, and the Earth also, as they orbit around the Sun. Our planet is moving three times faster as it follows its trail around the Sun. Here are some examples. Only, I ask your permission to express these values in kilometers, as the measurement units which Americans use are unfamiliar to me, and my head overheats trying to do the calculations."

What he asked for was simple and without much difficulty. The orator resumed his discourse:

"Here you are then, Gentlemen, the velocity of the different planets. I am obliged to avow that, and forgive my ignorance, I do not understand exactly the small details of astronomy; but within 2 minutes you shall know as much as I do. Therefore learn that Neptune moves at 5,000 kilometers an hour;

Uranus, 7,000; Saturn, 8,858; Jupiter, 11,675; Mars 22,000; the Earth, 27,000; Venus, 32,426; Mercury, 52,520; certain comets, 400,000 kilometers at their perihelion! As for ourselves, veritably strolling, at an embarrassing speed, our velocity will be 9,900 kilometers and constantly decelerating! And does that demand any rapture, when it is evident that all this will be surpassed one day with velocities much greater than these, when either light or electricity will probably become the agents powering future mechanics?"

No person doubted this affirmation of Michel Ardan.

"My audience of friends," he continued, "if we are to believe certain narrow-minded spirits- and this is the convenient qualification to give them- humanity is encircled in a containment that even Popilius could not escape from, and condemned to vegetate upon this globe without ever being able to launch into planetary space! This will never be true! We are soon to go to the Moon and on to the planets, and on to the stars; in the way today we travel from Liverpool to New York, easily, quickly, surely. And soon, through an atmospheric ocean, we will travel just as though we were traversing across oceans to go to the Moon! Distance is only a relative word; and when we are finished, it will be reduced to zero!"

The audience, though very much supportive of their hero from France, was slightly taken aback by these audacious theories. Michel Ardan seemed to comprehend this.

"You do not seem convinced, my brave hosts," he replied with an amiable smile. "Ah well! Let us reason a bit. Do you know how much time it would take an express steam-train to reach the Moon? 300 days. No more. The trajectory's distance would be 476,406 kilometers, but what is that really? That is the same as nine times around the Earth, and there is no experienced sailor or voyager who hasn't stretched their paths further than this in their lifetime. Imagine that I will be taking only 97 hours on my whole route! Ah! You may figure that the Moon is a long way from the Earth and that I should think twice and with tentative caution about this adventure! But what would you say therefore if I were to go to Neptune, which gravitates 1,147,000,000 kilometers from the Sun! Now there is a trip which not many gentlemen could afford the fare for, even if it cost a nickel per kilometer! Baron Rothschild himself, with his millions, could not buy for himself a place- he would be short $86,750,000, and would be ejected en-route!"

This line of argument appeared to please the assembly a lot. And then Michel Ardan, full of his subject, launched himself without restraint into a superb spirit; he sensed his avid listeners, and continued with admirable assurance:

"Ah well! My friends- that distance between Neptune and the Sun is nothing even, if we compare that to the stars; in effect, to evaluate the distance of the stars we enter into dizzying numerations where the smallest number has 9 figures, and we must use millions for our unit. I demand your pardon for wandering from the subject, but it is of palpable interest. Listen and you be the judges! Alpha Centauri is 8,000,000,000,000 kilometers, Vega 50,000,000,000,000, Sirius 50,000,000,000,000, Arcturius 52,000,000,000,000, the Polar Star is 67,000,000,000,000, Capella 660,000,000,000,000; and the other stars are thousands, millions, billions and billions of kilometers away! So how can we entertain talk about the distances which separate the planets from our Sun! How can we even maintain that distance even exists! Error! Falsehood! Aberration of the senses! Do you know what I think of a world with our radiant Sun, which is but another star, that finishes at Neptune? Would you like to comprehend my theory? It is really quite simple. For me, the solar system is a solid body, homogenous; the planets which compose it press, touch, adhere against each other in the same sort of space that separates molecules of the most compact metals; silver or iron, or platinum! I therefore have the right to affirm, and I repeat with conviction that will penetrate to all: the word distance is a vain word, because distance does not exist!"

"Well said! Bravo! Hurrah!" cried the assembly in a single voice, electrified by the gestures, by the accent of the orator, by the strength of his conceptions.

"No!" cried J.T. Maston, even more energetically than the others. "Distance does not exist!"

And, carried away by the violence of his movements, the surging momentum of his body was seen to trouble Ardan's self-control and he almost fell from the height of the stage to the ground. But he managed to recover his equilibrium, and evaded a plunge which would have brutally proven to him that distance was indeed not merely a vain word. Then the entraining discourse of the orator continued its course:

"My friends," said Michel Ardan, "I think that the question is now settled. If I have not convinced all, that is due to the timidity of my demonstrations, the feebleness of my arguments, and I must accuse my insufficient studies of the theories. Be that as it may, I repeat to you: the distance from the Earth to its satellite is really of little importance and an undignified preoccupation for those who are serious in spirit. Hence I think as we advance and develop we will next establish trains of projectiles, and there people will be ferried in comfortable commodes from the Earth to the Moon. There will be no crashes, no bumping about, no fear of derailment and those onboard will arrive with great speed, without fatigue, travelling in a straight line '*as the crow flies*' to employ the language of trappers. Within 20 years, half of the Earth will have gone to visit the Moon!!"

"Hurrah! Hurrah for Michel Ardan!" cried all those present, even the least-convinced.

"Hurrah for Barbicane!" responded the modest orator.

This act of recognition towards the promoter of the enterprise was accompanied by unanimous applause.

"Now, my friends," said Michel Ardan. "If you have any questions to address to me, you will evidentially embarrass a poor man like me, of course, however I will endeavor to respond to you."

Up until here, the president of the Gun Club had been entirely satisfied with the course of the discussion. It had delivered the speculative theories of Michel Ardan; carried with his vivid imagination, displayed brilliantly. Barbicane felt that he should deliver him from or divert any practical questions, as it would only serve to lessen the quality of his talk, without doubt. Barbicane hastened to occupy the subject of the speech, and asked his new friend if he thought the Moon or the planets were inhabited?

"This is a great problem you have posed to me, my dignified president," responded the orator cheerfully. "However, if I may use the ideas from men of great intelligence, Plutarch, Swedenborg, Bernardin de Saint-Pierre and many others, who have pronounced that concept affirmatively. Were I to satisfy a point of view from natural history, I am inclined to agree with them; I say to myself that nothing useless exists in the world, and, responding to your question with another question, friendly Barbicane, that if these worlds are habitable then they will be inhabited, or have been, or they will be."

"Very good!" cried the front rows of spectators, whose opinion carried the force of law for those towards the rear.

"Only a few could respond with more logic or justification," said the president of the Gun Club. "Hence the question essentially is this: are the other worlds inhabitable? I think so, for my part."

"For me, I am certain," responded Michel Ardan.

"However," replied one of the listeners in the audience, "there are contrary arguments concerning the habitability of worlds. It is evident that the majority of the principles of life would require modification. For example, to speak of the other planets, some must be exceedingly hot and the others incredibly cold, according to if they are closer or further away from the Sun."

"I regret," responded Michel Ardan, "that I do not know personally my honorable contradictor, for I would attempt to respond to him. This objection has some worthiness, but I think may be combatted with some success, as well as all other objections as to the habitability of other worlds.

"If I were a physicist, I would say, if less heat-energy is set in motion on the planets closer to the sun, and as well, to the contrary, on the planets further away, the simple phenomena would be sufficient for the equilibrium of heat to render the temperature of the worlds supportable for beings who are biologically organized like we are.

"If I were a naturalist, then I would say, as many scientists have illustrated, that the nature of life which forms on our own Earth gives us examples of animals living in conditions greatly diverse in habitat; for the fish respire in a medium which is lethal for other animals; and the amphibians have a double life which is difficult to explain; there are certain inhabitants of the sea that are maintained at layers of great depth and support their bodies at pressures of fifty or sixty atmospheres; and the diverse aquatic insects, insensible to temperatures, have been recovered from sources of boiling waters and in the glacial plains of polar oceans. Indeed, I'd suggest that in nature there is a diversity whose action is to us incomprehensible, but no less real, and which is almost pure omnipotence.

"If I were a chemist, I would say that meteorites, whose bodies were evidentially formed beyond our terrestrial world, have revealed in analysis the inscrutable traces of carbon; and that substance is known to originates in organisms, and which, according to the experiments of Reichenbach, are necessarily "animalized".

"And finally, if I were a theologian, I would say that divine redemption seems, as Saint Paul believed, is an application not only upon Earth, but throughout the entire celestial world.

"But I am not a theologian, nor a chemist, nor a naturalist, nor a physicist. And so, in my perfect ignorance of the grand laws which regulate our universe I will limit myself to this response: I do not know if there are habitable worlds, and because I do not know, I shall go there to see!"

Did the adversary of the theories of Michel Ardan hazard forth other arguments? It was impossible to say, because the frenetic cries of the crowd prevented any other opinions of the day. When the silence was eventually reestablished even amongst the groups furthest away, the triumphant orator to add these final scientific considerations:

"You well understand, my brave Yankees, this grand question has been hardly touched upon by me; I have not come to make a point about a public course or expound a thesis upon this vast subject. There are so many other series of arguments in favor of the habitability of other worlds. I leave them to the side. Permit me only to insist on one point.

"If someone maintains that the planets are not habitable, have this response: You may provide good reason, if you can demonstrate that the Earth is the best of all possible worlds, but this is not so, even what Voltaire says. We have only one satellite, whereas Jupiter, Uranus, Saturn, Neptune have plenty in their service, a point of advantage not to be scorned.

"But the main reason which renders our globe less than comfortable is the inclination of its axis in orbit. Here we have the inequality of the days and the nights; the unfortunate diversity of our seasons. On our destitute sphere, it is always too hot or too cold; one freezes in winter, one burns in summer. It is a planet of rheumatism, consumption, flus and pneumonia whereas the surface of Jupiter, for example, whose axis is very slightly inclined- their inhabitants possess the joy of invariable temperatures; there, perpetually, there is a zone of springtime, a zone of summer, a zone of autumn, a zone of winter; every Jovian may choose the climate which suits them best and keep that for their entire life without abrogation to the variations of temperature. You may suitably and without difficulty accept the superiority of Jupiter over our own planet, without even speaking of their years, whose length of duration are to a dozen of ours!

"In addition it is evident to me that, due to the auspicious conditions of that marvelous existence, the inhabitants of that fortunate world are entirely superior, their scholars are more scholarly, their artists are more artistic, their merchants are better merchants, and their good are actually the best. Alas! And what is lacking on our planet to attain such perfection? Hardly anything! An axis that rotates slightly inclined to the plan of its orbit."

"Very well!" cried an impetuous voice, "Unify your efforts, and invent a machine that redresses the axis of the Earth!"

A ton of applause acclaimed that proposal, whose author was none other than J.T. Maston. It is probable the spirited secretary had been carried away by his instincts an engineer to hazard such a strong proposition. However it must be said- and that is with sincerity- there were plentiful cries of support, and without any doubt, if they have had the supporting point as suggested by Archimedes, the resourceful Americans would have created a lever capable of lifting the world to redress its axis. But the point of support to rest their lever upon, it was this which was lacking for those temerarious mechanics.

Meanwhile, that idea of eminent practicality was an enormous success; the discussion was suspended for a good quarter of an hour, a long time, and for a good time afterwards in the United States of America, talking about the proposition formulated by the perpetual secretary of the Gun Club.

20. Thrust and Counterthrust

It seemed that final incident would consume and terminate the discussion- their decision to un-tilt the world's axis. If that was the final word, no one knew of a better way to complete it. However, when the agitation had calmed, these words were heard pronounced severely in a strong voice:

"Now that the orator has given us a large portion of fantasy would he mind returning to the subject, and with less theories discuss the practical parts of the expedition?"

All eyes turned towards the voice of the person who had spoken. It was a lean man, hard, who had an energetic figure, with an American style of beard that grew fuzzily underneath his chin. Making favorable use of the diverse agitations being produced throughout the assembly, he made his way little by little to the premier ring of spectators. There; with his arms crossed, his eyes brilliant and stern, he fixated his gaze on the heroes of the meeting. After having formulated this demand, he stood unwavering as thousands of gazes converged upon him, and murmurs of excited disapproval were uttered. When no forthcoming response occurred, he posed the question again in the same neat and precise accent, and then added:

"We are here to be involved with the Moon, not the Earth."

"You are right, sir," responded Michel Ardan. "The discussion had meandered. Let us return to the Moon."

"Sir," replied the incognito stranger, "you have presented that the Moon is inhabited. Excellent. But if there exist any Selenites living on the Moon, to be sure, they live without breathing, for- and I give this warning in your own interest- there is less than a molecule of air on the surface of the Moon."

At that affirmation, Ardan shook his mane of fawn hair; he comprehended the struggle that had been engaged by the man who had offered the question. He stared at him, then said:

"Ah! There is no air on the Moon! And who told you that, if I may ask?"

"'The scientists."

"Really?"

"Really."

"Sir," replied Michel, "all pleasant jokes aside, I have profound esteem for the scientists who are knowledgeable, but profound disdain for the scientists who are not scientists."

"And do you know any who are part of the latter category?"

"In particular. In France, there is one who claims that mathematically birds cannot fly, and another whose theories demonstrate that fish are unable to live in the water."

"I am not perturbed, sir, and I could cite names of whom support my proposition that you could not challenge."

"If you did, sir, I would be really embarrassed for my poor ignorance, and I only ask of you for a greater instruction!"

"Then why do you abound us with scientific questions if you have not done any study?" the stranger demanded brutally.

"Why!" responded Ardan. "For the reason that a man is certainly braver when he is unaware of the danger! I know nothing, that is true, but it is precisely that weakness which gives me my strength."

"Your feebleness turns to folly!" cried the stranger, with a tone of dark humor.

"Eh! Even better," countered the Frenchman, "if my folly takes me to the Moon!"

Barbicane and his colleagues scrutinized this intruder who was attempting so strongly to deter the course of the enterprise. No one recognized him, and the president, experiencing a lack of assurance about the suitability of the discussion which the Frenchman had now posed, regarded his new friend with a certain apprehension. The assemblage of spectators watched attentively and seriously, disquieted, as the results of this argument had drawn attention to the dangers or even the veritable impossibilities of their expedition.

"Sir," replied Michel Ardan's adversary, "the reasons are numerous and inscrutable which prove the complete absence of any atmosphere around the Moon. I may say *a priori* that if an atmosphere had ever existed, it would have been drawn away by the Earth. But there are better facts in opposition that are incontestable."

"Oppose me then, sir." responded Michel Ardan with perfect gallantry. "Oppose me as you will please!"

"You are aware," said the stranger, "when rays of light traverse the medium of air, they are deviated from a straight line, or, in other terms, this is a property of refraction. Ah well! When stars are occulted by the Moon, their rays, as they touch upon the Moon's disc, are proven to show not the amount least deviation- which is the key requirement for the indication of refraction. From this consequence that the Moon is not enveloped in an atmosphere."

They all regarded the Frenchman, in whom, if they observed an admission of folly, the consequences of the argument would be rigorously upheld.

"In effect," responded Michel Ardan, "if this is your best argument, and all you have to say, and a scientist might be embarrassed to respond; for me, all I have to say to that argument is one of absolute valor, because you suppose the diametric angle of the Moon is perfectly determined, and it is not. But let us move on, I say, my gentlemanly friend, if you will admit the existence of volcanoes on the surface of the Moon."

"The volcanoes that are extinct, yes; enflamed ones, no."

"Allow me to suggest an idea to you, and without extending beyond the boundaries of logic, if there are volcanoes present then they were active for a certain period!"

"That is certain, but since they could have provided in their fumes the necessary oxygen for combustion, the presence of an eruption does not actually prove the presence of a lunar atmosphere."

"The let us pass on," Michel Ardan continued, "and leave the direction of these sort of arguments to arrive at direct observations. But I must warn you that I am going to mention names."

"Mention them."

"I will. In 1715, the astronomers Louisville and Halley, observing the eclipse on 3rd May, remarked upon certain fulminations of a bizarre nature. These bright lights, rapid and repeating often, were deduced to be attributed to thunderstorms raging in the Moon's atmosphere."

"In 1715," replied the stranger, "the astronomers Louisville and Halley appraised purely terrestrial phenomena as lunar phenomena, such as meteorites, which were produced in our atmosphere. That was the response of scientists when this announcement was made, and I respond with that."

"Let us move on again," answered Ardan, entirely untroubled by this riposte. "Herschel, in 1787, is it not true, observed a great number of luminous points on the Moon?"

"Without a doubt; but without explaining the origin of these luminous points, Herschel then did not conclude this apparition was necessarily a product of the lunar atmosphere."

"Well answered," said Michel Ardan, complimenting his adversary. "I see that you are very strong when it comes to selenography."

"Very strong, sir, and I add of all the accomplished observers, the best who have studied the Moon, MM. Beer and Moelder, were in accordance their findings that there was absolutely no air on its surface."

There was a movement amongst the crowd of spectators, who appeared to be moved by the arguments of this single person.

"Let us pass on once more," responded Michel Ardan with even more great calmness, "and we now arrive at an important fact. The skillful French astronomer, M. Laussedat, when observing the eclipse on 18th July 1860, stated that the corners of the Sun's crescent were rounded and truncated. And, the phenomena which produced the deviation of the Sun's rays was the atmosphere of the Moon, because there is no other explanation possible."

"But is that fact certain?" asked the stranger vehemently.

"Absolutely certain!"

The movement in the assembly reversed itself in favor towards their hero, and his adversary rested in silence. Ardan replied by saying this, speaking without vanity as he recovered the advantage, simply: "So you therefore can well see, friendly sir, in fact it is not certain to pronounce absolutely that an atmosphere does not exist on the surface of the Moon; that atmosphere in probability has a low density, which is very subtle, but nowadays science generally admits that it exists."

"Not on the mountains, there I must disagree with you," argued the stranger, "where it would not remain."

"No, but it would lie in the valleys, where it does not pass higher than a few hundred feet."

"In either case, you would fare well to make precautions, for that air is sure to be terribly rarified."

"Oh! my brave sir, I declare it will be sufficient there for one man; besides, once rendered there, I shall economize as best I can, and only respire on grand occasions!"

A formidable burst of laughter thundered into the ears of the mysterious interlocutor, who ran his eyes over the assembly, with fierce bravery.

"Hence," continued Michel Ardan, clearing the air, "now that we have come to agree that a certain amount of atmosphere is present, this forces you to admit the presence of a certain quantity of water. That is a consequence in which I rejoice for my own count. Furthermore, my friendly contradictor, allow me to submit one last observation. We are only aware of one side of the Moon's disc, and whilst there is only a small amount of air on the face which we regard, it is possible that it is plentiful on the opposite face."

"And for what reason?"

"Because the Moon, from the attraction of the Earth's gravity, is formed in the shape of an egg and we perceive the little bit. This is a consequence of the calculations of Hansen, who found the center of gravity is situated in the other hemisphere. The conclusion is that all the masses of air and water were drawn to the other side of the satellite at the beginning of its creation."

"Pure fantasies!" cried the stranger.

"No! Pure theories, once you apply the mechanical laws of physics, and I think difficult to refute. I thereby appeal to this assembly, and to them I voice the question, do they think that life, just as it is seen to exist on the Earth, can be possible on the surface of the Moon?"

The 300,000 in attendance applauded the proposition. The adversary of Michel Ardan attempted to speak once again, but it was not possible for him to be heard. The cries, the threats arose from the crowd like hailstones.

"Enough! Enough!" cried many dissidents.

"Expel that intruder," repeated the others.

"Throw him out! Throw him out!" cried the irritated crowd.

But he stood there, firmly, grasping the stage, digging-in and waiting for the storm to pass; it grew to formidable proportions when Michel Ardan managed to appease them with an gesture. He was too chivalrous to abandon his arguer to such extremities.

"You desire to add a few words?" he asked graciously.

"Yes! A hundred, a thousand," responded the stranger with a temper. "Or rather, no- only a few! To persevere in your enterprise, it follows that you are..."

"Imprudent? How can you label me this way, when I have demanded a cylindrical-conical cannon ball from my friend Barbicane, so that I am not trundled about on my route like a squirrel?"

"But, you wretched person, the appalling repercussions when you depart will pull you into pieces!"

"My friendly contradictor, you have put your finger on the solely veritable difficulty; however, I have too good an opinion of the genius of the industrial Americans to believe they will not find a resolution."

"But what of the heat developed by the velocity of the projectile as it traverses through the air?"

"Oh! The walls are quite thick, and it will pass so rapidly through the atmosphere!"

"But your food? And water?"

"I calculate that I can carry enough for a year, and my journey is four days duration!"

"And what air will you breathe on route?"

"I can derive that from chemical processes."

"But what about your fall onto the Moon, if you arrive there?"

"It will be a sixth of the force of falling on the Earth, since the gravity is six times less on the surface of the Moon."

"But that will still be sufficient for you to break like glass!"

"And what is to prevent me retarding my plunge by igniting conveniently placed rockets at the correct moment?"

"But finally, supposing all those difficulties are resolved, all those obstacles ironed-out, and succeeding chances are in your favor, and we admit that you arrive safely on the surface of the Moon, how will you return?"

"I will not return!"

At this response, which touched upon sublime with its simplicity, the assembled crowd went demurely mute. This silence was more elegant in its essence than the earlier cries of enthusiasm. The stranger turned this to his profit by protesting one last time.

"You will be killed, infallibly," he cried, "and your death; not only will it be an insensitive death, it will have been of no service to science!"

"Continue, my generous stranger, with your veritable prognostications that are so agreeable."

"Ah! This is too much!" cried the adversary of Michel Ardan. "And I do not know why I continue this discussion which is not serious. Pursue your enterprise of folly! You are not the one who shall be held to blame!"

"Oh! You do not offend me!"

"No! It is another who will bear the responsibility for these acts!"

"And who will, if you please?" asked Michel Ardan in an imperious voice.

"The ignorant fool who organized this attempt who it is impossible to ridicule!"

The attack was direct. Barbicane, since the intervention of the stranger, had been making violent efforts to contain himself and was burning on his fumes as certain steam boiler furnaces do; but, with such a rude and outrageous designation, he leapt to his feet and proceeded to march towards his adversary to brave in the face, when he was quickly and suddenly separated from him.

The platform had been lifted by a hundred vigorous arms, and the president of the Gun Club duly partook with Michel Ardan the honors of their triumph. The stage was extremely heavy, however their porters were relayed unceasingly; because everyone disputed, struggled, combatted for the privilege of carrying them on their shoulders.

However the stranger had not taken advantage of the tumult to attempt to depart from the place. Would it have been possible, in the midst of that compacted crowd? No, without any doubt. In any case, he held his place in the premier row, his arms crossed, his eyes fixated upon Barbicane.

He never lost his view, and the two men regarded each of the other's gaze like two quivering swords.

The cries of the immense crowd maintained their maximum intensity throughout this triumphant march. Michel Ardan allowed himself to be taken with evident pleasure. His face was radiant. Sometimes the stage pitched and rolled like a ship battling waves. But the two heroes displayed their sea legs; they were unflinching, and eventually their vessel arrived safely in the port of Tampa Town. Michel Ardan was fortunately able to slip away from the last entreaties of his vigorous admirers; he ran into the Franklin Hotel, proceeding to his chamber and slipping rapidly therein, whilst an army of a hundred thousand men coagulated below his window.

During this time a scene that was curt, grave and decisive occurred there between that mysterious person and the president of the Gun Club.

Barbicane, liberated finally, went straight to his adversary.

"Come!" he said with a voice of brevity.

The stranger followed him to the quay, and soon the two were at the entrance to the wharf outside Jones' Fall.

There, the enemies, still unknown to one another, regarded themselves.

"Who are you?" demanded Barbicane.

"Captain Nicholl."

"I held no doubt. It is here that fate has brought our paths together..."

"I have come to cross yours!"

"You have insulted me!"

"Publically."

"And you will render me satisfaction for this insult."

"In an instant."

"No. I desire everything between us to be done with secrecy. There is a wood situated three miles from Tampa- Skersnaw Woods. Do you know it?"

"I know it."

"You will please to enter it on one side at 5 o'clock tomorrow morning?"

"Yes, if at the same hour you will enter from the other side?"

"And you will bring your rifle?" said Barbicane.

"If you will oblige and bring your own," responded Nicholl.

With these words coldly pronounced, the president of the Gun Club and the captain separated. Barbicane returned to his residence, but in lieu of spending a few hours in the repose of sleep, he passed the night searching for a way to evade the initial jolt caused by the projectile and in resolving the difficult problems posed by Michel Ardan during the discussion at the meeting.

21. How a Frenchman Settles a Matter

Whilst the conditions of the duel were discussed by the president and the captain- a duel that was terrible and savage, where each adversary descends into being a man hunter- Michel Ardan reposed from the fatigues of his triumph. Although reposing was evidentially not a justifiable expression, for the beds of Americans can rival in their hardness any tabletop of granite or marble.

Hence Ardan slept rather badly; he tossed and turned, and turned again between the serviette napkins that served for his sheets and he dreamed about installing a comfortable couch in the projectile when a violent noise interrupted his reverie. The door was being rained upon by blows. It sounded as though this was being done with an iron instrument. The formidable noise was being combined with a loud voice in those little hours of the morning.

"Open!" he heard the voice cry. "But, in the name of heaven, open up! Tarnation!"

Ardan had no reason to acquiesce to a demand posed so loudly. However he arose and opened his door at the moment it was about to cede regardless due to the efforts of his obstinate visitor. The secretary of the Gun Club erupted into the room. A bomb could not have entered with less ceremony.

"Here, yesterday evening," cried J.T. Maston explosively and abruptly, "our president received a public insult during the public meeting! The provocation came from an adversary, no other than Captain Nicholl! They will fight tomorrow morning in the Skersnaw Woods! I learned this from Barbicane's own mouth! If he is killed, it will be the annihilation of our project! We must interrupt this duel! There is only one man in this world who possesses the power to arrest Barbicane's intentions, and that man is Michel Ardan!"

As J.T. Maston was speaking to him, Michel Ardan, having abandoning the idea of interrupting, had already begun dragging his vast pantaloons on and less than two minutes after, the two friends engaged their legs rapidly through the suburbs of Tampa Town.

During their rapid course Maston told Ardan of the current situation. Ardan was appraised of the veritable causes of enmity between Barbicane and Nicholl, of how that enmity had grown from an earlier date, and how until then, thanks to their friends, the president and the captain had never seen one another face to face; he added that it was due to the unique rivalry between armor and cannon balls, and that final scene during the meeting had been nothing but an occasion that Nicholl had searched for a long time to satisfy his age-old animosity.

Nothing is more terrible than the duels particular to America, for during them the two adversaries search for one another as they traverse wild grounds, lying in wait with his weapon to shoot in the midst of the forest like a wild beast. It follows straightforwardly they must envy the marvelous qualities that are natural to the Indians of the Prairies, their quick intelligence, their ingenious ruses, their tracking abilities, their skill at sensing the enemy. One error, one hesitation, one false step and then you are dead. During these encounters, the Yankees are often accompanied by their dogs, and as each chase their prey, the pursuit can continue for entire hours.

"What diabolic gentlemen you all are!" cried Michel Ardan, when his companion had described with plentiful amounts of energy the entire production which entailed.

"That is how we are," responded J.T. Maston modestly. "But haste now."

Although Michel Ardan and his diligent compatriot hurriedly traversed the fields that were humid and dew-bespeckled, encountering rice paddies and over creeks, taking short cuts, they could not arrive earlier at the woods of Skersnaw than half past 5 o'clock in the morning. Barbicane was to have passed through its edge half an hour earlier.

From their viewpoint they saw a woodsman occupied at work cutting timber for firewood with his hatchet. Maston ran to him and cried:

"Have you seen enter into the woods a man armed with a rifle, Barbicane, the president... My best friend?"

The dignified secretary of the Gun Club naively assumed that the president was known to the entire world. But the bushman held the air of a lack of comprehension.

"A hunter," added Ardan.

"A hunter? Yes," answered the woodsman.

"A long time ago?"

"A little less than an hour before now."

"Too late!" cried Maston.

"And have you heard any rifle shots?" demanded Michel Ardan.

"No."

"Not one?"

"Not one. Your hunter doesn't seem to be having much good hunting!"

"What do we do?" said Maston.

"Enter the woods, at the risk of attracting a bullet that was not destined for us."

"Ah!" cried Maston with a powerful inflection as he heeded the idea. "I would take ten bullets in my head rather than let one hit Barbicane's head."

"Then we must go!" replied Ardan, gripping the one hand of his companion.

A few seconds later the two friends disappeared into the edge of the woods. It was an extremely thick forest; filled with giant cypresses, sycamores, tulip trees, olive trees, tamarinds, live oaks and magnolias. The diverse trees tangled their branches together in an inextricable melee that did not permit one's view to extend very far. Michel Ardan and Maston marched side by side passing silently through the high growth, fraying their shirts surrounded by vigorous liana vines, interrogatively peering into the dark bushes and branches lost into shadow thick with foliage and listening at every moment for the unmistakable detonation of rifles.

They were not able to discern any tracks which Barbicane might have left behind as he travelled through the woods, so it was impossible to determine his whereabouts; and they marched blindly on the scant trails- which surely an Indian would have seen and followed his adversary step by step.

After an hour of vain searching, the two companions rested. Their anxiety redoubled.

"It must be all ended," said Maston discouraged. "A man like Barbicane would not have used any ruses with his enemy, nor set any traps, nor make practical maneuvers! He is too straightforward, too courageous. He must have advanced, straight into danger, and without a doubt too far for the woodsman's to hear on the wind the detonation of arms being fired!"

"But no! No!" responded Michel Ardan. "Since we entered the woods, we would have heard!"

"Not if we arrived too late!" cried Maston, the despair sounding in his voice.

Michel Ardan had not a word in response; he and Maston returned to their interrupted march. Time after time they uttered great cries; they appealed to Barbicane, to Nicholl; but not one or the other of the adversaries responded with their voice. The joyous flocks of birds, startled and aroused by their noise, disappeared into the branches and sometimes frightened deer ran hastily away into the copses of trees.

For another hour more, their searching was prolonged. The greater part of the woods they had already explored. Nothing revealed the presence of the combatants. They were beginning to doubt the woodsman's affirmation, and Ardan was about to renounce their persevering for much longer in the futile reconnaissance, when, giving him a nudge, Maston stopped.

"Shh!" he said. "Someone is there!"

"Someone?"

"Yes! A man! He seems immobile. And his rifle is not in his hands. What is he doing?"

"Is he recognizable to you?" asked Michel Ardan. His bad eyesight was of little value in these circumstances.

"Yes! As he turns around," answered Maston.

"And it is?..."

"Captain Nicholl!"

"Nicholl!" cried Michel Ardan, sensing his heart beating violently.

For Nicholl was disarmed! Did it not follow that he had nothing to fear from his adversary?

"Let's walk up to him," said Michel Ardan, "and we can find out what has taken place."

But before he and his companion had taken fifty steps, they stopped to examine the captain more attentively. They had imagined a man altered and deranged with desire for the blood of vengeance! And what they saw held them stupefied.

A tightly-knit net stretched across two gigantic tulips, and, in the middle of the net, a little bird, its wings entangled and battered, struggled with plaintive cries. The bird was powerless to extricate itself from this dense web; which had not been put there by humans, but by a venomous spider, particular to that country, as big as the body of a pigeon and the weaponry it held in its limbs were enormous. This hideous animal, at the moment it was about to fall upon its prey, retreated from its foray into the high branches of the tulip tree, as redoubtable and menacing an enemy as it appeared below its trap.

In effect, Captain Nicholl, his gun left on the ground, oblivious to the dangers of his situation, was occupied in delivering as delicately as possible the victim held glued by the web of that monstrous arachnid. When he had finished the little bird took flight, beating its wings joyously as it disappeared.

Nicholl, attentively, sought to regard what it was that travelled along those branches? When a voice extended to him and pronounced emotionally:

"You are a brave man, you are!"

He turned around. Michel Ardan appeared before him, and repeated in the same tone:

"And a kind man."

"Michel Ardan!" cried the captain. "And what are you doing here, sir?"

"I have come to shake your hand, Nicholl, and prevent you from killing Barbicane or him from killing you."

"Barbicane!" cried the captain. "I have been searching for him for two hours without discovery. Where is he cowering?"

"Nicholl," said Michel Ardan, "this is not polite! One must always respect their adversary. You can relax, if Barbicane is alive, we will discover him; and especially because, if he is not amusing himself by securing the freedom of tiny birds, he will be searching for you. But when we do find him, as assuredly as Michel Ardan says this, there will be no duel between you both."

"Between president Barbicane and I," responded Nicholl gravely, "is a rivalry so telling, that there must be the death of one of us..."

"Come along! Come along!" reprimanded Michel Ardan. "The brave gentlemen you both are, as much as you detest one another, must also hold one's adversary in esteem. You and he will not fight."

"I fight, dear sir!"

"I disagree."

"Captain," along came J.T. Maston with plentiful feeling in his heart, "I am the friend of the president, his alter ego, another just as him; if you absolutely must kill someone, then kill me- it will be exactly the same thing."

"Sir," said Nicholl and he gripped the rifle in his hands convulsively, "these jokes..."

"My friend Maston is not kidding," responded Michel Ardan, "and I comprehend the idea to die for a man that is one's friend! But you and Barbicane will not shoot any bullets, Captain Nicholl, when you two rivals become aware of the proposition which will seduce and impress you both into acceptance."

"And that is?" demanded Nicholl with visible incredulity.

"Patience," responded Ardan. "I must communicate it in the presence of Barbicane."

"Then let us go find him," cried the captain.

Immediately the three men began to follow the path; the captain, after disarming his rifle, put it upon his shoulder and advanced smoothly, without speaking a word.

During the next half-hour, they searched in futile. Maston was taken by a sinister presentiment. He observed Nicholl severely, and he asked himself; had the captain taken satisfactory vengeance, and Barbicane received the misfortune of the bullet's touch, being left lying lifeless and bloodied in some tangled thicket? Michel Ardan felt the same pensive thoughts, and the two shot interrogative looks of suspicion at Captain Nicholl, when Maston stopped suddenly.

The immobile bust of the man leaned back with his feet against a gigantic catalpa tree, appearing twenty yards away, half-disappearing amongst the long grass.

"It is you!" said Maston.

Barbicane was unmoved. Ardan's eyes opened wide as he stared at the captain, but he was unflinching. Ardan stepped forward a few paces and cried out:

"Barbicane! Barbicane!"

No response. Ardan ran towards his friend; but, at the moment he was within arm's length, he stopped abruptly and uttered his surprise.

Barbicane, a crayon in hand, was tracing formulas and geometric figures into a paper pad, his rifle opened and lying abandoned on the ground.

Absorbed in his work, like a scientist, he had forgotten entirely the duel and vengeance, and had heard nothing, seen nothing.

When Michel Ardan put his hand onto Barbicane's, he leapt to his feet and considered him with an astonished eye.

"Ah!" he cried finally. "It's you! Here! I've found it, my friend, I've found it!"

"What?"

"My means!"

"What means?"

"The means to annul the effect of repercussion when the projectile departs!"

"Really?" said Michel as he regarded the captain from the corner of his eye.

"Yes! With water! The water will act as a simple spring... Ah! Maston!" cried Barbicane. "You also!"

"He is with me," responded Michel Ardan, "and permit me to present at the same time the dignified Captain Nicholl!"

"Nicholl!" cried Barbicane, rising to his feet instantly. "Pardon, captain," he said, "I had forgotten... I am prepared..."

Michel Ardan intervened without allowing the enemies the time to interact.

"Good heavens!" he said. "It is fortunate that you brave gentlemen had not met before now! We would now be crying tears of mourning over one or the other of you. But, thanks to the grace of God who has intervened in this melee, there is nothing more to fear. When one has forgotten to hate to plunge into the problems of mechanical physics and the other to steal a spider's morning breakfast, it strikes me that this hatred is not dangerous for any person."

And Michel Ardan recounted to the president the story of how he had found the captain.

"And so I ask you," he said in summary, "if two good men like you are intended by fate to reciprocate put bullets into your heads and bodies with a carbine?"

The situation became a little ridiculous, something unexpected, and Barbicane and Nicholl surveyed one another with guarded countenances; each was glancing towards the other. Michel Ardan sensed their apprehension well, and resolved to brusquely bring about resolution.

"My brave friends," said he, allowing his best smile to form upon his lips. "There is nothing between you both other than a misunderstanding. That is all it is. Ah well! To prove that this is now all finished between yourselves, and because both you gentlemen are willing to risk your lives over so little, accept the proposition I shall put before you."

"Speak," said Nicholl.

"My friend Barbicane believes his projectile will fly straight to the Moon."

"Yes, certainly," replied the president.

"And my friend Nicholl is persuaded that it will tumble to the Earth."

"I am so certain," cried the captain.

"Good!" continued Michel Ardan. "I do not have any pretentions of bringing you to an agreement; but you will both find this to your satisfaction: Leave with me, and we will all see if we reach our route."

"Hey!?" said J.T. Maston, stupefied.

The two rivals, at this sudden proposition, cast their eyes on the other. They observed with attention. Barbicane waited for a response from the captain. Nicholl lay in wait for the speech of the president.

"Well then?" said Michel Ardan in a most-engaging tone. "Since you have thought of how to solve the momentum difficulty."

"Accepted!" cried Barbicane.

Meanwhile with the same enthusiasm as he had pronounced the word, Nicholl also accepted at the same time.

"Hurrah! Bravo! Lively! Hip! Hip! Hip!" cried Michel Ardan and he offered his hands to the two adversaries. "And now the affair is arranged, my friends, permit me in the way of the French. Let us all go to have breakfast!"

22. The New Citizen of The United States

That day all of America became aware at the same time of the affair between Captain Nicholl and the president Barbicane, and it's singular development. The role played in this encounter by the chivalrous European, an unexpected proposition laced with difficulty, accepted simultaneously by the two rivals, that the conquest of the Moon would be performed with

France and the United States together, all combined to increase even more the acclaim and popularity of Michel Ardan.

It is known with what frenzy the Yankees can be passionate about an individual. In a country where grave magistrates can harness themselves to the carriages of dancers in a triumphant procession, one can judge the passion unleashed upon that audacious Frenchman! If any of his horses had been unharnessed, it is probably because he had none; but all other marks of enthusiasm were prodigiously bestowed upon him. Not one citizen did not unite with him in spirit and heart! *Ex pluribus unum*, which is the motto of the United States.

From the date of that day on, Michel Ardan never had a moment of repose. The local delegations from all corners of the United States harassed him endlessly. He was the receiver of goodwill, for better or worse. The hands he shook, the friendly greetings he was given went beyond computation- soon he was worn to the teeth. His voice, hoarse from the innumerable speeches, escaped from his lips unintelligibly; and he barely failed from getting gastroenteritis by the continuous toasts that he was given throughout all of the Union. This success would have greyed another by the first day; but he seemed contained within a semi-inebriation that was spirited and charming.

Of all the delegations the kind most-especially assailing, was the '*lunatics*' who never forgot to guard their future conqueror of the Moon. One day, several of these poor people, rather numerous in America, came and demanded they be returned with him to the country of their birth. Certain ones pretended to speak the words of the Moon's inhabitants, the Selenites, and volunteered to teach Michel Ardan. With his good heart he remained open to all of their innocent mania and was encharged with commissions and messages to their friends on the Moon.

"A unique madness!" as he said to Barbicane after dismissing the last of them. "A madness that strikes the sharp intelligences. One of the most illustrious scientists, Arago, told me that there are plenty of people very wise and very reserved who have allowed their conceptions to slip away and become greatly excited, an incredible singularity, when the Moon begins to occupy their minds. Do you think the Moon has an influence on our maladies?"

"Not really," the president of the Gun Club responded.

"I do not believe in it either, and yet however history has registered the facts which are slightly astounding. For instance, in 1693 during an epidemic, there were a great number more of people who perished on 21st January at the moment of an eclipse. The celebrated Bacon fainted during an eclipse of the

Moon and did not recover his consciousness until after the entire Moon's immersion had completed. The King Charles VI fell on six occasions into dementia throughout the year of 1399, during either a new Moon or a full Moon. There are medical physicians who have classified epilepsy as being due to the lunar phases. The nervous maladies are often ascribed to its influence. Mead tells of a child who entered into convulsions when the Moon entered into opposition. Gall had remarked that the excitement of weakened people increased twice per month, at the epochs of the new and the full Moon. And finally after more than a thousand observations of vertigoes, malignant fevers and somnambulism it all tends to prove that shining body of the night sky has a mysterious influence on terrestrial illnesses."

"But how? Why?" asked Barbicane.

"Why?" responded Ardan. "In faith, I'll offer you the same response which Arago repeated nineteen centuries after Plutarque: '*It is perhaps because it is not true*'."

In the midst of his triumph, Michel Ardan could not escape any of the drudgery inherent to the position of being a celebrity. The successful entrepreneurs tried to exhibit him. Barnum offered him $1,000,000 to promenade him from town to town throughout the United States displayed like an animal curiosity. Michel Ardan told him he was corny and sent him promenading away.

However although he refused to satisfy the public curiosity, his portraits, on the other hand, were couriered across the entire world and occupied the place of honor in people's albums; and these were printed in all dimensions, from the grandeur of life-sized to the microscopically-reduced postage stamps. Everyone could possess their hero in all the poses imaginable; his headshot, his bust, or full-body, in face, profile, three-quarters or from the back. There were more than a million examples- it was a wonderful occasion to deal in personal relics, but he profited not at all. Should he have sold his hairs at one dollar apiece, he still had enough for a fair fortune!

For all truth, the popularity did not displease him. On the contrary. He placed himself at the public's disposition and corresponded with the entire universe. People repeated his witticisms and propagated them, particularly the ones he did not say. Many were loaned, in accordance with the habit that one only lends to the rich.

Not only was he admired by men, but also by women. What an infinite number of '*good marriages*' could he have made, if he had taken into his head to indulge but a small number of the fantasy of his '*fixers*'. The unmarried women throughout, particularly those who had been waiting forty years for their husband, dreamed night and day in front of his photographs.

It is certain he could have had a hundred of companions, even if he had imposed the condition they must accompany him into the air. Women are either intrepid and without fear or entirely in fear of everything. However he had no intention to put down his roots on the lunar continent, and transplant a founding a crossed race of French-American. He thereby always refused.

"I am not going up there to play," said he, "the role of Adam with my wife Eve, please! All I would then need to do is encounter the serpents!...."

Then when he could finally sequester himself from the receptiveness of triumph, he went, joined by his friends, to visit the Columbiad cannon. He owed it his devotion. Moreover, he had developed a strong knowledge of ballistics since he had begun living with Barbicane, J.T. Maston and other Gun Club members. His grand pleasure consisted in repeating that these brave artillery men were no more than amiable and intelligent murderers. He never tired of making jokes at their expense.

On the days he visited the Columbiad, he admired it greatly and descended into the deep barrel of that gigantic mortar which soon would launch him to the Moon.

"On the one hand," said he, "at least this cannon was not cast to kill a person, and this is rather astonishing on the part of a cannon. But as for your engines that destroy, with incendiaries or explosions, and kill; do not speak to me about them, and I especially don't wish to talk about it inside the cannon's bore, or even think about it!"

It follows to report here a proposition that relates to J.T. Maston. When the secretary of the Gun Club heard Barbicane and Nicholl accept the proposition put forth by Michel Ardan, he resolved to join them and to form a party of four. One day he demanded to be included in the voyage. Barbicane disconsolately refused, understanding the projectile did not have the power to deliver so great a number of passengers. J.T. Maston, desperate, then approached Michel Ardan, who he invited to resign his place and valorously gave *ad hominum* arguments.

"Do you see, my old Maston," he said to him, "and please forgive my words for their offence; but between you and me, you are too incomplete to present to the Moon!"

"Incomplete!" cried the valiant invalid.

"Yes! My brave friend! Imagine the case we encounter those inhabitants on high. Would you wish to impart to them the extremely sad idea regarding your missing arm, when they would then apprehend that this is war, and show them how we employ the best of our time devouring, disarraying sets of arms and legs, and this on a globe that could provide nourishment for 100,000,000 inhabitants, and yet only 1,250,000 manage to live in such sorrow? Come along, my dignified friend, you would cause them to throw us out!"

"But if you arrive smashed into different pieces", replied J.T. Maston, "you would appear as incomplete as me."

"Without a doubt," responded Michel Ardan, "but we will not arrive smashed into different pieces!"

In effect, a preparatory experiment attempted 18 October had provided such superior results that it was legitimately conceivable to be in high spirits. Barbicane, desiring to render to account the effect of the counter-momentum force at the moment of the projectile's departure, had requested a mortar of 32 pounds sent from the arsenal at Pensacola. It was installed on the banks of the harbor at Hillsboro, fixed so the bomb would tumble into the sea and the downward plunge would be cushioned. The aim of the experiment was to observe the initial jolt and not the final impact. A projectile was hollowed out and prepared with great precision for the curious experience. The walls within were padded, and a network of springs were applied against the steel, doubling the size of the interior walls. It was a veritable nest tended with cotton wool.

"What a pity I cannot fit into such a space!" said J.T. Maston regrettably, knowing that he was not permitted to personally take part in the upcoming adventure.

Into that charming bomb, which could be sealed by a lid on the top, a big fat cat was introduced plus a squirrel that was cared for as a pet by the perpetual secretary of the Gun Club and one which J.T. Maston was particularly fond of. But it was required to be known how the little animal, who was not subject to vertigo, would be subjected to the experimental voyage.

The mortar was charged with 160 pounds of powder and the bomb was placed into the piece. It was then fired.

Immediately the projectile was sent with great velocity, describing a majestic parabola, attaining a height of a thousand feet in the air, and then curved gracefully down into the midst of the waves.

Without missing an instant, a small boat was embarked to the place of the fall; there skillful divers plunged into the water, and attached cables making small handles around the sides of the bomb, and rapidly hoisted it on board. 5 minutes had barely passed by from the moment the animals had been locked helplessly inside and when the lid to their prison was screwed open.

Ardan, Barbicane, Mason, Nicholl had travelled in the small boat, and they attentively watched the operation with an interested sentiment which was easy to understand. As soon as the bomb had been fully opened the cat launched itself out; slightly offended, but full of life, and without showing any perception of having experienced the aerial expedition. However the squirrel was not there. They searched. No trace. They well had to face the truth. The cat had eaten its companion of the voyage.

"Consarn' it." said J.T. Maston, very saddened on the part of the poor squirrel, and proposed to record his martyrdom for science.

After that experiment all hesitation, all fears had vanished; moreover, the plans Barbicane further developed to perfect the projectile and eliminate entirely the effects of inertia. There was nothing further to do but depart.

Two days later, Michel Ardan received a message from the President of the Union, an honor that he was particularly careful to receive.

As an example like his chivalrous compatriot, the Marquis de La Fayette, the government had bestowed upon him the title of an honorary citizen of the United States of America.

23. The Projectile Carriage

After the achievement of constructing that celebrated Columbiad cannon, the interest of the public threw itself immediately on the projectile- the new vehicle destined to transport the three hardy adventurers to, and travel through, interplanetary space. No person had forgotten that, as per the telegram dispatched 30th September, Michel Ardan had asked for a modification to the plans created by the members of the committee.

The president Barbicane had thought with good reason the shape of the projectile was of little importance, for, after traversing the atmosphere in a few seconds, it would then effectively be moving through an absolute vacuum. The committee had therefore adopted a round form, allowing the bullet to turn and spin on itself as it wished whilst it moved. But, the instant it was transformed into a vehicle, things were an entirely different affair. Michel Ardan did not wish to pass the voyage in the fashion of a squirrel; he wanted to have his head held high, his feet on the floor, and all the dignity as if he had been cradled by the wicker carriage of a hot-air balloon; admittedly with much more velocity, no doubt, but something more respectable than being delivered in a succession of somersaults.

The new plans had been relayed to the house of *Breadwill and Co.* in Albany, with the recommendation they be executed without delay. The projectile, in its modified form, was cast on 2nd November and expedited immediately to Stone Hill along the eastern railways. On the 10th it arrived without accident at the place of its destination. Michel Ardan, Barbicane and Nicholl waited with lively impatience for the projectile carriage which would deliver them their passage to fly them to the discovery of a new world.

It has to be acknowledged that it was a magnificent piece of metal, a product of metallurgy which gave great honor to the genius of American industry. It was the first time such a considerable mass of aluminum had been obtained and this in itself justified it as a prodigious result. The precious projectile glittered in the rays of the sun. The impression it gave with its imposing form and conical top, reminded one of those turrets in the fashion of pepperboxes, which the architects of the Middle Ages suspended at angles on the edges of their fortresses. It only lacked shooting-windows and a weathervane.

"I am only waiting for," declared Michel Ardan, "a group of armed soldiers with halberds and corsets of armor to emerge. We will be inside there like feudal lords, and, with our little artillery shell we will be able to head-off all the armies of the Selenites, if there are any on the Moon!"

"And so you find the vehicle to your pleasure?" Barbicane asked his friend.

"Yes! Yes! Without a doubt," answered Michel Ardan, examining it like an artist. "My only regret is that its shape was not slightly more elongated, which would make the cone more graceful; it might also have been finished with some tufted ornaments in metal clusters, with a chimeric, for example, or a gargoyle, or a salamander escaping from fire with wings deployed and mouth opened."

"For what good?" interjected Barbicane, who was not possessed with that positive spirit which is sensitive to the beauties of art.

"For what good, Barbicane my friend? Alas! Since you have asked me, I well-fear that you will not comprehend my response."

"Tell me anyway, my brave companion."

"Very well! To my mind, one should always mete a small amount of art in all that we do, that gives it better value. Do you know an Indian play called *The Infant's Chariot*?"

"I do not know that name," answered Barbicane.

"That does not astonish me," replied Michel Ardan. "Then I will explain to you. In that play there is a thief who, at the moment he is to cut a hole into the mansion, asks himself if it should be in the shape of a lyre, a flower, a bird, or an amphora? Very well! Tell me, my friend Barbicane, if at that time you had been a member of the jury, would you have condemned that thief?"

"Without hesitation," responded the president of the Gun Club. "He had aggravated the circumstances with unlawful entry."

"And for me, I would have acquitted him, Barbicane! And this is why you'll never understand me!"

"I do not even attempt to, my valiant artist."

"But on the other hand," replied Michel Ardan, "because the exterior of our carriage-projectile is less than to be desired, permit me a piece of furniture for my comfort, one with all the luxury which is appropriate for ambassadors of the Earth!"

"For those considerations, my brave Michel," answered Barbicane, "you may aggrandize it however you imagine, I leave to you to do as you please."

However, before passing on to pleasant aesthetics, the president of the Gun Club had been focused on the aspects of utility and had invented a means to absorb the initial force of being fired with perfect intelligence.

Barbicane had said to himself, not without reason, that no spring would be sufficiently resistant to soften the shock, and, during that famous walk in the Skersnaw woods, he had finally resolved that great difficulty in an ingenious fashion. It was water that he would count upon to render the distinguished service. Here is how:

The projectile was to be filled to a height of 3 feet around its sides with water intended to support a disk of wood perfectly watertight, which slid along a running-groove on the interior side of the projectile. It was a veritable raft in which the voyagers would take their place. Regarding that mass of liquid, it was divided into horizontally partitioned sections which the shock of departure would concurrently smash apart. Each layer of water, from the lowest to the uppermost, would escape through clearance pipes running out from the superior part of the projectile, performing as a spring would; and the disk, dampened from the extreme power, would be prevented from striking the inner walls of the projectile until after crushing successively each of the layer divisions. Without a doubt the voyagers would be afflicted by the violent inertial shock after completely shifting the mass of liquid, but the first impact would be entirely amortized by this dampening-spring of exceptional strength.

It is true that 3 feet of water with a surface area of 54 square feet created a weight of 11,500 pounds; but the triggered gas accumulating in the Columbiad was sufficient, Barbicane figured, to overcome the increased weight; additionally the blast would press all the water out within a second, and the projectile would return promptly to its normal weight.

That is how by making use of his imagination the president of the Gun Club quelled the grave question of shock from the initial blast. The rest of the work was intelligently completed by the engineers of the house of *Breadwill and Co.*, and marvelously executed. The effect of force produced and the water flushed away, the voyagers could then do away with the sections and disassemble the mobile disk which had supported them at the moment of departure.

As for the walls in the superior part of the projectile, their surface was thickly padded with leather, applied above spirals of quality steel, which had the suppleness of clock springs. The pipes allowing the water used in dampen the impact of the initial blast to escape were concealed beneath this padding and would not allow anyone to suspect of their existence.

Hence every precaution imaginable for cushioning the initial blast had been taken. "If we still manage to be crushed," reflected Michel Ardan, "it will be the fault of our having weak compositions."

The projectile measured nine feet across its large exterior and a dozen feet in height. In order not to exceed the assigned weight they had slightly diminished the wall's thickness and reinforced the lowest part, which was required to support the entire violence developed from the gas when igniting the guncotton. This is the way in which bombs and cylindrical-conical shells are made, with their lowest parts thickened.

To enter the tower of metal a narrow opening was housed in the wall of the cone. It resembled the manholes in a steam boiler; hermetically sealed by means of an aluminum steel plate, retained on the interior side with strength to offset the pressure. Thus the voyagers were provided with a way to leave their mobile prison, when they had attained their destination upon the Moon.

But it was not sufficient for them to go, they must be able to see along their route. Nothing was easier. In effect, underneath the padding four portholes of extremely thick lenticular glass were added; two piercing the circular walls of the projectile, the third in the lowest part and the fourth in the conical hat. Hence the voyagers would each be able to observe during the journey their abandoning of the Earth, the Moon approaching, and whilst in space the constellations of the heavens. Not only this, the portholes were protected from the blast on departure by being encased in solid plates that could be removed from by interior screws. In that fashion, the air contained within the projectile would not escape, and made observations eminently possible.

All these mechanisms, admirably established, functioned with great facility. And the engineers had displayed the same intelligence in fitting the arrangements for the projectile-carriage.

There were solid reciprocals welded in-place that were designed to contain the water and the food necessary for the three voyagers; they had even provided a means to procure a flame and light from a special gas canister kept under several atmospheres of pressure. All that was required was to turn a faucet and six days' worth of gas was provided to light and warm this comfortable vehicle. One may see, nothing in the manner of essential things for life had been left out. As well, thanks to the instincts of Michel Ardan, agreeable aspects were joined to utility in the form of objects of art- and in fact the projectile was to become a veritable atelier, an artist's studio, if not for the lack of space. Moreover, one would be deceived to suppose the three persons were perceived as a little cramped within that tower of metal. It had a surface area of 54 square feet and a little over 10 feet in height, and this would permit the guests a certain liberty of movement. In essence, it was as nice within as any of the most comfortable carriages in the United States.

The question of food and interior lighting being resolved, there still remained the question of air. It was evident that the air encased within the projectile would not be sufficient for 4 days' worth of breathing by the voyagers; each man, in effect, consumes in one hour all the oxygen contained in 25 liters of air. Barbicane, his two companions, and two dogs taken in compliment, would consume over 24 hours 2,400 liters of oxygen, or, in weight, little over 7 pounds. Hence it followed they must renew the air in the projectile. How? By a very simple process, that of MM. Reiset and Regnault, as indicated by Michel Ardan during the discussion in the meeting.

We all know that air is composed principally 21% oxygen and 79% nitrogen. What occurs in the act of respiration? The phenomenon is exceedingly simple. The man absorbs oxygen in the air, necessary to entertain life, and rejects the nitrogen entirely. The air which is expired has lost approximately 5% of its oxygen and now contains an equal amount of carbonic acid, definitively produced by the combustion of the elements in the blood with the oxygen that was breathed in. Within an enclosed space, after a certain time, the oxygen in the air is replaced by carbonic acid, or carbon dioxide, a gas that is essentially deleterious to our constitution.

The question was reduced to this: with the nitrogen conserved intact, how could replenished oxygen be absorbed into the air, and how could the expired carbonic acid be destroyed?

Nothing was more simple than by means of potassium chlorate and caustic potash.

The potassium chlorate is a salt which presents itself in the form of white flakes; when it is brought to a temperature above 24° it transforms into potassium chloride and the oxygen it contains is released completely. So, 18 pounds of potassium chlorate renders 7 pounds of oxygen, that is to say the quantity necessary for the voyagers during 24 hours. There you have it- the oxygen is replenished.

As to the caustic potash; it is a material that quite avidly mixes with carbonic acid in the air, if sufficiently agitated to take hold and form potassium bicarbonate. And there you have it- the carbonic acid is absorbed.

In combining these two methods, one is certain to the restore the tainted air with its life-giving qualities. However it must be said, this experiment had only been performed on lower animals. And although performed with scientific precision, everyone was ignorant as to how it would support men.

These facts had been explained during the meeting in relation to that grave question. Michel Ardan did not wish to leave any doubt about living on artificial air, and he offered to test it before the departure. But the tentative honor of proving the process was claimed by the energetic J.T. Maston.

"Since I may not be part of the journey," said the brave artillery man, "in the very least I can live in the projectile for eight days' duration."

It would have been ill-mannered to refuse. His wish was granted. A quantity of sufficient potassium chlorate and caustic potash was outlaid for his disposition with food provisions for 8 days. Then, after shaking hands with his friends, on 12th November at 6 o'clock in the morning, after expressing his recommendations not to be released from the prison until the 20th, at 6 o'clock in the evening, he slid into the projectile and the hatchway plate was hermetically sealed. What transpired during those 8 days? It is impossible to know. The thickness of the walls of the projectile totally prevented any sound from the interior being heard outside.

The 20th November, at 6 hours precisely, the plate was taken away; the friends of J.T. Maston not just a little worried. But they were promptly reassured at the joyous voice and formidably powerful hurrahs emerging.

Soon the secretary of the Gun Club appeared at the summit of the cone in a triumphant attitude. He had put on weight!

24. The Telescope on the Rocky Mountains

On the 20th October the preceding year, after the subscription had been closed, the president of the Gun Club had credited the Cambridge Observatory with the sums necessary to construct a vast optical instrument. That apparatus, either a reflecting or refracting telescope, was to be powerful enough to render visible on the Moon's surface an object the size of 9 feet in diameter.

It is an important difference if a telescope is refracting or reflecting; and best to discuss this here. A refracting telescope is composed of tubes which deliver an image from its upper end through a convex lens called the objective, and at the lowest extremity a second lens named the ocular; to which the eye of the observer is applied. The rays of light emanating from the object traverse the first lens and are seen, from refraction, to form a reverse image. That image is observed with the ocular lens, which enlarges it exactly like a magnifying glass. The tube of a refracting is hence closed at each extremity by the objective and the ocular.

On the contrary, the tube of a reflecting is opened at its upper extremity. The rays from the observed object penetrate freely and strike a concave metallic mirror, that is to say, one that is convergent. Here those rays encounter a smaller mirror which relays them to the ocular, and by this fashion an enlarged image is produced.

And so in the refracting telescope, as the name suggests, refraction enjoys the principle role and in the reflecting telescope, it is reflection. The name refactors are often simply used for the first kind, and the second attributed as reflectors. All the difficulty in executing these optical apparatuses is in the construction of the objective lens, that is the same if it is a lens telescope or one which makes use of a metallic mirror.

Meanwhile, in the period when the Gun Club tendered their grand experiment these instruments had been singularly perfected and delivered magnificent results. The times had come a long way from when Galileo observed the stars with a poor lens that enlarged an image seven times. Since the 16th Century, optical telescopic instruments have progressed in their proportionate power considerably, and permit stellar space to be gauged into inconceivable depths.

Amongst the refracting telescopes functioning at these times one must cite the lens at the Pulkovo Observatory, in Russia, whose objective lens measures 15 inches; the lens made by the French optician Lerebours, with an objective lens the same size as the previous example, and finally the lens at the Cambridge Observatory, with an objective lens 19 inches in diameter.

Amongst refracting telescopes, there are some known both with remarkable power and gigantic dimensions. The first ever constructed, by Herschel, was 36 feet long and possessed a mirror the size of 4 and a half feet in diameter; this permitted him to obtain a magnification of 6,000. The second refracting telescope was erected in Ireland, at Birr, in the park at Parsontown, and was owned by Lord Rosse. The longer tube attained a length of 48 feet, with a larger mirror of 6 feet in diameter; its magnification was 6,400, and it followed that an immense construction in masonry needed to be built to allow the necessary movements of the instrument, which weighed 28,000 pounds.

However, in terms of viewing, despite the terribly colossal dimensions, the magnifications never exceeded the power of 6,000, in round numbers; so, a magnification of 6,000 brings the Moon to within 39 miles, and it permits one to perceive objects 60 feet in diameter, unless the objects are very narrow or elongated.

Using a projectile 9 feet wide and 12 feet in length, it followed the Moon must be rendered to a visual distance of 5 miles or less; and, for that, it must produce a magnification of 48,000 times.

Here was the difficulty posed to the Cambridge Observatory. They would not be arrested by financial questions, however they were restrained by the difficulties in their materials.

And so accordingly the option needed to be chosen between a refraction or a reflection telescope. Refraction lens telescopes have an advantage over reflection mirror telescopes. Being equally objective, they permit one to obtain considerable magnifications, because the light rays when passing through the lenses produce less absorption than the metallic mirror in a reflection telescope. But the thickness which can be given to the lens is limited; if it is too thick it will allow rays of light to pass straight through, unaffected. In its production, the construction of vast lenses is excessively difficult and demands a considerable time, which can be measured in years.

Hence, even though the images are rendered clearer in a refractor lens; an appreciable advantage when observing the Moon, whose luminosity is simply reflected- it was decided to employ a reflector telescope, which can be executed more-promptly and permits one to obtain a greater magnification. Only, because the light rays lose a great portion of their intensity as they travel through the atmosphere, the Gun Club resolved to establish their instrument on one of the highest mountains in the Union, which would diminish the thickness of the atmospheric layers.

In the reflection telescopes, as we have seen, the ocular, that is to say the magnifying glass where the eye of the observer is placed, produces the enlargement; the object is displayed in greater magnification, and the greater the diameter and the more considerable the length for the focusing distance, the larger the power of magnification. To obtain a magnification of 48,000 times, they needed to exceed the grand size of the objectives used by Herschel and Lord Rosse. Therein lay the difficulty: for the casting of mirrors is a very delicate operation.

Fortunately a few years before, a scientist from the Institute of France, Leon Foucault, invented a procedure which rendered the polishing of the objective mirrors very easily and very quickly by replacing the metallic mirror with mirrors of silver. It was sufficient to cover the parts of cast glass with a great volume of metallizer to ensure it sealed with the silver. This procedure, whose results were excellent, was employed in the fabrication of the objective.

Accordingly they followed the method which Herschel had imagined for his telescopes. In the grand apparatus of the astronomer Slough, images in the objective, reflected by the mirror at the end of the tube, were formed at the other end in the situated ocular lens. And so the observer, instead of being placed at the lowest end of the telescope, would be seated at the topmost part; and there, with his magnifying glass lens, would look into the depths of that enormous cylinder. This combination gave the advantage of superseding the requirement of using a small mirror to re-invert the ocular image. It subjected the image to only one reflection instead of two. Hence a lower number of light rays were absorbed, the image was not as weakened, and therefore, finally, one obtains a greater clarity; a precious advantage when observing the fate of the projectile.

Once these resolutions had been passed, the work of construction commenced. After the calculations performed by the bureau of the

Cambridge Observatory, the tube of the new reflector telescope needed to be 280 feet in length, and the mirror 16 feet in diameter. Something so colossal for such an instrument as this might be, it was not comparable to a telescope of 10,000 feet long which the astronomer Hooke proposed to construct a few years back. Nevertheless establishing this apparatus presented great difficulties.

As to the question of emplacement, this was promptly resolved. They were required to choose a high mountain and high mountains are not so numerous in the United States.

In effect, the system of orography - which is the science that studies mountains- in this grand country is reduced to two chains of medium height and between these flows the magnificent Mississippi; which the Americans would name "the king of rivers", if they admitted any kind of royalty.

In the east are the Appalachians, whose tallest summit in New Hampshire is 6,600 feet, which is still quite modest.

In the west, on the contrary, one encounters the Rocky Mountains; an immense chain that commences at the Straits of Magellan, running along the occidental coast of South America under the name of the Andes of the Cordilleres, encountering the isthmus of Panama, it then traverses North America until it reaches the banks of the Arctic Sea.

These mountains are not very elevated, and the Alps of the Himalayas regard them with supreme disdain from the heights of their own grandeur. In effect, the tallest peak of the Rocky Mountains is 11,771 feet high whereas Mont Blanc in France measures 15,787 feet high and Kanchenjunga of the Himalayas extends for 29,454 feet above the level of the sea.

However because the Gun Club wished for their telescope to be established in the United States, as it had been for the Columbiad Cannon, they needed to content themselves with the Rocky Mountains. All the materials necessary for the construction of this enterprise were sent to Long's Peak, in the territory of Missouri.

To speak of the many kinds of difficulties which the American engineers encountered and valiantly defeated, the prodigious audacity and skill with which this was accomplished, neither pen nor speech could adequately describe. There were mountains of enormous stones, heavy pieces of forged metal whose corners weighed considerably, several vast pieces of the telescopic cylinder and an objective which weighed 30,000 pounds that had to be brought above the perpetual snow line, over 10,000 feet high; after being brought across deserted prairies, impenetrable forests, frightening rapids, far from centers of population in the midst of wild, savage regions where every detail of existence developed into almost unsolvable problems.

And nevertheless, with a thousand obstacles, the genius of the Americans triumphed. Less than a year after commencing the work, during the final days in the month of September, the gigantic reflector was pointed into the air by its telescopic tubes of 284 feet in length. It was supported by an enormous scaffolding of iron; an ingenious mechanism permitting easy maneuvering to all points of the sky in order to survey the stars from one horizon to the other, scientifically attending to those mysterious presences as they traversed their somnolent march across space.

The cost had been more than $400,000. On the first time it was turned to point at the Moon, the observers were apprehensive with emotion and at the same time as curious as they were worried. What would they discover in the field of that enormous telescope that magnified any observed objects to a power of 48,000? Populations, herds of lunar animals, cities, lakes and oceans? No, there was nothing that science had not already encountered; and on all points of the disk the volcanic nature of the Moon was able to be determined with absolute precision.

But the telescope of the Rocky Mountains, before serving the Gun Club, rendered immense service to the science of astronomy. Thanks to its powerful penetration the depths of the sky were seen beyond any of their previous limits, and the apparent diameter of a great number of stars was rigorously measured. Mr. Clarke, from the bureau at Cambridge, decomposed the Crab Nebula in Taurus, which the reflection telescope of Lord Rosse had never been able to accomplish.

25. Final Details

It was 22nd November. The supreme departure was to take place ten days later. Only one operation still remained to be completed; an operation delicate, perilous, demanding infinite precaution and against which success the Captain Nicholl had engaged a third part of his wager. It was, in effect, to charge the Columbiad cannon by introducing 400,000 pounds of guncotton. Nicholl had considered, not without reason perhaps, that the manipulation of such a formidable quantity of pyroxylin could entertain grave catastrophes, or in any case so huge a mass was eminently explosive and would ignite by the pressure of the projectile.

The grave dangers were further accentuated by the insouciance and carefree nature of the Americans, who had not hesitated during the Civil War to load their bombs with lit cigars in their mouths. But Barbicane heartily refused to allow failure; he therefore chose his greatest workmen, and, forcing every prudence and precaution upon them weighed the chances of success towards his favor.

They protected themselves by not bringing the charges inside the enclosure of Stone Hill all at once. They brought them in bit-by-bit, in perfectly sealed cases. The 400,000 pounds of guncotton was divided into packets of 500 pounds, and these were placed into 800 cartridge bags produced by the most skilled artificers in Pensacola. Every 10 cartridge bags were placed into a container and arrived along the railroad from Tampa Town; in this fashion there was never more than 5,000 pounds of guncotton at any one time inside the enclosure surrounding the Columbiad cannon. As they arrived, every cartridge bag was unloaded by laborers who walked about barefoot and every packet was transported directly into the mouth of the gargantuan Columbiad; where it descended and was maneuvered about by hand cranes.

All steam-powered machinery had been carted away and all fires extinguished for two miles around. It was then the difficult task to preserve the mass of guncotton from the ardors of the Sun, even in November. Therefore they preferred to work during the night, underneath the bright lights produced from the Ruhmkorff apparatus; which created artificial day even into the lowest portion of the Columbiad. There the packets were arranged with perfect regularity with metal wires pressed into each of them, and these were destined to send simultaneously an electric charge to ignite the explosives all at once.

In effect it was by these means that a battery would distribute the firing to that mass of guncotton. All wires, wrapped in isolating material, were united into a single electric cable running through a hole in the walls of the cannon that had been pierced just beneath the height which the projectile would maintain; this then traversed through the supporting stone framework into a tunnel constructed for that purpose and up through the soil. When the wire cable arrived at the summit of Stone Hill, supported upon electricity poles for two miles, it was joined into a powerful Bunsen battery after passing through an interrupter switch. Hence it was sufficient to press with one finger this apparatus which would then instantly relay an electric signal firing 400,000 pounds of guncotton. It does not need saying that the battery would not be actively connected to the system until the final moment.

On the 28th November the 800 cartridge bags had been disposed into the bottom of the Columbiad cannon. This part of the operation had been successful. But the worries, the apprehensions, the struggles that had been suffered by the president Barbicane! He had vainly attempted to defend the entrance to Stone Hill; every day the curious climbed the palisades, and some of them, possessed by imprudence and stupidity, had smoked standing above the bales of guncotton. Barbicane had daily scenes of rage and fury. J.T. Maston had assisted to his best ability, chasing away the intruders with that great vigor and collecting ends of the cigars lit by Yankees and then discarded. A rough endeavor, when more than 300,000 people pressed around the enclosure palisades. Michel Ardan had offered to escort the cases of guncotton as they were brought into the Columbiad; but to Barbicane's surprise he himself had an enormous cigar in his mouth and at the same time as he chased away the imprudent intruders he had set a disastrous example, and the president of the Gun Club realized that he could not count upon that intrepid smoker- in fact he would require special surveillance.

And finally, because there is a God for artillerymen nothing exploded and the charges were eventually finished successfully. Hence the third part of Captain Nicholl's wager seemed risky. It still required the introduction of the projectile into the barrel of the cannon and to be placed upon the cushion of guncotton.

Meanwhile, as they proceeded with their operation the objects necessary for the voyage were methodically stowed into the projectile-carriage. There were a great number of these, and if it had been left to Michel Ardan, they would soon have occupied the entire space reserved for the voyagers. It was a sizeable figure, the number of items which the amiable Frenchman wanted to bring along to the Moon. But a veritable pile of useless things, and Barbicane intervened so that the list was reduced to what had been strictly necessary.

Many thermometers, barometers and telescopes were stored in the instrument chest.

The voyagers were curious to examine the moon during their trajectory, and, to facilitate the reconnaissance of this new world, they brought an excellent selenographic map of the Moon's surface done by Beer and Moedler, published in four printed plates- which is regarded as a veritable masterpiece of observation and patience. This reproduced with scrupulous accuracy the smallest of details of that portion of the Moon which turns its face towards the Earth. Mountains, valleys, cirques, rocky outcrops, rills, were portrayed in exact dimensions, their orientation faithful; all named, from the *Doerfel Mountain* and *Leibnitz Mountain*, whose high summits tower above the oriental part of the lunar disk, to the *Mare Frigoris* which extends through the circumpolar regions to the north.

It was a precious document for the travellers because they could study the country from where they were, without ever having stepped a foot upon it.

They also brought with them three rifles and three repeating carbines that worked from a system of exploding bullets; as well, a great quantity of powder and lead bullets.

"We don't know what we will meet during this affair," explained Michel Ardan. "Men or beasts which may feel evilly about our rendering them a visit! We therefore must prepare with precaution."

Along with the instruments of personal defense were picks, mattocks, handsaws and other indispensable tools; to say nothing of the clothing suitable for all the temperatures, from the coldest polar regions to the heat of the torrid meridian zone.

Michel Ardan had expressed his wish to bring on their expedition a certain number of animals. Not a couple from every species; for he saw no need to acclimatize the Moon to serpents, tigers, alligators and the other malfeasant beasts.

"No," he told Barbicane, "but some beasts of burden, such as oxen or cows, donkeys or horses would fare well in that countryside and not to say be greatly useful, either."

"And I agree, Ardan my friend," responded the president of the Gun Club. "But our projectile-carriage is not Noah's ark. It has neither the capacity nor the same destination. And so we must restrict ourselves to within the limits of possibility."

And finally after long discussions it was agreed amongst the voyagers to content themselves by taking an excellent female hunting dog belonging to Nicholl and a vigorous Newfoundland dog that was prodigiously strong. They included several cases of useful seeds amongst the number of indispensable items. If it had been left entirely to Michel Ardan, he would also have packed several sacks of soil to germinate them in. In any case, he brought along a dozen small plants which were wrapped in a covering of straw and placed in a corner of the projectile.

There still remained the important question of food provisions, in foresight of the case they would berth in an absolutely sterile portion of the Moon. Barbicane saw well to ensure a sufficient quantity for a year. This is not so incredulous, to the astonished persons, when their food consisted of canned meat and vegetables reduced to their smallest volume by the action of a hydraulic press, and which retained a great quantity of nutritious elements; it was not very varied, but one cannot be too particular in such a difficult expedition.

They also packed fifty gallons of brandy and sufficient water for two months only; in effect, as a consequence of the most-recent observations of the astronomers, no one had any doubt of the presence of a certain quantity of water of the Moon's surface. When it came to food, it would have not been sensible to think that these Earthly inhabitants would not be able to find nourishment of some kind. Michel Ardan held no doubt in that regard. If it had been so, he would not have decided to participate.

"Besides," he said one day to his friends, "we shall not be completely abandoned by our friends on the Earth, and they will not forget about us."

"No, certainly," replied J.T. Maston.

"What are you thinking about?" asked Nicholl.

"Nothing is more simple," answered Ardan. "The cannon will be here, yes? Ah well! Every time the Moon presents the favorable zenith conditions, otherwise in perigee, that is to say about once per year, couldn't our friends send a charged shell filled with food, which we will look out for on a certain day?"

"Hurrah! Hurrah!" cried J.T. Maston like a man whose idea was his own. "That is excellently said. Certainly, my brave friends, I will oblige you all by doing so!"

"Then it is complete! And so, we shall have regular news from the globe, and, for our part, we shall be seriously amiss if we do not find means to communicate with our good friends on Earth!"

These words were given so confidently, by Michel Ardan, with such an air of determination and superb aplomb, that it would have entrained the entire Gun Club to follow suit with their purpose. What he had said seemed so simple, elementary, easy, so assured of success, that one would have been a veritable miser to wish to maintain a hold onto that miserable earthly globe and not accompany the three voyagers on their lunar expedition.

When the diverse objects had been stored within the projectile, the water destined to act as a spring was introduced into its sections and then the gas designed to clear the contents compressed above this. With the potassium chlorate and the caustic potash, Barbicane, fearing unforeseen delays along their route, decided to carry a quantity sufficient for renewing the oxygen and absorbing the carbonic acid in the air for two months. An extremely ingenious apparatus was installed; responsible for rendering the air purified and imparting it with the suitable qualities for life, it functioned automatically. The preparations for the projectile were then completed and there was nothing more to be done than to lower it into the Columbiad. An operation that would be full-enough of difficulties and perils.

The enormous shell was brought to the summit of Stone's Hill. Here, powerful cranes seized and held it suspended above that pit of metal.

It was a palpating moment. If the chains holding that enormous weight were to break, the impact of the falling mass was certain to ignite the guncotton.

Fortunately nothing occurred and several hours later the projectile-carriage, having been sweetly lowered into the arm of the cannon, reposed on its cushion of guncotton; a veritable eiderdown of explosive material. The pressure of it above had no other effect than to compress the charge of the guncotton in the Columbiad cannon more tightly.

"I have lost," said the captain, remitting to president Barbicane the sum of $3,000.

Barbicane did not wish to receive the money from the hands of his companion on the voyage; but he had to cede to the obstinacy of Nicholl, who wanted to have completed all his engagements before quitting the Earth.

"Accordingly," said Michel Ardan, "I have only one more thing to wish for, my brave captain."

"Which are?" asked the captain.

"That you lose the two other bets! In that fashion, I will know that we are resting along our route."

26. Fire!

The first day of December arrived, a fateful day; for if the departure of the projectile that same evening was not affected, at 10 hours, 46 minutes and 40 seconds in the night, more than 18 years would endure before the Moon would represent the same conditions where the zenith and the perigee occurred simultaneously.

The temperature was magnificent; in spite of the approach of winter, the Sun was resplendent and swimming in this abundance radiance the Earth which was soon to lose three of inhabitants to a new world.

How many had slept badly during the preceding night with impatient desire for the day! How many chests had been oppressed by the burdensome weight of worry! All were the hearts which palpitated with apprehension and anxiety, but for the heart of Michel Ardan. That impassive person attended to things as if they were habitual affairs, there was nothing in his demeanor that suggested any preoccupation. His slumber had been peaceful, the slumber of Turenne, on the way to battle, asleep upon his cannon.

During the morning an un-reckonable crowd had covered the prairies extending around Stone's Hill as far as the eye could see. Every quarter past the hour, the railroad trains from Tampa delivered new curious spectators; that immigration soon grew to fabulous proportions, and, according to the articles by the *Tampa Town Observer*, during that memorable journey 5,000,000 spectators in that crowd stood upon the Florida soil.

Throughout that month the greater part of that crowd had bivouacked around the enclosure, and they lay the foundations of a town that would later be called Ardansville. The sheds, the cabins, the shanties and the tents bristled upon the plains; and these ephemeral habitations accommodated a population so numerous as to be envied by the very grand cities of Europe.

All the people of the Earth were represented here: all the dialects of the world were spoken at once. They spoke a confusion of languages like biblical times in the Tower of Babel. Here the diverse classes of American society intermingled in absolute equality.

Bankers, cultivators, commissionaires, brokers, cotton planters, merchants, boatmen, and magistrates went shoulder to shoulder with primitive geniality. The creoles of Louisiana fraternized with the farmers of Indiana, the gentlemen of Kentucky and of Tennessee, the Virginians elegant and haughty gave replies to the half-savage trappers from the Great Lakes and cattle merchants of Cincinnati. Broad-rimmed white beaver hats, or classic panamas, wearing pants in tough blue cotton fabricated in Opelousas, unbleached linen jackets, ankle boot slippers of all brilliant colors; they exhibited extravagant batiste shirt fronts, and on their shirts, their shirt cuffs, their cravats, on their ten fingers and displaying the same from all their ears was an entire assortment of rings, pins, diamonds, chains, buckles, earrings, whose expensiveness was only equaled by their bad taste. Women, children, servants- all dressed with an opulence and were accompanied, attended, proceeded and surrounded by the husbands, the fathers; men who resembled chiefs of tribes in the midst of their innumerable families.

At the hour for meals, it was a sight for all the world when they fell upon their particular plates particular to the Southern states and devoured, with an appetite that menaced the entire provisions of Florida, elements that would have been repugnant to a European's stomach; such as fricasseed frogs, braised monkey, fish chowder, roast opossum and grilled raccoon.

But as well, what a varied array of liquors and other drinks to aid in the alimentation of those ingestions! What cries of excitement, what engaging vociferation echoed throughout the bar rooms and taverns adorned by glasses, mugs, flasks, carafe decanters; the bottles shaped incredibly, the polished granite mortars for breaking sugar and the decanter-packets of drinking straws!

"Here is a mint julep!" cried out one bartender in a loud voice.

"Here is a Burgundy sangria!" replied another in a yelling tone.

"And a gin sling!" repealed a voice nearby.

"And a cocktail! A brandy smash!" cried a voice further along.

"Who wishes to try an authentic mint julep, in the latest style?" cried the last adroit bartender; passing the mixing-glass rapidly from one hand to another, like a conjurer with the nutmeg, the sugar, the lemon, the green mint, the ice finely-crushed, the water, the cognac, and the pineapple which altogether composed that refreshing cocktail.

And so, skillfully, these incantations were addressed to all throats altered from the action of hot spices and repeated; they crossed through the air producing a resounding uproar. But on this day, the 1st of December, these cries were exceedingly rare. The bartenders fussed and could have vainly shouted themselves hoarse without provoking any customers. No person could think of eating or drinking, and, at 4 o'clock in the afternoon, how many spectators circulated in the crowd who were still without their lunch!

There were even more significant symptoms: the violent passion of the Americans for gambling and games had been vanquished by their emotions. The sight of quills of tenpins left lying on their sides, the craps dice sleeping in their throwing-cups, the roulette wheel listless and still, cribbage board games left abandoned and the cards for whist, twenty-one, red and black, and monte and faro left intact tranquilly enclosed in their envelopes; one could well comprehend that every person was absorbed in that day's event and there was no place left for any other distractions.

By the evening, a hidden agitation without clamor, like the kind of which precedes the great catastrophes, moved through the anxious crowd. An indescribable uneasiness reigned over their spirits, a painful torpor, an indefinable sentiment had taken ahold of their hearts. Everyone wished that it was already finished.

However, towards 7 o'clock, the heavy silence dissipated brusquely. The Moon levitated on the horizon. Several million hurrahs saluted the apparition. It had arrived at the time exactly appointed. The clamor mounted to the sky, the applause shattered on all parts, while the blonde Phoebe shone peacefully in the wonderful sky and caressed that crowd enveloped by its rays of deep affection.

At that moment the 3 intrepid voyagers appeared. Unanimously, instantly, the national anthem of the United States escaped from the crowds heaving chests; and the Yankee doodle, expressed in a chorus of five million executants, rose like a sonorous tempest from there unto the limits of the atmosphere.

Then, after that irresistible surge of spirit, their hymn was sung, the final harmonies died away little by little; the sounds dissipated, and a murmuring silence floated above that crowd producing a profound impression. Meanwhile, the Frenchman and the two Americans had entered within the enclosure around which the immense crowd pressed. They were accompanied by the members of the Gun Club and the delegations sent from the European observatories.

Barbicane, cold and calm, remained tranquil as he gave his final orders. Nicholl, his lips pressed serenely closed, his hands crossed behind his back, walked with firm, measured steps. Michel Ardan, nonchalant, dressed like the perfect traveller, with leather boots on his feet, a leather hunting bag slung on his shoulder, his brown velvet clothes floating loosely upon him, cigar in mouth, distributing as he walked by warm poignant handshakes with prodigiousness of a prince. His inexhaustible witty eloquence, his gaiety, laughter, jokes, farcical games on the dignified J.T. Maston- in a word, he was French, and to make it even worse, Parisian, right up to the last second.

10 hours sounded. The moment had arrived for them to take their place in the projectile; the maneuvering necessary to descend, to have the entrance plate firmly locked into place and the disengagement of the scaffolding above the Columbiad cannon required a certain amount of time.

Barbicane had regulated his pocket watch to a tenth of a second of the timepiece held by the engineer Murchison, who was encharged to set the fire by means of the electric spark; the voyagers encased within the projectile were able supervise with their eyes the impassive needle ticking towards the mark of the precise instant of their departure.

Hence the moment for goodbyes had arrived. The final scene was touching; and despite his feverish gaiety, Michel Ardan could sense the emotions. J.T. Maston retrieved from underneath his eyelids a single tear which he had without doubt reserved for that kind of occasion. It fell upon the front of his brave friend and president.

"I may still not be a part?" said J.T. Maston. "There is still time!"

"Impossible, my dear Maston," responded Barbicane.

A few instants later, the three companions followed one another down and installed themselves in the projectile and then they screwed shut from the inside the plate covering the entrance. The mouth of the cannon, entirely cleared, opened freely to the sky.

Nicholl, Barbicane and Michel Ardan were definitively encased in their carriage of metal.

Who could portray that universal emotion, that now reached to a paroxysm?

The Moon advanced through the firmament above in pure movement, extinguishing along its passage the scintillating fire of stars left in the path's sway; it passed towards the constellation of Gemini, travelling between the horizon and zenith. Everyone there could easily understand that they aimed ahead of the Moon's position, like a hunter who has aimed ahead of the hare he chases.

A silence fell frighteningly over that entire scene. There was not a breath of wind over the Earth! Nor a breath in anyone's chest! Their hearts no longer dared to beat. All alarmed stares were fixated on the gruesome beam of the

Columbiad.

Murchison kept his eye on the ticking needle of his watch's hand. There was only 40 seconds to the instant of departure, and each took the duration of a century.

At the 20th second, there was a universal tremor, and all in that crowd understood that the audacious voyagers encased within the projectile counted the same terrible seconds! Isolated cries escaped:

"35!... 36!... 37!... 38!... 39!... 40! Fire!!!"

Immediately Murchison pressed his finger to the switch of the ignition apparatus, sending a current along the electric wire and into the depths of the Columbiad cannon.

A detonation dreadfully appalling, fantastic, superhuman, there was nothing to compare it with, no explosion, nor any fracas from a volcanic eruption, was produced instantaneously. An immense bursting cloud of fire jettisoned in the projectiles entrails of the soil as though it were a mountainous crater. The ground revolted; and it was but a few people only who caught a glimpse of the fiery projectile as it sped victoriously through the air surrounded by its flaming, flamboyant vapors.

27. Cloudy Weather

At the moment the incandescent plume elevated towards the sky to a prodigious height, the blossoming flames lit the entirety of Florida. During that incalculable instant, the day was substituted for night over a considerable extension of the countryside. That immense panache of fire was seen a hundred miles out at sea in the Gulf of Mexico and in the Atlantic Ocean, and more than one ship's captain noted in their logbook the apparition of that gigantic meteoric.

The detonation of the Columbiad was accompanied by a veritable earthquake. Florida was shaken to its foundations. The gas of the guncotton, dilated by the heat, created a repercussion with an incomparable violence against the layers of atmosphere; and that artificial hurricane, a hundred times faster than their tempest hurricanes, passed like a whirlwind though the medium of air.

   Not one spectator had remained standing; men, women, children, all were put upon the ground like stalks of grain in a storm and in that inexplicable tumult, a grand number of persons were gravely injured. J.T. Maston, who, contrary to all prudence, had stood too far forward, was jettisoned 50 feet behind and passed like a cannon ball over the heads of some citizens. 300,000 people were momentarily deafened and held fast in a stupor.

   That atmospheric current of destructive wind, after knocking over the worker's huts, tumbling the cabins, uprooting trees in a radius of twenty miles, pushed the trains along their rails all the way to Tampa and hit that city like an avalanche. It destroyed over one hundred houses as well as the Church of Saint Mary and the new stock exchange building, which was cracked completely along its length. Certain numbers of ships in the port smashed against one another and sank from leaks; and ten or so boats, lying at anchor in the harbor, were blown against the coast with their chains snapped as though they were made from cotton threads.

   Yet the circle of devastation extended further still, onto the limits of the United States. The effects of the concussive blast, aided by winds from the west, reached onto the Atlantic more than 300,000 miles from the shores of America. An artificial tempest, an unexpected tempest that could not have been predicted by Admiral Fitzroy, stuck his ships with an insensible violence. Many vessels seized in those terribly turbulent cyclones had no time to bring in their sails and began to sink, including as well the *Childe Harold* of Liverpool- a regrettable catastrophe which became on the part of the English a subject of sharp recriminations.

   And finally, to say it all, given that the sources are guaranteed only by natives, in half an hour after the departure of the projectile the inhabitants of Goree and Sierra Leone claimed to have experienced the sound of that commotion, the final displacement of the sound waves, which, after traversing the Atlantic Ocean, died out along the African coast.

   [see introductory comments*].

   But we must return to Florida. The first instant the tumult passed the blessings, the sighs, and finally as the crowd emerged from their reverie, the frenetic cries: "Hurrah for Ardan! Hurrah for Barbicane! Hurrah for Nicholl!" elevated into the sky. Several million men across the continent- their noses in the air, armed with telescopes and binoculars- interrogatively peered into space, forgetful of their contusions and emotions when necessary, in their preoccupation of the projectile. But they searched in vain. It was no longer possible for one to perceive it. They were reduced to waiting to receive a telegram from Long's Peak. The director of the Cambridge Observatory stood at his post in the Rocky Mountains, and there, the skillful astronomer persevered with the observations he had been entrusted to perform.

Then came an unexpected phenomenon. Though easily perceptible, about which nothing could control, it was soon to test the patience of the public in a rude trial.

The weather which had been fine changed suddenly: the sky turned somberly and covered itself with clouds. How could it have been any other way, after the terrible displacement of the atmospheric layers, in that dispersion of the enormous quantity of vapors were produced by the deflagration of 400,000 pounds of pyroxylin guncotton? The whole natural order had been troubled. It was nothing to be astonished by; because it is known that in the past, during combat upon the sea, the atmospheric state has been brutally modified by artillery discharges.

The following day the sun leavened itself over the horizon thickly-laden with clouds; a heavy and impenetrable curtain entirely covering the sky from the ground, and which, unfortunately, extended into the regions of the Rocky Mountains. It was completely inevitable. Concerted cries of protest were made all over the globe. But nature paid little heed and decided, because men had troubled the atmosphere with their detonation, they would be subject to the consequences.

During the first day of that journey, everyone searchingly tried to penetrate with their eyes the opaque clouds, but this was for no purpose; because while everyone had pointed their vision towards the sky, due to the diurnal movement of the globe, the projectile by necessity was following a line above the antipodes.

So that was how it was and when night enveloped the Earth, a night impenetrably deep, when the Moon mounted over the horizon it was impossible to perceive; it was as though it deliberately hid from the temerity of those who dared shoot at it. Hence there was no observation possible, and the dispatches from Long's Peak confirmed the anger of the inopportune moments.

Therefore if the experiment had been successful, the voyagers, departing on the 1st December at 10 hours, 46 minutes and 49 seconds in the evening were due to arrive on the 4th at midnight. Hence in the meantime, as it would have been difficult to observe the small shell during the conditions of its flight, all patiently awaited that date without uttering a single complaint.

On the 4th of December, between 8 o'clock and midnight, it was possible to seek for a trace of the projectile; which would have appeared like a black dot on the bright lunar disk. But the weather remained mercilessly clouded, exciting a paroxysm of exasperation from the public. There were some who hurled insults at the Moon just to demonstrate their point. A sad change of things!

J.T. Maston, desperate, departed for Long's Peak. He wanted to observe things for himself. He was without any doubt his friends had arrived safely at the termination of their voyage. There had been no word received that the projectile had tumbled back onto some island or continent on the Earth, and J.T. Maston refused to admit for an instant that it was possible for it to have fallen into one of the oceans which cover three quarters of the globe.

On the 5th of December, the same weather conditions. The grand telescopes of the old world- those of Herschel, Rosse, Foucault- were invariably trained upon the lunar surface, for the weather there was precisely magnificent; but the relative feebleness of those instruments meant that observation was useless.

The 6th of December: the same weather conditions. Impatience raged across three-quarters of the globe. There were some who spoke out, proposing very insensible ideas to dissipate the clouds which had accumulated in the air.

On the 7th of December the sky seemed to modify itself a little. There was hope, but the hope was not very long in duration; and by the evening, the clouds thickly defended the starry vault from view.

And so things had become grave. In effect on the 11th, at 11 minutes past 9 in the morning, the Moon was scheduled to enter its final quarter. After the delay, as it entered its decline, when even if the sky returned to its clear serenity the chances of observation were greatly reduced; in effect, the Moon would display a constantly-reducing portion until it's disk became a diminishing crescent, and then it would eventually become new- that is to say it would rise and set level with the Sun, whose rays would render it absolutely invisible. It would then not be full again until the 3rd January, at 47 minutes past midnight, and only when it had returned completely could they recommence with their observations.

The journals and newspapers published these reflections with a thousand commentaries, and did not conceal the point to the public that they must arm themselves with an angelic patience.

The 8th: nothing. By the 9th the Sun appeared for an instant, briefly, as though to annoy the Americans. It was received with jeers, and, without a doubt blessed by excellent vision, decided in response to avert it's rays.

The 10th, there was no change. J.T. Maston almost became mad, and there were fears for the mind of that dignified man, which had been well conserved until now by his rubber skull.

But on the 11th of December there was a powerful tempest in the intertropical regions which loosened the chains binding the atmosphere. Great winds from the east swept away the clouds that had accumulated there for such a long time; and that evening, the half-rounded disk of the Moon, that shining body of the night, passed majestically in the midst of the sparkling constellations in the sky.

28. A New Star

That same night, the thrilling news which had been sought impatiently for so long exploded like a bursting bomb over the United States; and then onwards, launched into transit across the Oceans, running in currents along telegraphic wires throughout the globe. The projectile had been sighted, thanks to the gigantic reflection telescope situated on Long's Peak.

Here is the note which was written by the director of the Cambridge Observatory. It formulates the scientific conclusion to that grand experiment of the Gun Club.

Long's Peak, 12 December.

To All Members of the Bureau of the Cambridge Observatory.

The projectile launched by the Columbiad cannon at Stone's Hill has been sighted by J.M. Belfast and J.T. Maston, the 11th December, at 8:47pm, as the Moon entered into its final quarter.

The projectile did not arrive at its intended point. It passed to one side, but closely enough, however, for it to be affected by the Moon's gravitational attraction.

There, its rectilinear trajectory was changed into a circular movement along a rapidly vertiginous path, and is now entrained in an elliptical orbit around the Moon, where it has become a veritable satellite.

The elements of this new star have not been entirely determined. We have not yet measured the velocity of its transition, nor the speed of its rotation. The distance which separates it from the surface of the Moon is evaluated at 2,830 miles or thereabouts.

Now, there are two hypothesis possible, only one of which could produce any modification to its current state:

If the attraction of the Moon's gravity is sufficient, it will eventually draw the projectile onto its surface, and the voyagers will have reached their intended destination;

otherwise, if it's angle and distance is immutable, it will maintain its orbit around the lunar disk in its current state until the end of time.

Continued observations will determine the outcome one day, but for now the tentative result of the Gun Club's experiment has been to donate a new star within our solar system.

J.M. Belfast.

All the questions which now remained unanswered! What circumstances of immense mystery were now reserved for the investigation of science! Thanks to the courage and dedication of the three men, that enterprise to send a cannon ball to the Moon, although futile in appearance, had produced an immense result whose consequences were incalculable.

The voyagers, imprisoned in the new satellite, had not attained their goal; however at least they were a part of the lunar world; they gravitated around the Moon, that shining body of the night sky, and, for the very first time human eyes could penetrate its mysteries.

Henceforth the names of Nicholl, Barbicane, and Michel Ardan were celebrated in the records of astronomy as hardy explorers; who avidly aggrandized the levels of human understanding, audaciously launching themselves into the traverse of space and joyfully putting their lives at risk in the strangest and most tentative undertaking of modern times.

When the time came about for the note of Long's Point to be understood, an entirely universal sentiment of surprise and dread occurred. Was it possible to provide aid to those hardy Earthly inhabitants?? No, there was no doubt, for they had removed themselves from humanity by passing beyond the ordinary limits God imposed upon terrestrial beings. It was known they had only enough air procured for two months. They had enough provisions of food for one year. But afterwards?... All hearts were insensibly fearful of this terrible question.

Only one man would not voluntarily admit that the situation was desperate. Only one soul had confidence and faith- that was their devoted friend, as audacious and resolute as the voyagers themselves were, the brave and incomparable J.T. Maston.

Thereafter, he was keeping his eyes on them. His domestic residence was now at the disconsolate post on Long's Peak; his horizon, the mirror of that immense reflector telescope. When the Moon levitated above the horizon he surrounded it within his telescopic field, and did not allow an instant of his attention to stray from its assiduous survey as he regarded that slow lunar processional march through the void of stellar space. He observed with eternal patience the passage of the projectile across the silver disk and by these veritable means, the dignified man remained in constant, perpetual communication with his three friends; and he desperately hoped to see them again one day.

"We'll correspond with them again one day," he said to anyone who would entertain him. "When the circumstances permit it. They shall hear our news, and we will apprehend theirs! You see, I know them- they are ingenious men. Amongst those three we've sent into space the entire resources of art, science and industry. With that they can accomplish anything, and you will see that this is not the end of the affair!"

Interlude

Excerpts- Christopher Brennan [1897-1902]

Beneath the kindly vaulted gloom
that gather'd them in quickening ease,

they saw the rose of heaven bloom,
alone, in heights of musky air,
with many an angel's painted plume.

So, shadowing forth their dim-felt prayer,
the daedal glass compell'd to grace
the outer day's indifferent stare,

where now its disenhallow'd face
beholds the petal-ribs enclose
nought, in their web of shatter'd lace

save this pale absence of the rose.

THE QUEST OF SILENCE

What gems chill glitter yon, thrice dipt,
in dusky Styx, or tears unshed
the spheres, in icy exile stript,
congeal in midnight's gaze of lead?

O thou crow'd caitiff, o'er our head
whereon thine agelong wounds have dript
the dark arms of thy passion spread
dwarf the vast vault to a hard crypt.

Round thine eternal hour of woe
the abyss urges, a rigid throe,
whose woeful dark see nought emerge,

save these, their consolation vain
and frozen on the helpless verge,
lonely, ecstatic fires of pain.

IV

O vanish'd star, fall'n flower, O god deceas'd
and deep in marble night sepulchred, where
rises the might that sank, disastrous flare,
in the agonizing dream thy latest priest?

Far hence in the awful vault another East
blossoms ecstatic rose and Eden air
is sweet on singing flesh that knows no share
in thy void grave whence all springs have ceas'd.

Stars that with all our glory laden shift
aimless, what term is set unto this drift?
All dawns are split along the hopeless way,

and far the white hour when our darkling prayer
must be consumed and wraithful love shall slay:
- Ye are but jewels in her scatter'd hair.

THE LABOUR OF NIGHT

Around the Moon
[1870]

Jules Verne

Chapters

Preliminary Chapter………………………....….…................……158

I. From Ten O'clock to Forty-Six Minutes Past Ten and Forty Seconds……………………………………………………..……...….159

II. The First Half-Hour……………………………....……....164

III. Their Place of Shelter…..175

IV. A Small Amount of Algebra……………………..…….…183

V. The Coldness of Space………..…………………….….…191

VI. Demanding Questions and Answers..…………......….…199

VII. A Moment of Drunkenness…..……………………...….…207

VIII. At 78,114 Leagues……..…………………….....….…215

IX. The Consequences of a Deviation……………………….223

X. The Observers of the Moon..……………………..….…228

XI. Fantasy and Realism……………….….………....….…233

XII. Orthographical Details……………..………...….…237

XIII. Lunar Landscapes……………..….……………….....…..244

XIV. The Night of Three Hundred and Fifty-Four and One Half Hours……………………………………………………...…..251

XV. Hyperbola or Parabola…………….………….....….…259

XVI. The Southern Hemisphere………..…………....…..….268

XVII. Tycho…………………………………....…….....…..….272

XVIII. Grave Questions…………..………..………...….….279

XIX. Struggle against the Impossible………..………..…..….286

XX. The Soundings of the *Susquehanna*..……………....….….295

XXI. The Recall of J.T. Maston…..….…………….....….….....300

XXII. The Rescue Attempt………..……………….....….….307

XXIII. For the End………………………………...….….….314

Preliminary Chapter

The telegram which J.M. Belfast had sent, dated 11th December, had been erroneous.

In effect, the telegram contained errors of two sorts, which were verified later.

1. Error of observation which concerned the distance of the projectile from the surface of the Moon, and which at that date on the 11th December, it had been impossible to perceive and which J.T. Maston had thought he had seen- that it was not actually the cannon ball of the Columbiad.

2. Errors in theory regarding the examination of the projectile, that is it had become a satellite of the Moon, which was in absolute contradiction of the laws of rational mechanical physics.

One sole hypothesis of the observers at Long's Peak was capable of being realized, that was the possibility for the case of the voyagers- if they still existed- to combine their efforts with the attraction of the Moon in a manner which would enable them to reach the surface of that lunar disk.

So, these men, as intelligent as they were hardy; had they survived the terrible repercussive counter-shock upon their inertia on departure? Their voyage in that cannon ball carriage will be recounted here with all the high drama and the many singular details. This recitation will destroy the plentiful illusions and predictions; but it will deliver a just idea of the kind of journey reserved for such an unparalleled enterprise and it will put into relief the scientific instincts of Barbicane, the industrial resources of Nicholl and the humorous audacity of Michel Ardan.

Besides which it will prove their dignified friend J.T. Maston lost time when, leaning over that gigantic telescope, he observed the march of the Moon traversing through stellar space.

1. From Ten O'clock to Forty-Six Minutes Past Ten and Forty Seconds

When 10 hours sounded Michel Ardan, Barbicane and Nicholl gave their goodbyes to the numerous friends whom they were leaving behind on the Earth. The two dogs, destined to condition a canine race on the lunar continents, had already been imprisoned within the projectile. The three voyagers approached the great orifice of that enormous tube of cast iron, and with one last look towards the crowd descended through the conical cap atop the cannon ball.

Then, as an overture to that effect, they began their descent in their aluminum carriage. The hoists of the crane were removed from the exterior, and the cranes around the Columbiad were instantly disengaged from the last of the scaffolding.

Nicholl, after waiting for his companions to enter into the projectile, shut the opening by manipulating a strong plate from within which maintained the pressure inside. Other plates, solidly adapted, covered the lenticular glass of the portholes. The voyagers, hermetically sealed in their prison of metal, were plunged into a profound and obscure darkness.

"And now, my friendly companions," said Michel Ardan, "make yourselves at home. I am the interior decorator, and am very good in the housekeeping aspects. I have tried as best as possible for our new lodgment to be most comfortable. Now we are aboard, I shall endeavor to make it a little clearer to see. What a devil! This gas mechanism must have been invented by moles!"

Having spoken thus, the insouciant bachelor created a flame by striking a match against the sole of his boot. Then he approached the gas lamp and fixed it to the receiver, which ran by hydrogen carbon stored under high pressure that could provide sufficient light and heat for 146 hours, or 6 days and 6 nights.

The gas lit. The projectile, now illuminated, appeared like a comfortable chamber with padded walls, furnished with circular divans and surrounded by the vault-like dome.

The objects which it contained- arms, instruments, utensils- were stowed solidly, maintaining their places against the padded walls, sensibly supported and locked into place against the shock of the departure blast. All the precautions humanely possible had been taken to create a good finish and not leave it as a reckless attempt.

Michel Ardan examined all around and declared his strong satisfaction at the installation.

"It is a prison," he said, "but a prison for a voyage, and so long as I can put my nose up against a window, I could bail up in here for one hundred years! What do you say, Barbicane? Are you feeling mental reservations? Or are you thinking this prison could easily become our tomb? Tomb, so be it, but I would not change it for that of Mahomet's- as we shall be floating through space, without taking a step!"

Whilst Michel Ardan spoke this way, Barbicane and Nichol made their final preparations.

Nicholl's pocket watch marked 10 hours and 20 minutes when the three voyagers were definitively enclosed by the cannon ball. All their watches had been regulated to within a tenth of a second of the hand-piece held by the engineer Murchison. Barbicane consulted his.

"My friends," he said, "it is 10 hours 20. By 10 hours 47, Murchison will have activated the electrical wires switch that communicates with the loaded charge in the Columbiad. At the moment precisely, we leave our sphere. Hence in 27 minutes we will no longer rest upon this Earth."

"26 minutes and 13 seconds," responded the methodical Nicholl.

"Ah well," cried Michel Ardan in a tone of good humor, "in 26 minutes, that is nothing! A small discussion on the grave questions of morality or politics, which we would have resolved! 26 well employed minutes are better value than 26 years of doing nothing! Several seconds to Pascal or Newton is far more precious than the total existence than an indigestible crowd of imbeciles..."

"And what do you conclude, eternal talker?" asked the president Barbicane.

"I conclude that we have 26 minutes to go," responded Ardan.

"25 minutes actually," said Nicholl.

"24, if they hold, my brave captain," responded Ardan. "24 minutes during which one can go into deeper discussion..."

"Michel," said Barbicane, "during our traverse, we shall have all the time necessary profound questions of great ardor. Now we should occupy ourselves with our departure."

"You are not ready?"

"Without a doubt. But there are still some precautions we should mitigate as much shock as possible before the detonation!"

"With the layers of water filled in each section, surely therefore that will have enough elasticity to provide us sufficient protection?"

"I hope, Michel," responded Barbicane gently. "But I am not entirely sure!"

"Ah! The farce!" cried Michel Ardan. "He hopes!... He is not sure!... And he waits for the moment we are encased to express that deplorable confession! But I demand to be let out!"

"And by what means?" replied Barbicane.

"In effect!" admitted Michel Ardan. "That is difficult. We are in the train and the conductor's whistle is ready to blow in 24 minutes..."

"20," said Nicholl.

For several instants, the three voyagers regarded one another. Then they examined the objects they had imprisoned with them.

"Everything is in its place," said Barbicane. "We must now decide how to best place ourselves to support against the shock of departure. The position we choose is not a matter of indifference; and as much as possible, we should seek to keep our blood from rushing too violently to our heads."

"Just so," said Nicholl.

"Then," responded Michel Ardan, ready to follow the example of what had been spoken, "we should keep our head upside down and our feet up high, like the clowns of the Great Circus!"

"No," said Barbicane, "but we should extend ourselves along on our sides. This will better resist against the shock. Note well that the moment the cannon ball departs, whether we are standing inside of it or in front of it, is almost the same thing."

"If it is only 'almost the same thing', then I am reassured," replied Michel Ardan sardonically.

"Do you approve of my idea, Nicholl?" asked Barbicane.

"Entirely", responded the captain. "13 and a half minutes to go."

"There is no man like Nicholl," cried Michel. "He is chronometer of seconds, an escape mechanism, with eight holes..."

But his companions were not listening closely, and they took their last positions with an unimaginable cold-blooded-ness. They displayed the airs of methodical travellers, raising themselves in their carriage, who sought to make themselves as comfortable as possible. We may demand truthfully as to what material the hearts of Americans are made of, as they approach the most terrifying dangers without one additional pulse!

Three couches, thickly and solidly conditioned, had been placed in the projectile. Nicholl and Barbicane moved them into the center of the disk which formed the mobile wooden floorboards that would protect them against the shock of the blast. On these the three voyagers reclined for the several moments until the departure.

Throughout that time, Ardan, who was never able to rest still, turned about in that cramped prison like a wild beast held within a cage; chatting with his friends, calling to their dogs, Diane and Satellite, and to whom, one can see, he had already given during that time names of significance.

"Hey! Diane! Hey! Satellite!" he cried, exciting them. "You are going to show the Selenite dogs the good ways of the dogs of Earth! That is quite an honor for the canine race! By god! If we ever return to here, I will bring with me a crossbreed of 'moon-dogs'; which will cause quite a furor!"

"That is, if there are dogs on the Moon," said Barbicane.

"They are there," affirmed Michel Ardan. "As there are horses, cows, donkeys, and fowls. I wager we shall find fowls there!"

"One hundred dollars that we come across none," said Nicholl.

"I meet you, my captain," responded Ardan and he shook hands with Nicholl. "But you have already lost three bets with our president; that the funds necessary for the enterprise have been found, that the operation of casting was a success, and finally that the loading of charges into the Columbiad cannon was without accident, namely six thousand dollars!"

"Yes," replied Nicholl. "10 hours, 37 minutes and 6 seconds."

"It is agreed, captain. Ah well, within a quarter of an hour, you will soon count $9,000 to the president, $4,000 when the Columbiad does not fragment from the explosive blast, and $5,000 when the cannon ball is sent over 6 miles through the air."

"I have the dollars," and he tapped on the pocket of his jacket. "I only demand that I may pay."

"Come now, Nicholl, I see you are an orderly man, which I myself could never be; but in summary, you have made a series of bets that are of little advantage to you, allow me to say so."

"And why?" questioned Nicholl.

"Because if you gain on the main wager, that is that the Columbiad cannon shall burst apart, and the cannon ball with it, Barbicane shall not be there to reimburse your dollars."

"My stakes have been deposited in the Bank of Baltimore," Barbicane responded simply, "And if the default of Nicholl, it will be returned to his heirs!"

"Ah! Practical men!" cried Michel Ardan. "And of positive spirits! I admire you even more for not being able to understand you!"

"10 hours 42!" said Nicholl.

"Five more minutes!" added Barbicane.

"Yes! Five little minutes!" continued Michel Ardan. "And we are locked encased in a cannon ball inside a cannon nine hundred feet long! And beneath this cannon ball have been crammed 400,000 pounds of guncotton equivalent to 1,600,000 pounds of ordinary gunpowder! And our friend Murchison, with his timepiece in hand, eye fixed to the hand of its needle, his finger poised above the electrical apparatus switch; counting the seconds before he launches us into interplanetary space!..."

"Enough, Michel, enough!" said Barbicane in a grave voice. "Prepare yourself. A few instants only separate us from the supreme moment. One handshake, my friends."

"Yes," cried Michel Ardan, with more emotion than he had wished to show.

The three hardy companions joined together for one last embrace.

"God protect us!" said the religious Barbicane.

Michel Ardan and Nichol lay down on the couches moved into the center of the disk.

"10 hours 47!" murmured the captain.

Twenty seconds more! Barbicane rapidly extinguished the gas and took his position on the couch amongst his companions.

The profound silence was only interrupted by the battering ticks of the hand watches counting the seconds.

Suddenly, a terrifying, dreadful shock was produced! And the projectile, under the power of the 6,000,000 liters of gas developed by the explosion of the pyroxylin guncotton, was sent into interplanetary space.

2. The First Half-Hour

What precisely had happened? What effect was produced by that horrifying shock? Had the genius of the projectile's constructors brought about a fortunate result? Had the shock been deadened thanks to the springs, to the four buffers, the cushions of water and the disintegrating-sections? Had they tamed the fearful power of that initial velocity of 11,000 meters per second, which was sufficient to traverse New York or Paris within a moment? It was evidentially these questions that were posed by the thousands of witnessing spectators at that moving scene. They had forgotten about the voyage in their concern for the voyagers. And if there were any of them- J.T. Maston, for example- could have cast one look into the projectile, what would they have seen?

Nothing at all. The dark obscurity inside the cannon ball was profound. But these walls of cylindrical-conical shells possess superior resistance. They do not tear or split, they do not bend, they do not deform. In the same way, the admirable projectile did not alter from the intense explosion of the guncotton; nor liquefy into molten metal, as some had feared, into tears of raining aluminum.

And the interior: only slightly disordered all in all. Some objects had been launched violently throughout the vault but the most important of these did not appear to have suffered from the shock of the blast. Their fixtures remained intact.

Upon the mobile disk reduced at the base of the projectile, after the disintegrating sections of water had escaped, three bodies lay without movement. Barbicane, Nicholl and Michel Ardan- did they breathe still? Or had the projectile become a coffin of metal, exporting three corpses into space?...

A few minutes after the departure of the cannon ball, one of the bodies started to move! Their arms agitated, their head straightened out and they managed to get to their knees. It was Michel Ardan. He felt himself, expressing a sonorous "Ahem", and then he said:

"Michel Ardan, complete. How are the others!"

The courageous Frenchman attempted to rise, but he could not hold himself upright. His head was faint from the blood that had been violently injected into to it; he was blind, and like a man who was drunk.

"Brr!" he uttered. "This has produced the same effect of two bottle of Corton. Only, it is slightly less agreeable to swallow!"

Then, passing his hand several times over his forehead and the sides of his temples, he cried in a firm voice:

"Nicholl! Barbicane!"

He waited anxiously. No response. Not even a sigh to indicate the hearts of his companions battered still. The same silence.

"The devil!" he said to himself. "They seem as though they have tumbled through the air from a fifth story onto their heads! Bah!" He spoke with that imperturbable confidence which nothing could halt. "If a Frenchman can pull himself onto his knees, two Americans should remit themselves to their feet without trouble. But, I shall shed some light on the situation."

Ardan sensed the life returning to him in ebbs. His blood calmed and restored to the circulation he was accustomed to. The new efforts regained his equilibrium. He managed to stand, and sought in his pocket for a match which he lit by scratching at the phosphorus. Then, approaching the gas burner he ignited a flame. Its receiver had not suffered. The gas had not escaped. Besides, an odor was not perceptible- if it had been that case, Michel Ardan would not have recklessly promenaded himself about with a lit match in the midst of room filled with hydrogen. That gas, combined with air, would have produced an explosive mixture whose detonation would have achieved what perhaps the shock had commenced.

With the burner's flame illuminated, Ardan peered over the bodies of his companions. Their limbs were spread one over the other, like inert masses. Nicholl above, Barbicane underneath.

Ardan straightened out the captain against the verge of the divan, and began to massage him vigorously. The friction, intelligently-practical, reanimated Nicholl; who opened his eyes and they instantly recovering their cold-blooded aspect. He seized the hands of Ardan. Then he looked around himself:

"And Barbicane?" he asked.

"Each in turn," responded Michel Ardan calmly. "I commenced with you, Nicholl, because you were lying above him. And now I shall attend to Barbicane."

Saying that, Ardan and Nicholl lifted the president of the Gun Club and deposited him on the divan. Barbicane seemed to have suffered more than his companions. He was bleeding, but Nicholl reassured them both by reporting that the hemorrhage was not serious; only a slight wound at his shoulder. A simple skin lesion which he compressed carefully.

Nevertheless Barbicane was still some time to resuscitate and his frightened two friends were unsparing in their attentions.

"He breathes, however," said Nicholl, placing his ear on the chest of the invalid.

"Yes," responded Ardan. "He breathes like a man who has somewhat of a habit in that daily operation. Massage, Nicholl, massage with vigor!"

And the two improvised physicians worked upon him so well, that Barbicane recovered the use of his senses. He opened his eyes, he straightened himself, taking the hands of his friends, and his first words were:

"Nicholl," he demanded. "Are we moving?"

Nicholl and Barbicane regarded one another. No one had to this point worried about the projectile. Their first preoccupation had been for the voyagers, and not their carriage.

"Are we, in fact, moving?" repeated Michel Ardan.

"Or do we lie in tranquil-repose upon Florida soil?" asked Nicholl.

"Or at the bottom of the Gulf of Mexico?" added Michel Ardan.

"What an example!" cried the president Barbicane.

And that double hypothesis suggested by his companions had instantly returned Barbicane to his immediate sentiments.

In any circumstance, they were still unable to determine the cannon ball's location. It was apparently immobile; and the absence of communication with their exterior permitted no resolution to the question. Perhaps the projectile was unwinding in its trajectory as they traversed through space; perhaps, after a short ascent, it had tumbled back towards ground, or even into the Gulf of Mexico- a fall which the small size of the Floridian peninsula rendered possible.

The case was exceedingly grave, the problem interesting. It would be resolved very soon. Barbicane, whose over-excitement triumphed over his weakened physique by its moral energy, rose. He listened. Outside, the silence was profound. But the padded walls were sufficient to insulate all the noises of Earth. However, one circumstance struck Barbicane. The temperature of the interior of the projectile was remarkably high. The president took a thermometer from out of its protective envelope and consulted it. The instrument marked 45° centigrade.

"Yes!" he cried loudly to the others. "Yes! We are moving! That suffocating heat is transferring through the walls of the projectile! It is being produced from abrasion with the atmospheric layers. It will soon diminish, because we are now floating through the void and after this heat fails us, we shall be subject to an intense cold."

"What have you determined, Barbicane?" Michael Ardan asked. "Are we at present outside the limits of the terrestrial atmosphere?"

"Absolutely without a doubt, Michel. Listen here. It is 10 hours and 55 minutes. We have been travelling since 8 minutes earlier. So, if our initial velocity had not been diminished by abrasion against the air, six seconds was already sufficient to cross the 16 leagues of atmosphere which surrounds our spherical planet."

"Perfect," responded Nicholl. "But what do you estimate as the proportion of diminution in velocity due to air-friction?"

"In the proportion of a third, Nicholl," answered Barbicane. "That diminution is considerable, but after my calculations, those are my findings. So then, if we had an initial velocity of 11,000 meters per second, as we pierce through the atmosphere that velocity should have reduced to 7,332 meters per second; which in any case, we should now have crossed that interval and..."

"And accordingly," said Michel Ardan, "my friend Nicholl has lost the two wagers: $4,000 because the Columbiad cannon did not burst and explode; $5,000, because the projectile has ascended to a superior height than six miles. Therefore, Nicholl, you must execute them."

"Observe it as fact," answered the captain, "and after which I will pay. It is highly possible that the reasonings of Barbicane are exact and I will lose my $9,000. But a new hypothesis has presented itself to my mind, and it would annul the agreement."

"Which is?" demanded Barbicane in a lively tone.

"The hypothesis is, for one reason or another, the fire was never sufficiently set to the guncotton and we have not actually departed."

"By God, captain," cried Michel Ardan, "that is a hypothesis dignified for my brain! You cannot be serious! Were we not stunned half-unconscious by the explosion? And did I not restore you back to life? And is not the president's shoulder bleeding still from the counter-shock when he was struck?"

"I concur, Michel," replied Nicholl, "but I only have one question."

"Make it, my captain."

"Did you actually hear the detonation, which was certain to be formidable?"

"No," responded Ardan, very surprised. "In effect, I did not notice the detonation's sound."

"And you, Barbicane?"

"No, I did not either."

"And well?" said Nicholl.

"In fact," murmured the president, "why did we not hear the detonation?"

The three friends regarded one another with an air of disconcertion. It presented an inexplicable phenomena. The projectile had, however, departed and in consequence the detonation would have been produced.

"Let us see where we are," said Barbicane, "and un-batten the panels."

The operation was extremely simple, for it was also practical. The nuts which maintained the bolts of the exterior plates covering the portholes ceded under the pressure of an english wrench. Those bolts were pushed outwards and indian rubber shutters surrounding the holes sealed the resulting passage. As soon as the exterior plates were pushed away from their hinges as though scuttled, the lenticular glass in the portholes appeared. There was an identical porthole in the padded walls on the other side of the projectile and another where the dome terminated, and finally a fourth in the middle of the floor. These therefore provided observation in four opposing directions; the firmament most-directly through the lateral glass viewpoint, and the Earth or the Moon through the uppermost and lowest points of the cannon ball.

Barbicane and his two companions immediately fell upon the uncovered glass window. No rays of light animated the outside. The projectile was enveloped by a profound obscurity. This did not prevent the president from descrying:

"No, my friends, we have not fallen back upon the Earth... No, we are not immersed at the depths of the Gulf of Mexico! Yes! We have mounted into space. Do you see the stars, shining brilliantly in the night, and that impenetrable obscurity which is the entire mass of the Earth beside us!"

"Hurrah! Hurrah!" cried the communal voices of Michel Ardan and Nicholl.

In effect, the dense compacted darkness proved that the projectile had left the Earth; for the soil, brilliant and bright beneath the Moon's shining clarity, would have appeared to the eyes of the voyagers, should they have reposed on the surface. That obscurity demonstrated that the projectile had surpassed the atmospheric layer, for otherwise the luminosity would diffuse, shedding through the air and reflected onto the metallic walls and reflected inside in that manner. That light would have lit the glass in the portholes, and that glass had been left empty. Doubt was no longer permissible. The voyagers had left the Earth.

"I have lost," said Nicholl.

"I offer you my congratulations," Ardan told him.

"There is nine thousand dollars," said the captain, as he withdrew from his pocket a bundle of paper dollars.

"Do you wish to have a receipt?" asked Barbicane, taking the sum.

"If you would oblige me," responded Nicholl. "It is more correct."

And, seriously, phlegmatically, as though he had been beside a treasury-case, the president Barbicane took out his notebook and detached a blank page; writing in his crayon a legal receipt which he dated, he signed, he initialed; and which he then he remitted to the captain, who shut it carefully within his wallet.

Michel Ardan, removing his cap, bowed without speaking towards his two companions. So much formalism in unparalleled circumstances had left him stunned for words. He had never seen anything so 'American'.

Barbicane and Nicholl, that operation terminated, had returned to their places by the glass portholes and regarded the constellations. The stars were detached in crisp points onto the deep black of the sky. But, from this side, they could not perceive that shining body of the night sky, the Moon, which, moving from east to west, elevated little by little towards the zenith. And its absence provoked a reflection from Ardan.

"And the Moon?" he said. "Is it, by chance, going to miss our rendezvous?"

"Reassure yourself," answered Barbicane. "Our future sphere is at its post, but we cannot perceive it from this side. Open the other lateral porthole."

At the moment when Barbicane was about to abandon the glass window and proceed to disengage the plating from the opposite porthole, his attention was attracted by the approach of a brilliant object. It was an enormous disk whose colossal proportions could not be entirely estimated. The face which turned towards the Earth was vividly bright. One may have said it was a little Moon reflecting the light of its greater. It advanced with prodigious speed and the path it described around the Earth was in an orbit that would impact with the trajectory of the projectile. The movement of translation of the mobile was completed with a movement of rotation upon itself. Hence it comported itself like all celestial bodies abandoned to space.

"Eh!" cried Michel Ardan. "What is that? Another projectile?"

Barbicane did not respond. The apparition of the enormous body was amazing and disconcerting. A collision was possible, which would bring about a deplorable result as this would cause their projectile to deviate from its route or otherwise the shock against it, breaking the surge of their progress, would cause them to precipitate to the Earth; or finally it might irresistibly entrain them in the powerful attraction of the asteroid's own gravity.

Vigorously, president Barbicane reviewed the consequences of these three hypotheses which- one way or the other- facilitated their experiment towards a deadly failure. His companions, mute, regarded the empty traverse of space. The object became prodigiously huge as it approached and by a certain illusion of optics it seemed as though the projectile itself hastened towards it.

"A thousand gods!" cried Michel Ardan. "These two trains shall encounter one another!"

Instinctively, the voyagers threw themselves backwards. Their fatal sense of fear was extreme but it did not endure for a long time; several seconds in full. The asteroid passed several hundreds of meters from the projectile and disappeared, not so much from the rapid speed of its course, but because the face opposing the Moon was suddenly confounded into absolute obscurity by the darkness of space.

"Bon voyage!" cried Michel Ardan and uttered a sigh of relief. "Pardon! Isn't infinity grand enough for a poor tiny cannon ball to promenade itself about under its own power without fear! Ah then! What was that pretentious globe who was too weak to hit at us?"

"I know," answered Barbicane.

"Good heavens! You know everything."

"It is," said Barbicane, "a simple meteorite, but an enormous meteorite which gravity's attraction has turned into a satellite."

"Is it possible!" cried Michel Ardan. "The Earth has two moons like Neptune?"

"Yes, my friend, two Moons, although it passes generally for possessing only one. But this second Moon is so small and it's velocity is so great, that the inhabitants of the Earth fail to perceive it. It was by taking account of certain perturbations that a French astronomer, M. Petit, could determine the existence of the second satellite and calculate its elements. From his observations the meteorite accomplished a revolution around the Earth in only 3 hours and 20 minutes, which implied a prodigious velocity."

"Do all the astronomers," asked Nicholl, "admit the existence of this satellite?"

"No," responded Barbicane; "but if, like us, they have an encounter with it they would have no further doubt. In fact I think the meteorite, which would have greatly hindered us should it have collided with the projectile, permits us to locate our precise position in space."

"How?" said Ardan.

"Because its distance is known and, so, at the point where it was encountered we were exactly 8,140 kilometers above the surface of the terrestrial globe."

"More than 2,000 leagues!" exclaimed Michel Ardan. "This breaks the records of the express trains on some pitiful globe called the Earth!"

"I can well believe it," responded Nicholl consulting his pocket watch. "It is 11 o'clock, and we have been gone from the American continent for 13 minutes."

"13 minutes only?" said Barbicane.

"Yes," responded Nicholl. "And if our initial velocity of 11 kilometers is held constant, we shall have made close to 10,000 leagues within the hour!"

"Everything is very good, my friends," said the president. "But there still remains that insoluble question. Why did we not hear the detonation in the Columbiad?"

In default of response the conversation ended and Barbicane, lost in reflection, occupied himself in removing the protective plate over the second lateral porthole. This operation succeeded and through the window, now unencumbered, the Moon lit the interior with its brilliant light. Nicholl, a man of economy, extinguished the gas which was now useless and whose glare had become a nuisance to observing the interplanetary space.

The brilliant lunar disk came through with an incomparable purity. Its rays, which were un-subdued by the atmosphere of the terrestrial globe, filtered through the glass and saturated the interior air of the projectile with reflected silver. The black curtain of the firmament veritably doubled the splendor of the Moon, which, in a void of ether that made diffusion inappropriate, did not eclipse the nearby stars. The heavens, thus seen, presented totally new aspects to the human eye it had never suspected were possible.

One may conceive the interest with which these audacious men contemplated the Moon, that shining body of the night sky, the supreme goal of their voyage. The satellite of the Earth through its movement of translation impassively approached zenith, the mathematical point which it would attain 96 hours later. Its mountains, its plains, all its characteristics were exposed into very clear relief before their eyes as though their gaze were considering some point on the Earth; but the luminosity, traversing through void, developed an incomparable intensity. The disk was resplendent like a mirror of platinum. Of the invisible Earth receding beneath their feet, the voyagers had then quite forgotten all of their remembrance.

It was the Captain Nicholl who was first to call their attention onto the disappearing globe.

"Yes," answered Michel Ardan. "We should not be ungrateful that it inverts us. Since we have abandoned our lands, let us regard this apparition for one last time. I wish to look upon the Earth and say goodbye before it completely eclipses beneath my eyes!"

Barbicane, to satisfy the desires of his companion, detached the plate covering the window at the base of the projectile which then permitted direct observation of the Earth. The wooden disc, designed to shatter from the force of the initial ejection in order to suppress the counter shock, had been rammed into the floor and without pain it was dismantled. Its fragments were placed tidily against the walls where they could be of further service, should such a case develop. Below them appeared a circular bay 50 centimeters in size, hollowed into the inferior part of their aluminum cannon ball. A sheet of glass fifteen centimeters thick was reinforced by the armature of the metal, which sealed it. Outside of this was a plate, retained by bolts, the same design of aluminum metal which had covered the lateral windows. The nuts were unscrewed, the bolts dropped away, the plate was jettisoned and visual communication was established between the interior and the exterior.

Michel Ardan fell to his knees upon the glass. It was dark and gloomy, as though opaque.

"Ah well," he cried. "Where is the Earth?"

"The Earth," said Barbicane, "is there."

"What!" exclaimed Ardan. "This miniscule filament, that silver crescent?"

"Without doubt, Michel. In four days, when the Moon is seen fully- at the same time when we attain our destination- the Earth will be seen as new. It appears underneath us in the shape of a delicate crescent, and will soon entirely disappear, and then be submerged for a few days within an impenetrable shadow."

"There! The Earth!" repeated Michel Ardan, with all of his eyes regarding the thin sharp edge that was his native planet.

The explanation provided by the president Barbicane was just. Earth, in relationship to the projectile, had entered its last phase. It was in its octant and displayed a fine crescent that traced onto the black background of the sky. Its luminosity, rendered blue-ish by the depth of the atmospheric layer, offered a reduced intensity to the lunar crescent.

This crescent presented below offered considerable dimensions. One might say it was an enormous arc that strained against the firmament. Several parts, vividly lit, especially upon the concave part, announced the presence of high mountains; but they often disappeared beneath thick dark clumps that are never seen upon the surface of the lunar disk. These were rings of cloud concentrically disposed around the terrestrial sphere.

However, by a particular sort of natural phenomenon identical to that which was produced on the Moon when it was in its octants, it was possible to see the contours of the entire terrestrial globe. The entire disk could be visibly appraised by the effect of an ashen light, less-appreciable than the Moon's ash-light. And the reason that intensity is reduced is easy to comprehend.

When the reflection is produced upon the Moon it is due to the solar rays which the earth reflects onto its satellite. Here, by an inverse effect, it is the solar rays reflected by the Moon onto the Earth. So the terrestrial luminosity is approximately thirteen times more intense than the lunar luminosity, which is due to the difference in volume between the two bodies. Hence from that consequence, in the phenomenon of the ashen light the part of the disk of the Earth that is obscured is by its design less clear than the disk of the Moon, since the intensity of the phenomenon is proportionate to the power of the clarity of the two astral bodies. It should also be added that the terrestrial crescent resembles the shape of a more-elongated curve than that of a disk. Purely an effect of irradiation.

Whilst the voyagers searchingly tried to pierce the profound unending darkness of space a bouquet of sparkling filaments of stars burst before their eyes. These were hundreds of meteors, inflamed from the contact of the atmosphere, their shadows radiated into luminous trains of fiery streaks across the ashen portions of the Earth's disk. At that epoch, the Earth was in its perihelion, and the month of December is propitious for the apparition of these starry filaments of which the astronomers have counted as many as 24,000 in one hour. But Michel Ardan, disdainful of scientific reasoning, rather preferred to believe that the Earth had saluted with that exceptionally brilliant fiery artifice the first-ever departure of its three children.

In summary, that was all which they saw of the Earth's sphere before it perished into complete shadow; an inferior heavenly body in that solar world, which, for the grand planets, had set like a simple star of the morning or evening! An imperceptible point in space, which was nothing more than a fugitive crescent, this globe where they had left behind all of their heartfelt affections!

For a long time, the three friends, without speaking, but united in heart, stared outwards whilst the projectile launched away with a uniform velocity from the diminishing crescent. Then an irresistible somnolence invaded their minds. Could it be fatigue of the body, or of the spirit? Without doubt, for after the over-excitement of the final hours passed on the Earth, their reaction was an inevitable product.

"Ah well," said Michel, "since we must sleep, then sleep."

And, extended upon the couches, the three were soon ensphered by profound slumber.

But they had not even dozed for half an hour's duration when Barbicane sat up excitedly and revealed to his companions in a formidable voice:

"I have it!" he cried!

"What do you have?" asked Michel Ardan, still sauntered across the couch.

"The reason for which we did not hear the detonation of the Columbiad!"

"And that is?..." muttered Nicholl.

"Because the projectile was moving faster than sound!"

3. Their Place of Shelter

That explanation was curious, but certainly exact. Once given, the three friends were plunged into deep slumber. Was there ever, for sleeping, anywhere more calm, more peacefully quiet? On the Earth, the houses in their cities, the cottages in their countryside, feel all the effects of every blow imparted to the outer skin of the globe. On the sea, the ships, buffeted by the waves, are never shocked by their constant movement. In the air, the balloon oscillates incessantly on fluid layers of diverse turbulent densities. Only here, in the projectile, floating in absolute void in the midst of absolute silence, could its residents be offered an absolute repose.

And so the sleep of the three adventurers may have slowly prolonged indefinitely, if not for a surprising noise which disturbed them towards 7 hours in the morning, the 2nd December, 8 hours after their departure.

The noise was a very characteristic barking.

"The dogs! It is the dogs!" cried Michel Ardan, who rose immediately.

"They are hungry," said Nicholl.

"Good heavens!" responded Michel. "We had forgotten them!"

"Where are they?" asked Barbicane.

On searching they discovered one of the animals huddled beneath the divan. Terrified, overwhelmed by the initial shock of the blast; it had rested in the corner until the moment when its voice had revived by famished sentiment.

It was the amiable Diane, still sufficiently contrite, who emerged from her retreat- although not without being coaxed. However, Michel Ardan encouraged her with caring words.

"Come, Diane," he said, "come, my girl! You, whose destiny will be marked in the annals of the cynegetics, that great history book for all dogs; you who the pagans would have donated for the consort of the god Anubis, and the christians as a friend to Saint Roche! You, as though cast in that legendary unbreakably alloy of brass and iron by the king of infernal hell, like the little puppy Jupiter presented to beautiful Europa for the price of one kiss! You, whose celebrity effaces that hero of Montargis and the hero of Mount Saint Bernard! You, who have launched into interplanetary space, perhaps you will become the Eve of all selenite moon-dogs! It is you who justifies that high speech of Toussenel; '*In the beginning, God created man, and seeing how feeble he was, he gave him the dog!* Come, Diane! Come here!"

Diane, flattered or otherwise, advanced little by little, uttering plaintive entreaties.

"Good!" said Barbicane, "I can see Eve, but where is Adam?"

"Adam!" responded Michel. "Adam is not very far! He is here, in some part! We must use the name Satellite! Here, Satellite!"

But Satellite did not appear. Diane continued to whimper. On inspection however she was not injured anywhere, and once served some appetizing mash she had finished with her cries.

As for Satellite, he appeared un-locatable. There followed a search for a long time before he was discovered in one of the compartments in the upper part of the projectile where the repercussions from the initial blast, rather inexplicably, had violently thrown him. The poor beast, badly damaged, was found to be in a pitiful state.

"The devil!" said Michel. "There it is- our acclimatization program has been compromised!"

The sick dog was cautiously brought down. His skull had fractured against the vault, and it seemed difficult to revive him from that shock. Nevertheless, he was comfortably laid out on cushions and once there, he let out a sigh.

"We will nurse you," said Michel. "We are the ones responsible for your survival. It would be better for me to lose an arm than a paw of my poor Satellite!"

And, this spoken, he offered some mouthfuls of water to the injured dog, which was taken avidly.

This medical attention having been administered, the voyagers attentively observed the Earth and the Moon. The Earth's great figure was a disk of ash terminated by a crescent that traced along its veil; but it's volume still remained enormous, which they compared to the Moon that, as they approached, became more and more a perfect circle.

"Good heavens!" then said Michel Ardan. "I am really angered that we did not leave at the moment when the Earth was full, that is to say when our globe was travelling in opposition with the Sun."

"Why?" asked Nicholl.

"Because then we might have surveyed with our eyes beneath a new day our continents and our seas, lying resplendently there beneath the extension of the Sun's rays- far more than the gloomy depictions that are reproduced on certain world-maps! I wish to have seen the poles of the Earth on which the eyes of man have never rested!"

"Without doubt," responded Barbicane. "But if the Earth had been full, the Moon would be new, that is to say, invisible in the midst of the Sun's irradiation. So, it is best for us to see the point where we aim to arrive, rather than our point of departure."

"You speak reasonably, Barbicane," responded the Captain Nicholl. "And after we have reached the Moon, we shall have the time during those long lunar nights, to consider at leisure the Earthly globe swarming with our fellow creatures."

"Our fellow creatures!" cried Michel Ardan. "But now, they are no more our fellow creatures than the Moon people, the Selenites! Now we are the inhabitants of a new world, peopled solely by us, citizens of the projectile! I am a fellow creature of Barbicane, and Barbicane is a fellow creature of Nicholl. It is we who are here, and outside of us humanity ends. At the moment we are the only population in this microcosm until we convert into pure Selenites!"

"In approximately 88 hours," completed the captain.

"What are you intending to say?..." asked Michel Ardan.

"That it is 8 and a half hours," responded Nicholl.

"Ah well," Michel parried, "then it is impossible for me to find even the appearance of a reason we hesitate to take breakfast."

Indeed the inhabitants within that new star could not survive without eating, and their stomachs accordingly suffered by the imperious laws of hunger. Michel Ardan, as a Frenchman of quality, was declared the chef of cuisine- an important function which no one else wanted to compete for. The gas gave them certain degrees of heat sufficient for their culinary affectations and the basket of provisions furnished all the elements needed for their first feast.

The breakfast began with three cups of soup from excellent stock, liquefied heated water and those precious cubes of *Liebig*, prepared with the best morsels of bison meat, those ruminants of the Pampas. This bouillon was succeeded by several slices of beef-steak hydraulically compressed, so tender, so succulent they thought it had come from an English cafe. Michel, a man of imagination, even maintained they were "rare".

The conserved vegetables, "and more fresh than nature," as the amicable Michel endorsed, followed their plate of meat and after these several cups of tea with sliced bread and butter were eaten in the American fashion. Their beverage, declared exquisite, was an infusion of leaves of premium choice which the Emperor of Russia had gifted several cases for the disposition of the voyagers.

Finally, to crown that repast, Ardan unearthed a fine bottle of Nuits, which he had found "by chance" in the provisions compartment. The three friends drank to the union between the Earth and its satellite.

And as if it had not been generous enough by providing the sunshine for that wine distilled upon the fair hills of Burgundy, the Sun decided to meet their party. The projectile came at that moment to the cone of shadow being cast by the terrestrial globe; and the shining rays of our star struck directly against the disc at the cannon ball's base, caused by the angle that the orbit of the Moon made with that of the Earth's.

"The Sun!" cried Michel Ardan.

"Without doubt," responded Barbicane. "I was waiting."

"However," said Michel, "does the cone of that shadow left by the Earth extend into space all the way beyond the Moon?"

"Well-past it, if we do not consider the atmospheric refraction," answered Barbicane. "But when the Moon is enveloped in that shadow, this is where the centers of the 3 astral bodies- the Sun, the Earth, and the Moon are in a straight line. At the moment when this bond coincides with the phases of the full Moon there is an eclipse. If we had departed during the Moon's eclipse, our entire trajectory would have been accomplished in shadow, which would have been unfortunate."

"Why?"

"Because even though we are floating in the void, our projectile, when bathed within the solar rays collects its light and warmth. Hence, by economizing gas, we economize precious resources."

In effect, underneath these rays where no atmosphere can temper the heat of their clarity, the projectile was heated and its interior illuminated like the sudden passing of winter into summer. With the Moon on high, and the Sun beneath, they were inundated by its fire.

"It is quite agreeable in here," said Nicholl.

"I think it is great! cried Michel Ardan. "With a little composted earth spread upon the floor of our aluminum planet, we should possess the first sprouts of peas in twenty-four hours. I do have one fear, though, and that is the walls of the cannon ball begin to melt!"

"Reassure yourself, my dignified friend," counseled Barbicane. "The projectile has withstood a more highly-elevated temperature, during the moments when we slipped through the atmospheric layers. I would not even be astonished if we looked to the eyes of the spectators in Florida like a fiery meteor."

"But then, J.T. Maston will fear we are roasted."

"It is my astonishment," Barbicane replied, "that we do not appear to have been. It was a danger that I had not foreseen."

"That fear was mine," responded Nicholl simply.

"And you had said nothing to us, sublime captain!" cried Michel Ardan and he shook the hands of his companion.

Then Barbicane proceeded to install himself in the projectile as though he were to never leave it. One should recall their aerial carriage offered from its base to its ceiling 54 square feet. As high as a dozen feet at the summit of its vault the interior was skillfully arranged, with little encumbrance by the instruments and utensils. The journey allowed each to occupy their particular place, and gave the three residents a certain liberty of movement. The thick window, gouged from part of the floor, supported a considerable weight with impunity. And so Barbicane and his companions walked upon its surface as though it were a solid plank; however the Sun, which struck directly with its rays, illumined the interior of the projectile from below producing an unusual effect of light.

They commenced to verify the state of their case of water and their container of provisions. The receptacles had not suffered at all, thanks to the arrangements employed to absorb the shock of the initial blast. And the abundant provisions were plentiful enough to nourish the three voyagers for the duration of an entire year. Barbicane had wanted this precaution in case they arrived onto an absolutely sterile portion of the Moon. As to the quantity of water and water-of-life, brandy; their reserve of fifty liters was for two months only. But in rapport with the most-recent observations of the astronomers; the Moon conserved a low, dense, thick atmosphere, at least in its deep valleys and along the streams, so their sources would not be empty. Hence, throughout the duration of their trajectory and throughout their first year installed on the lunar continent, the adventurous explorers would suffer no distress from hunger nor from thirst.

Regarding the question of the air in the interior of the projectile- once again, totally secure. The apparatus of Reiset and Regnaut, intended for the production of their oxygen, had 2 months' supply of potassium chlorate. They would necessarily consume a certain quantity of gas, for they needed to maintain the temperature of this material above 400° centigrade for it to be productive. But it was there still, held onto their floor. The apparatus demanded from them but a small level of supervision, it functioned automatically. At that elevated temperature, the potassium chlorate changed into potassium chloride, abandoning all the oxygen the chemical contained. So, how much would 18 pounds of potassium chlorate donate? The 7 pounds of oxygen necessary for their daily consumption during their stay in the projectile.

But it was not sufficient to renew the oxygen that was consumed, it further followed they must absorb the carbon dioxide produced through expiration. So, during a dozen hours, the state of the atmosphere in the cannon ball would become charged with that absolutely harmful gas, produced definitively by the combustion of the elements in the blood when breathing in oxygen. Nicholl recognized the condition of their air when he saw Diane panting difficultly.

In effect, the carbonic acid- by a phenomenon identical to that which is produced in the famous Grotto del Cane- had started to mass towards the base of the projectile, and this was the reason her breathing was burdened. The poor Diane, her head being lower, would begin to suffer before her masters from the presence of that gas. However Captain Nicholl hurried to remedy the state of things. He disposed onto the floor of the projectile multiple packets containing caustic potash which he agitated for a certain time; and that material, highly attracted to the carbonic acid, or carbon dioxide, absorbed completely and thereby purified the air of the interior.

Then commenced an inventory of the instruments. The thermometers and the barometers had maintained their resistance, but for one minimum thermometer whose glass had smashed. An excellent aneroid barometer, withdrawn from a box lined with cotton wool, was hung from the wall. Naturally, it was subject to and marked with precision the air of the interior projectile. But it also indicated the quantity of water vapor which was forming. At the moment the needle oscillated between 760 and 765 millimeters. It was '*fine weather*'.

Barbicane had also brought with him several compasses which had remained intact. One can understand that in those conditions, their needles were throwing themselves about in a panic; that is to say without holding a constant direction. In effect, due to the distance with the cannon ball had travelled from the Earth, the magnetic poles could not exercise on the apparatus any sensible result. But the magnetized instruments, when transported to the lunar disk, might report some peculiar phenomena. In any case, it stood to be interesting to verify how the Earth's satellite was subjected to magnetic influence.

An hypsometer to be used to measure the altitude of lunar mountains, a sextant destined to apprehend the height of the Sun, a theodite which was a geodesic instrument used to survey the level and reduce the plan of the horizon to an angle and sets of field binoculars and small collapsible telescopes which would be used to great appreciation as they neared their approach to the Moon- all these delicate optical instruments were carefully examined and found to be in working order despite the jolt from the initial blast when they had taken off.

As for the utensils, the pick-axes, the mattocks, and the diverse tools which Nicholl had chosen specially; as for the varieties of sacks of grain and the plants which Michel Ardan had brought to transplant into the lunar ground; these had stayed in their place in the upper corners of the projectile. Evidentially this had become a sort of attic encumbered by the objects which the prodigious Frenchman had piled there. What had been brought, no one was quite sure, for the joyous bachelor was inexplicit about their inventory. From time to time, he mounted the foot-holds riveted into the walls beneath that cornucopia, which he had reserved for his inspection. He arranged, rearranged, he plunged his hands rapidly into certain mystery boxes, and whilst doing this sang in a voice badly out of tune old French refrains which amusingly lightened their situation.

Barbicane noted with interest that his flare rockets and other similar artifices had not been damaged. These were important pieces, powerfully charged, whose duty was to slow the projectile's fall once solicited by the lunar gravitational attraction, after passing beyond the point of neutrality and they began to tumble towards the surface of the Moon. A plunge which would be with a force six times less-rapid than onto the surface of the Earth, thanks to the difference in mass of the two astral bodies.

Hence the inspection was terminated with general satisfaction. Then each returned to observing space by the lateral windows and through the lowest glass porthole.

The same spectacle. This whole expanse of the celestial sphere, swarming stars of constellations of marvelous purity, would render an astronomer mad. On one side the Sun, like the mouth of a flaring kiln, a dazzling disk without its halo, detached from the bottomless distance of black heavens. On the other, the Moon ejected its own reflective fire; it seemed unmoving in the midst of that stellar world. Then, a rather great stain, which resembled a hole in the firmament with its edge followed by threads of silver: that was the Earth! Here and there, nebulous masses like large flakes of ethereal snow; and from the zenith to the opposing nadir, an immense ring formed from the impalpable dust of astral worlds, that Milky Way- in the midst of which the Sun is counted as a star of the fourth magnitude of grandeur!

The observers were unable to remove their gaze from that novel spectacle, whose description could not compose an accurate idea. What imaginations it suggested! What emotions hitherto incognizable stirred and awakened within their souls! Barbicane wished to immediately commence writing in his journal the records of the voyage whilst under the influence of these impressions, and he noted hour by hour the facts which signified the debut of their experiment. The writer, deliberate and tranquil, inscribed in his notebook with large writing in a slightly business-like style.

During this time, the calculator Nicholl revisited his formulas of trajectory and manipulated the figures with an unparalleled dexterity. Michel Ardan chatted now with Barbicane, who barely responded, now with Nicholl who would not entertain him, with Diane who could never comprehend his theories, and finally with himself; to whom he offered both questions and responses, coming, going, being occupied by a thousand details, chattering away against the curve of the lowest glass porthole, chattering perched on the highest point of the projectile, and endlessly humming beneath his breath. In that microcosm he represented the French's agitation and loquacity, and one prays that you will believe he was a dignified representative.

The day, or rather- for the expression is unjust- the lapse of 12 hours which shaped a day on Earth, was terminated with a copious supper, finely prepared. Thus far they were without any of the incidents being produced whose nature that might have altered the confidence of these voyagers. And so, full of hope, already sure of their success, they slept peacefully whilst the projectile, under a speed that was uniformly declining, crossed its path of sky.

4. A Small Amount of Algebra

The night passed without incident. Strictly speaking, the word 'night' is inappropriate.

The position of the projectile did not change in its relationship to the Sun. Astronomically; it was day on the inferior part of the cannon ball, night on the superior part. During the recital of this story whenever those two words are employed, they express the period of time between the Sun's rising and setting on Earth.

The slumber of the voyagers was rendered more pleasant, despite their excessive velocity, because the projectile seemed absolutely immobile. They were without movement as they progressed through the traverse of space. Displacement, however rapid it might be, does not produce an effect upon the organism when it is in a vacuum or when the mass of air circulating around the body is brought along with it. What inhabitant of the Earth apprehends their velocity, when they are being moved according to scientific reasoning at 90,000 kilometers an hour? Movement, in those conditions, does not 'feel' anything more than indolent repose. And so all bodies are indifferent to it. When a body is unmoving, it will remain that way until a foreign force displaces it. And if it is experiencing movement, it will not be halted until an obstacle interrupts its forward momentum. The indifference to motion or rest, that is known as inertia.

Hence Barbicane and his companions thought themselves absolutely immobile, having enclosed their travel inside the projectile. The effect to them would have been the same, however, if they had taken their places on the outside of the projectile. Without the Moon, which increased in size above them, they would have sworn they were floating in complete stagnation.

That next morning of the 3rd December, the voyagers were awakened by a joyous noise, however unexpectedly. It was the crowing of a rooster which reverberated throughout the interior of the wagon.

Michel Ardan, the first on his feet, clambered to the summit of the projectile and half-opened a case:

"Can you keep quiet?" he entreated in a low voice, muttering: "This animal is mangling my plans!"

However Barbicane and Nicholl had emerged from their reverie.

"A rooster?" asked Nicholl imploringly.

"Eh no! My friends," said Michel convincingly. "It is I who wished wake you both by that rural vocalization."

And once speaking, he unleashed a splendid cock-a-doodledoo which would have given honor to the most proudest of fowls.

The two Americans could not prevent themselves from breaking into laughter.

"A jolly talent," said Nicholl, regarding his companion with an air of suspicion.

"Yes," responded Michel, "a pleasant joke from my countryside. It is very Galois. In fact, over there, the rooster is maintained by the highest of societies!"

Then, turning the conversation around:

"Say, Barbicane," said he, "do you know what I had thought of all night?"

"No", answered the president.

"Of our friend at Cambridge. You had previously remarked that I am an admirable ignorant in the field of mathematics; and hence it is impossible for me to discern how the scientists at the observatory had calculated what initial velocity needed to develop for the projectile to leave the Columbiad cannon and reach the Moon."

"You meant to say," replied Barbicane, "for us to reach the neutral point where the gravitational attractions of the Earth and the Moon are in equilibrium; that is, that position situated at nine-tenths of the complete journey, where the projectile will tumble onto the Moon simply in virtue of its gravity."

"Very well," agreed Michel. "But, for one more time, how had they calculated the initial velocity?

"Nothing would be more delightful to explain," replied Barbicane.

"And you as well understood the calculation?" questioned Michel Ardan.

"Perfectly. Nicholl and I together could have established the requirements if the note from the Cambridge Observatory had not saved us that pain."

"Ah well, my old Barbicane," responded Michel, "they may have rather cut off my head, and commenced with my feet, to cause me to solve that problem!"

"Because you do not know about algebra," replied Barbicane calmly.

"Ah! There you have it well- you and your ilk, the eaters of the x! You believe you have said it all when you use the word 'algebra'."

"Michel," Barbicane asked him, "do you think you produce from a forge without a hammer or labor in the fields without a plough?"

"With difficulty."

"Ah yes, well- algebra is a tool, like the plough or the hammer, and it is a good tool for those who understand how to employ it."

"Seriously?"

"Very seriously."

"That is interesting."

"And you would be able to use it like a tool before me?"

"If it is of interest."

"And I will be able to watch how to calculate the initial velocity of the carriage?"

"Yes, my dignified friend. One must encounter all the elements of the problem, the distance from the center of the Earth to the center of the Moon, the radius of the Earth, the mass of the Earth, the mass of the Moon; only then I establish exactly what the initial velocity of the projectile would be, it is by a simple formula."

"Show me the formula."

"You shall see it. Only, I shall not give to you the curb traced in reality between the Moon and the Earth, as they perform their movements of translation around the Sun. No. I will consider the two astral bodies, that is to say the Earth and the Moon, as being without motion, which for our purposes is sufficient."

"And why?"

"Because then we would be searching for a solution to that problem which is called 'the problem of three bodies' which integral calculus which is as yet not advanced enough for resolving."

"Hold on," said Michel Ardan, in a slightly-derisive tone, "mathematics has not said the final word?"

"Certainly not," answered Barbicane.

"Excellent! Perhaps the Moon's inhabitants, the Selenites, have taken integral calculus further than us! And if I may ask, what is integral calculus?"

"That is the calculation which is the inverse of differential calculation," Barbicane responded seriously.

"Much obliged."

"Otherwise speaking, it is the calculation by which one searches for finite quantities when only the differential is known."

"At least, that much is clear," responded Michel, with an air of not being completely satisfied.

"And now," replied Barbicane, "a bit of paper, a tip of crayon, and within half an hour you shall have before you the formula you demand."

Barbicane, having said that, absorbed himself in the work; whilst Nicholl observed space, leaving to his companions the care of preparing breakfast.

A half-hour had not yet passed by before Barbicane, lifting his head, showed to Michel Ardan a page covered with algebraic signs, which in the midst of these sequences a general formula stood out:

"And that signifies?..." asked Michel.

"This here signifies," interjected Nicholl, "that: one half of V two minus V zero square equals $G.R.$ multiplied by R upon X minus 1 plus $M\text{*}Prime$ upon M multiplied by R upon D minus X minus R..."

"X on Y on Z riding on P," cried Michael Ardan and his laughter shattered as it echoed throughout that vaulted space. "And you understand this, captain?"

"Nothing is more clear."

"How it is!" said Michel. "But it jumps before my eyes, and yet I demand more."

"Eternally laughing!" replied Barbicane. "You wished to see algebra, and you shall have it up to your chin!"

"I would be better to be hung!"

"In effect," said Nicholl, who explained the formula like a connoisseur, "this appears to be a good solution, Barbicane. That is the integral of the equation of the forces of life, and I do not doubt that it has given you the results you had searched for."

"But I wish to understand!" cried Michel. It would have taken ten years from Nicholl's life for him to have comprehended.

"Listen here," reprimanded Barbicane. "One half of V two less V zero squared, this is the formula which gives us the half-variation of the force of life." [Verne's literal depiction. The astute reader will be aware that zero squared remains zero, and that anything multiplied by zero will result in zero, '*naturellement*'. In fact in this instance the '*zero*' is a non-numerical, nominal term used to express an output of the algebraic computation.]

"Good, and Nicholl knows what that signifies?"

"Without doubt, Michel," Nicholl answered on Barbicane's behalf. "All these signs, which to you seem cabalistic, form however a very clear language, that is most-definite, most-logical for those who know how to read it."

"And you pretend, Nicholl," demanded Michel, "that by means of these hieroglyphics, more incomprehensible than the Egyptian's Ibis, you can deduce what initial velocity must be conveyed and imparted onto the projectile?"

"Incontestably," responded Nicholl, "and by that same formula, I can definitively say what the velocity would be at any particular point of its travel."

"You give your word?"

"On my word."

"So, you are as clever as our president?"

"No, Michel. The aspects which are difficult, that is what Barbicane has accomplished. It is establishing an equation which takes account of all the different conditions that is the problem. The rest is no more than a simple question of arithmetic, and demands merely your cognition of its four rules."

"This is something beautiful!" replied Michel Ardan, who, for his life, could never perform addition correctly, and defined that rule as: 'a Chinese puzzle which permitted one to obtain infinitely varied totals'.

However Barbicane affirmed that Nicholl, had he considered it, would certainly have arrived at that same formula.

"It is nothing I understand how to do," denied Nicholl. "For, the more I study it, the more I find it is marvelously derived."

"Now, listen," said Barbicane to his ignorant comrade, "and you will see all these letters have their own significance."

"I am listening," said Michel with an air of resignation.

"D," said Barbicane, "that is the distance from the center of the Earth to the center of the Moon, and from these centers we can perform the calculations of their attractions."

"That much I can comprehend."

"R is the radius of the Earth."

"R, radius. Admittedly."

"M is the mass of the Earth, and M' is the mass of the Moon. In effect, you need to take account of the mass of the two attracting bodies, because the gravitational attraction is proportionate to their masses."

"That is agreed."

"G represents gravity, the velocity acquired over the period of one second by a body which falls to the surface of the Earth. Is that clear?"

"As clear as water from a spring."

"Now, I represent by X the variable distance which separates the projectile from the center of the Earth, and by V the velocity of the projectile at that distance."

"Good."

"And finally, the expression V zero which in the equation is the figure of the velocity by the cannon ball as it emerges beyond the atmosphere."

"In effect," said Nicholl, "it is at that point where you need to calculate the velocity, because we know already the speed at departure is seen to be three times less the velocity when it escapes the atmosphere."

"I can comprehend no more!" said Michel.

"And yet is quite simple," said Barbicane.

"It is not simple for me," replied Michel.

"It is to say that when our projectile has arrived at the limits of the terrestrial atmosphere, already at that position it has lost a third of its initial velocity."

"As much as that?"

"Yes my friend, nothing is more abrasive than the atmospheric layer. You well comprehend the more rapidly we are moving, the function of resistance by the part of the air becomes higher."

"That, I admit," answered Michel, "and can understand, given that your V zero two and your V zero squared rattles around in my head like nails in a paper bag!"

"The first effect of algebra," replied Barbicane. "And now, for your ending, we will now establish the given numerical values for these diverse expressions, that is to say figure their values."

"End me!" Michael Ardan responded.

"Of these expressions," continued Barbicane, "there are some known, the others are calculated."

"I will take charge of the latter," Nicholl volunteered.

"Let us look at R," said Barbicane. "R, that is the radius of the Earth which, underneath the latitude in Florida were we departed, equals 6,370,000 meters. D, that is to say the distance from the centers of the Earth to the center of the Moon, has a value of 56 terrestrial radii, so..."

Nicholl rapidly did the figures:

"So," he said, "356,720,000 meters, at the moment when the Moon is at its perigee, that is to say the closest distance as it approaches Earth."

"Excellent," said Barbicane. "Now *M*Prime* on *M*, that is to say the rapport between the mass of the Moon and the mass of the Earth, is equal to 81 units."

"Perfect," said Michel.

"*G*, the gravity, is at Florida is 9 meters and 81 centimeters. There our result is that *G.R.* equals..."

"62,426,000 meters squared," Nicholl answered.

"And now?" demanded Michel Ardan.

"Now these expressions have figures," responded Barbicane, "I will discover the velocity of V zero, that is to say the velocity which the projectile in a straight line leaves the atmosphere to attain the point of equal attraction, with its velocity annulled. Because, at that moment, the velocity is zero, I will put that as equal to zero, at which X, the distance that is travelled to that neutral point, found to be represented by nine-tenths of D- that is to say the distance which separates the two centers."

"I have a vague idea this is how it should be," said Michel.

"Hence it follows: X equals nine-tenths of D, and V equals zero, and my derived formula..."

Barbicane scribbled rapidly on the paper. Nicholl looked on almost with avarice in his eyes.

"That's it! That's it!" he cried.

"It is clear?" demanded Barbicane.

"It is written in letters of fire!" answered Nicholl.

"These brave gentlemen," murmured Michel.

"And you comprehend finally?" Barbicane asked him.

"Do I understand!" cried Michel Ardan. "But I must say that my head is in fragments!"

"And so," Barbicane continued, "V zero two equals two $G.R.$ multiplied by one, less ten over nine D, less one unit of eighty-one multiplied by ten R on D less R on D less R."

"And now," said Nicholl, "for obtaining the velocity of the cannon ball as it pierces through our atmosphere, there is one more calculation."

The captain, as a practical man with a wide range of experience in all difficulties, started to enter figures with frightening erratic speed. Divisions and multiplications extrapolated beneath his fingers. The figures fell like hailstones upon that blank page. Barbicane surveyed the scene of activity, while Michel Ardan compressed with two hands an emerging migraine.

"And well?" demanded Barbicane, after several minutes of silence.

"And well, total calculations are in fact," said Nicholl, "V zero, that is to say the velocity of the projectile as it leaves the atmosphere, to attain the point of equal attraction, ought to be..."

"Be..." encouraged Barbicane.

"11,051 meters at the first second."

"Eh?!" said Barbicane, leaping to his feet. "You say!"

"11,051 meters."

"Curses!" cried the president affecting gestures of despair.

"What has happened to you?" asked Michel Arden, very surprised.

"What has happened to me! Why, if at this moment the velocity has diminished by the hold of friction, the initial velocity should ought have been..."

"16,576 meters," Nicholl completed.

"And the Cambridge Observatory, who declared 11,000 meters was sufficient at our departure, and our cannon ball was only imparted with that velocity when it was launched!"

"And well?" demanded Nicholl.

"And well, that was insufficient!"

"Good."

"We will not attain the point of neutrality!"

"Good heavens!"

"We shall not even make half of the way!"

"In the name of the cannon ball!" cried Michel Ardan, who sauntered about in different directions as if the projectile was on the point of colliding with the terrestrial sphere.

"And we shall tumble back onto the Earth!" Barbicane exclaimed

5 The Coldness of Space

That revelation struck like a bolt of lightning. Who would have expected such an error of calculation? Barbicane was not willing to believe it. Nicholl revisited his figures. They were exact. As to the formula which they had used to determine their results, they could not suspect that it was not an exact and verifiable fact; for it was consistently evident that an initial velocity of 16,576 meters in the first second was necessary to attain the point of neutrality.

The three friends regarded one another silently. Of breakfast, the question had escaped them. Barbicane, his teeth clenched, his brows knitted, his fists clenching convulsively, observed their travel through the porthole. Nicholl sat thinking with his arms crossed, examining the calculations. Michel Ardan murmured to himself:

"And there you have our excellent scientists! They never do anything else! I would give twenty pistoles to fall upon the Cambridge Observatory and crash into it and all those contained within fiddling with the figures sent to hell!"

Struck with an idea, the captain shared it directly with Barbicane.

"Ah that!" said he, "it is 7 hours in the morning. Hence we have been travelling for the past 32 hours. More than half of our trajectory has been run, and we have not yet tumbled, from my knowledge!"

Barbicane did not answer. But, after a rapid glance at the captain, he took up a compass which he surveyed with to measure the angular distance from the terrestrial globe. Then moving to the lower-most window, he made an observation that was very exact, due to the apparent immobility of the projectile. He then rose, wiping from his the forehead pearls of sweat that had formed, and put some figures onto paper. Nicholl comprehended that the president wished to deduce by measuring the terrestrial diameter the distance of their cannon ball from the Earth. He watched him anxiously.

"No!" cried Barbicane after several instants. "No, we shall not tumble back! We are already more than 50,000 leagues from the Earth. We have passed the point where the projectile would have halted, if our velocity had been 11,000 meters per second when it departed! We are still travelling upwards!"

"It is evident," responded Nicholl, "and in fact must conclude our initial velocity, beneath the power of that 400,000 pounds of guncotton, exceeded the 11,000 meters advertised. Now I can explain accordingly how we intercepted, after 13 minutes only, the second satellite which gravitates at over 2,000 leagues above the Earth."

"And that explanation is also more than probable," said Barbicane adjunctively, "when we rejected the water contained in the breakable sections that absorbed from the shock of our initial departure, as it moved the projectile's weight was suddenly alleviated considerably."

"Right!" said Nicholl.

"Ah! My brave Nicholl," cried Barbicane, "we are saved!"

"Ah well," responded Michel Ardan calmly, "since we are saved, let us breakfast."

In effect, Nicholl's earlier declaration was incorrect. The initial velocity had been, very fortunately, above the velocity indicated by the Observatory of Cambridge, but the Observatory of Cambridge had nevertheless been less than correct.

The voyagers, delivered from that false alarm, took their seats by the table and breakfasted joyously. They ate plentifully, and spoke even more. Their confidence had been heightened after their '*incident of algebra*'.

"Why should we not succeed?" repeated Michel Ardan. "Why should we not arrive there? We have launched. There are no obstacles before us. There are no stones in our way. The road is free, more free than that of a ship which battles against the sea, more free than that of a balloon struggling to control the wind! And, if a ship arrives where it wants to, and a balloon rises according to its own tastes, then why shan't our projectile attain the end of which it has been aimed towards?"

"It will attain it," said Barbicane.

"If for nothing else but the honor of the American people," added Michel Ardan. "The only people who were capable to lead so well such an enterprise, the only ones who could produce a Gun-Club president such as Barbicane! Ah! I think, now that we no longer have this disconcerting worry, about what will happen to us? We shall soon become royally bored!"

Barbicane and Nicholl each fired off gestures of denigration.

"But I am prepared for that case, my friends," replied Michel Ardan. "You only have to say so. I have at your disposition chess, draughts, cards, dominoes! All we are lacking is a billiards table!"

"What!" demanded Barbicane. "You brought along such silly trifles?"

"Without a doubt," answered Michel, "and not only for your distraction, but also with the laudable attention to equip the taverns of the Selenites with."

"My friend," said Barbicane, "if the Moon is inhabited, its inhabitants would have appeared several thousands of years before those of the Earth, for there is little doubt that astral body is much older than ours. Hence if the Selenites existed on the Moon for hundreds of thousands of years, and if their brains are organized like the human brain, they will have already invented all that we have invented and the same inventions which we might invent over the future centuries. They have nothing to learn from us, and we have everything to learn from them."

"What?" responded Michel. "You think that they have their own artists like

Phideas, Michelangelo and Raphael?"

"Yes."

"Their poets like Homer, Virgil, Milton, Lamartine, and Hugo?"

"I am sure."

"Their philosophers like Plato, Aristotle, Descartes, Kant?"

"I have no doubt."

"Their scientists like Archimedes, Euclid, Pascal, Newton?"

"I could swear on it."

"Their comics like Arnal and the photographers like... like Nadar?"

"I am sure."

"Then, friend Barbicane, if they are also as strong as us, and even more strong, these Selenites, why have they not tentatively attempted to communicate with Earth? Why have they not launched a lunar projectile into our terrestrial regions?"

"And who said to you they have not tried?" responded Barbicane seriously.

"In effect," interrupted Nicholl, "it would be more easier for them than us, and for two reasons; the first because the attraction is six times less on the surface of the Moon than on the surface of Earth, which would permit a projectile to be launched more easily and comfortably; the second, because it would be sufficient to send the projectile only 8,000 leagues instead of 80,000, demanding a force of projection ten times less."

"Then," asked Michel, "I repeat: Why have they not attempted it?"

"And I," replied Barbicane, "I repeat: Who told you they have not tried?"

"When?"

"Thousands of years earlier, before the appearance of man on the Earth."

"And the cannon ball? Where is the cannon ball? I demand to see a cannon ball!"

"My friend," responded Barbicane, "the sea covers five-sixths of the globe. From this, five good reasons for supposing that the lunar projectile, if it was launched, is now submerged at the bottom of the Atlantic or the Pacific. In the least it might be buried in some crevice, in the ages before the ground had sufficiently-formed into hardened crust."

"My old Barbicane," responded Michel, "you have an answer for everything and incline my head before your wisdom. However there is one hypothesis which cheers me better than the others; that is the Selenites, being older than we are, are more wise and have not invented gun powder!"

At that moment Diane disturbed their conversation with a resonant bark. She required her breakfast.

"Ah!" said Michel Ardan, "in our discussion, we have forgotten Diane and Satellite!"

Soon, a respectable mash was offered to the dog who devoured it with a grand appetite.

"Do you see, Barbicane," said Michel, "we might have made this projectile into a second Noah's Ark and imported onto the Moon a couple of all the domesticated animals."

"There is no doubt," answered Barbicane, "but the space is lacking."

"Good!" said Michel. "We might have squeezed in a few!"

"The fact is," responded Nicholl, "that oxen, cows, bulls, horses, all the ruminants would have served us very usefully on the lunar continent. It is our misfortune the carriage could not be developed into a cow shed or a stable."

"But at least," said Michel Ardan, "we could have taken along a donkey, nothing but a little one, that courageous and patient beast which was the mount of old Silenus. Those I love, the poor donkeys! The most excellent of animals least favored by creation. Not only are they beaten during their lives, but they are even beaten after they are dead!"

"How do you entertain that?" demanded Barbicane.

"Damn!" said Michel. "Because they are skinned into drums!"

Barbicane and Nicholl erupted into peals of laughter at that preposterous reflection. But a cry from their joyous companion arrested their mirth. He was bending over the niche where Satellite lay and said:

"Right! Satellite is no longer ill."

"Ah!" said Nicholl.

"No," replied Michel, "he is dead. There it is: an awkward difficulty. I fear, my poor Diane, that you will leave no progeny in the lunar regions!"

In effect, the unfortunate Satellite had not survived his injuries. He was dead and very dead. Michel Ardan was quite disconsolate as he regarded his friends.

"I present one question," said Barbicane. "We cannot keep the cadaver of the dog with us during the next 48 hours."

"No, without doubt," responded Nicholl, "but these portholes are fixed in their hinges. They might be un-shuttered. We open one and then two of us jettison the corpse into space."

The president reflected for several moment's duration. Then he said:

"Yes, we have to proceed thus; but we must take the most-minute precautions."

"Why?" asked Michel.

"For two reasons that you will understand," Barbicane answered. "The first relates to the air trapped within the projectile. Here we must lose the least amount possible."

"But since we manufacture that air?"

"In part only. We refresh the oxygen, my brave Michel. And in that regard we must watch closely that the apparatus supplies us with a moderated quality, for an excess brings about for us physiological troubles that are very grave. Although we refresh the oxygen, however, we do not refresh the nitrogen, which acts as a chemical vehicle the lungs do not absorb and remains intact. So that nitrogen which we need will escape rapidly through the opened porthole."

"Oh! The time to throw out poor Satellite," mourned Michel.

"Agreed. But we must act quickly."

"And the second reason?" asked Michel.

"The second reason, we must not allow the exterior cold, which is excessive, to penetrate into the projectile, under the sentence of being frozen alive."

"However, the Sun..."

"The Sun warms our projectile which absorbs the rays, but it does not heat the empty void we are floating through at the moment. Where there is not any air, there is no more heat than the diffusing light, and the same with black darkness; it is superlatively cold where the rays of the Sun do not directly reach. The temperature in those places is nothing other than the temperature produced by the stellar rays, that is to say suffered by the terrestrial globe if the Sun extinguished one day."

"Which is not to be feared," responded Nicholl.

"Who knows?" said Michel Ardan. "Moreover, in admitting that the Sun shall not extinguish, could it not occur that the Earth moves away from it?"

"Really!" said Barbicane in exasperation. "There you are Michel with your ideas!"

"Eh!," replied Michel. "Did not the Earth pass through the tail of a comet in 1861? Or, suppose a comet whose attraction was superior to the solar attraction, and the terrestrial orbit was curbed by this errant body and the Earth, becoming a satellite, was drawn to such a distance that the rays of the Sun no longer produced any action on its surface?"

"That possibly could occur, in effect," responded Barbicane, "but the consequences of such a displacement might well be not as formidable as you suppose."

"And why?"

"Because the cold and the heat on our globe would afterward redistribute into an equilibrium. It was calculated that if the Earth had become entrained by the comet in 1861, and no longer under the effects of the Sun by becoming moved a great distance away, a heat would have occurred sixteen times superior that that sent by the Moon. A heat which, concentrated by the focus of the strongest lens, could not have produced an appreciable effect."

"And well?"

"Wait a little," answered Barbicane. "It was also calculated that whilst the Earth's orbit was altered, the comet's magnitude was not strong enough to break our gravitational bond with the Sun, and so hence Earth would have remained a member of this solar system. However in its new orbital path, when at the closest point of approach to the Sun, at perihelion, the Earth would have undergone a heat equal to twenty-eight thousand times that of summer. That heat, capable of vitrifying terrestrial materials and vaporizing the water, was expected have formed a thick ring of clouds that would have reduced the excessive temperatures. And there, compensation between the colds of the aphelion and the heats of the perihelion, probably produced a supportable average."

"By how many degrees is the temperature of interplanetary space estimated to be?" asked Nicholl.

"In older times," Barbican answered, "it was believed that the temperature was excessively low. In calculating the thermometric decrease, they arrived at a figure of $-1{,}000{,}000°$ below zero. It was Fourier, a compatriot of Michel's, the illustrated scientist of the Academy of Sciences, who reduced the numbers to a more just estimation. According to him, the temperature of space does not fall below 60° Celsius."

"Peuh!" expressed Michel.

"It is a bit closer," replied Barbicane. "The temperature which is observed in the polar regions, at Melville Island or at Fort Reliance, are environments of -56° Centigrade below zero."

"It remains to be proven," said Nicholl, "that Fourier did not overestimate his evaluations. If I must say, another French scientist, M. Pouillet, estimated the temperature in space at -160° Centigrade below zero. It is for us to verify."

"Not in this moment," Barbicane answered him. "for the solar rays, striking directly on our thermometer would deliver to us, contrarily, a highly-elevated temperature. But when we arrive on the Moon, during the nights of fifteen days which each of the faces alternatively undergo, we shall be at leisure to perform that experiment, for our satellite is bound by void."

"But what do you mean by the void?" Michel questioned. "Is that an absolute vacuum?"

"That is the void, absolutely deprived of air."

"And then that air is replaced by nothing?"

"Yes. By the ether." responded Barbicane.

"Ah! And what is that, the ether?"

"The ether, my friend, that is an agglomeration of imponderable atoms, which, relative to their dimensions, that is to say the artifice of molecules, are also as far from one another as the celestial bodies are in space. Their distance, however, is inferior to one three-millionth of a millimeter. It is these atoms, by their mysterious vibrational movement, produce light and heat, making in one second four hundred and thirty trillion oscillations- that is an amplitude of four to six ten thousandth parts of a millimeter."

"Millions and millions!" cried Michel Ardan. "And have they measured and counted these oscillations! All these, my friend Barbicane, are the figures of scientists which are appallingly dreadful to the eye and that is to say nothing of what they do to one's spirit."

"It needs only simple calculation..."

"No. It seems better to compare. A trillion signifies nothing. An object of comparison says all. Example: When you repeat to me that the volume of Uranus is 76 times more than the size of Earth, the volume of Saturn is 90 times bigger, the volume of Jupiter is 1,300 times greater, the volume of the Sun is 1,300,000 times even larger, my knowledge has not advanced very much. And so, I prefer, a great deal more, the old comparisons of the Double Liegeois who will tell us basically: The Sun, that is a pumpkin two feet in diameter; Jupiter, an orange; Saturn a Greek apple; Neptune, a small cherry; Uranus, a big cherry; the Earth is a pea; Venus, a little pea; Mars, a pin's head; Mercury a grain of mustard and the moons of Juno, Ceres, Vesta, and Pallas are tiny grains of sand! At these are scales at least one can grasp!"

After that tirade of Michel Ardan against the scientists and their trillions which he had strung together without batting an eyelid, they proceeded with the burial of Satellite. It simply required them to jettison his body into space in the same manner that sailors lever a corpse into the sea.

But, as had been recommended by president Barbicane, they needed to operate quickly; to ensure they lost the least amount of air as possible whose elastic nature would escape rapidly into the vacuous void. The bolts of the porthole were drawn, of which the opening measured 30 centimeters, were unscrewed with care; while Michel, entirely sad, prepared to launch the dog into space. The glass, manipulated by a powerful lever which permitted them to overcome the pressure of the interior air against the weight on the walls of the projectile, turned rapidly on its hinges and Satellite was projected outwards. It was difficult for more than a few scarce molecules of air to escape, and the operation went so successfully that later Barbicane did not fear using the same method to rid themselves of the debris of rubbish which encumbered their carriage.

6. Demanding Questions and Answers

The 4th December, their pocket watches marked 5 hours of Earthly morning when the voyagers emerged from sleep, after 52 hours of their journey. At that time, they had exceeded by 5 hours and 20 minutes the halfway point of their assigned sojourn in the projectile; but of the distance of their trajectory they had accomplished seven-tenths. That peculiarity was due to deceleration caused by Earth's gravitational attraction, which they continued to draw away from.

When they observed the Earth through the inferior glass porthole it appeared to them more like a somber, shadowy stain flooded by the solar rays. No longer the crescent, no longer the ashen light! The following day, at midnight, the Earth would become new, at the precise moment the Moon entered its full phase. Above them the Moon, that shining astral body of the night sky, approached more and more the line followed by the projectile; in a manner that would encounter it at the appointed hour. All around, a vault of black punctured by brilliant points of constellations that moved with slowness. But at such considerable distance from their progression, their relative size remained unmodified. The Sun and the stars appeared exactly to them as they would on the Earth. As to the Moon, it had become considerably larger; however the voyager's binoculars, not powerful in their magnification, could not yet return a descent observation of the surface, and thus still they were unable to reconnoiter the topography and geology of the lunar disposition.

And so the time was passed with interminable conversations. They talked about the Moon especially. Each contributed his own contingent of particular knowledge that they were acquainted with. Barbicane and Nicholl, always serious; Michel Ardan, always fantastic. The projectile, the situation, their direction, the incidents which could possibly arise, the precautions which were necessary as they plunged onto the Moon- these were matters of inexhaustible conjecture.

Precisely, as they breakfasted, a question by Michel relating to the projectile provoked a curious response from Barbicane, that dignifies reporting.

Michel, supposing their cannon ball would be brusquely halted when it impacted with the Moon's surface, while it was still being acted upon by that formidable initial force, wished to know the consequences of such as sudden arrest.

"But," answered Barbicane, "I do not see how the projectile will arrive at a sudden stop."

"Supposing it did?" Michel asked, maintain his line of thought tenaciously.

"It is a supposition that is unrealizable," replied the practical Barbicane. "Unless the force of impulsion was wrong. But then, the velocity has decreased bit by bit, and it will not arrive in a brusque halt."

"Allow for it to have collided with another body in space."

"Such as?"

"That enormous meteor which we had encountered."

"Then," said Nicholl, "the projectile would have shattered into a thousand pieces, and us with it."

"More than that," responded Barbicane, "we would have been burned to a crisp."

"Burned!" Michel cried. "Pardon! I regret that case did not present itself, just to see."

"And you would have seen," Barbicane told him. "It is now known that heat-energy is but a modification, a transference, of the energy of motion. When in fact water is heated, that is to say when heat is applied to it, what you see happen before you is created by the movement of its molecules."

"Hold on!" said Michel. "There is one ingenious theory!"

"And fair, my dignified friend, for it explains entirely the theory of the phenomena of calories. That heat is but molecular movement, and a simple oscillation of particles that comprise any material body. When a brake is applied to a train, the train stops. But what became of the movement which had previously animated it? It has been transformed into heat, and the brake is heated. For why do they apply grease to axles moving along the road? To prevent their heating, attenuating that heat-energy, which would otherwise cause the energy of their movement to be lost by that transformation. Do you understand?"

"Yes I understand!" responded Michel, with admiration. "And so, when I am running for a long time or out exercising on the water rowing and sweating large drops of perspiration, what is the force that arrests me? It is totally simple, because my movement has transformed into heat!"

Barbicane could not conceal the smile which formed at Michel's reply. Then, recapturing the theory:

"Thus as well" said he, "in the case of a sudden shock with our projectile it would have been like the heated ball which falls after striking a metal plate. Its movement has been changed into heat-energy. In consequence, I can affirm that if our cannon ball had collided with that meteorite, the velocity, abruptly obliterated, would have created a heat capable of instantly volatizing us into vapor."

"Then," demanded Nicholl, "what henceforth would occur if the Earth was suddenly stopped in the movement of its translation?"

"The temperature would be raised to such a point," answered Barbicane, "that it would be immediately reduced to vapors."

"Good," said Michel, "there is a means to end the world which greatly simplifies things."

"And if the Earth tumbled into the Sun?" said Nicholl.

"According to the calculations," responded Barbicane, "the fall would develop a heat equal to the heat produced by 1,600 globes of coal equal in volume to our terrestrial globe."

"A good increase in temperature of the Sun," mused Michel, "and one which the inhabitants of Uranus or Neptune would receive pleasantly, no doubt, for it must be deathly cold on their planets."

"And so hence, my friends," replied Barbicane, "all movement which is brusquely arrested produces heat. And that theory permits the admission that the heat of the solar disk is augmented by the hailstorms of meteors which rain incessantly upon its surface. It has even been calculated..."

"Defend us," murmured Michel, looking upwards: "here comes the advance of more figures."

"It has even been calculated," continued the imperturbable Barbicane, "that the sudden impact of meteors on the Sun directly produces a heat equal to that of 4,000 masses of coal of equal volume."

"And what is the heat of the Sun?" Michel demanded to know.

"It is equal to that which would be produced by the combustion of one layer of coal completely covering the sun to a thickness of 27 kilometers."

"And that heat?..."

"It would be capable of easily boiling in an hour 2,900,000,000 cubic myriameters of cubic water."

"A myriameter is equal to ten kilometers, apparently," added Nicholl, who would have been willing to admit, if he were asked twice, that even he wouldn't have wished to calculate such extraordinary figures.

"And still it does not roast us!" cried Michel.

"No," answered Barbicane, "because the terrestrial atmosphere absorbs four-tenths of the solar heat. Moreover, the quantity of heat intercepted by the Earth is but two-billionths of its total rays."

"I can see well that this is all for the best," replied Michel, "and that the atmosphere is a useful invention; for not only does it permit respiration, but it also prevents us from being baked!"

"Yes," said Nicholl, "and, unfortunately, it won't be the same on the Moon."

"Bah!" said Michel, forever confidant. "If there are inhabitants, they have respiration. And if there aren't any left, well that should leave enough for three persons, if only at the bottom of ravines where gravity has caused them to accumulate! So what, we have no need for studded mountain-boots to climb the mountains! That is all there is to it!"

And Michel, standing up, moved his viewpoint so that he could see the lunar disk so brilliant and insouciantly clear.

"Sapristi!" said he. "It must be so hot up there!"

"Without counting," replied Nicholl, "that the day there lasts 360 hours!"

"By compensation," said Barbicane, "the nights are of the same duration; and as the heat is only constituted by the solar radiation, the temperature goes to the same level as interplanetary space."

"A jolly countryside!" said Michel. "It is of no importance! I will be happy when we get there! Hey! My friendly comrades, it will be curious to view the Earth from the Moon, to see it rise above the horizon, and to recognize the configuration of the continents and exclaim: there is America, there is Europe- and then to survey it when it becomes lost in the rays of the Sun! And regarding that, Barbicane, do you know if there are eclipses for the Moon's inhabitant's, the Selinites?"

"Yes, there are eclipses of the Sun," answered Barbicane, "when the centers of the 3 astral bodies have travelled onto the same line, and the Earth exactly in the middle. But these are only eclipses of a third, during which the Earth, projected like a screen upon the solar disk, leaves the most part of it remaining for viewing."

"And why," demanded Nicholl, "is it not a total eclipse at that point? Does not the cone of the shadow projected by the Earth extend past the Moon's form?"

"Yes, if we have not taken account of the refraction produced by the terrestrial atmosphere. Not if we include the refraction. And so, if we let the *delta* be the horizontal parallax, and *P* the half-diameter apparent..."

"Ouf!" said Michel. "A half of *V* zero squared...! Speak in everyday language, you algebraic man!"

"Very well, in vulgar language then," Barbicane conceded. "The average distance from the Moon to the Earth is 60 terrestrial radii, the length of the cone of shadow, by the action of refraction, reduces to less than 42 terrestrial radii. Hence the result of which is, during the eclipse, the Moon is delivered beyond the cone of pure shadow, and the Sun provides its rays not only from the borders around the Earth's sphere, but the rays additionally meet at the center."

"Then," said Michel in a mocking tone, "why is there an eclipse, when there are not any seen?"

"Uniquely because, when the solar rays are weakened by that refraction, the atmosphere through which they traverse has tainted them to a great extent!"

"That reason has satisfied me," replied Michel. "We shall see for ourselves well-enough when we get there."

"Now, I say, Barbicane, do you think that the Moon was actually an ancient comet?"

"And now, there is an idea!"

"Yes," replied Michel with amiable conceit. "I have several ideas of that kind."

"But it is not from Michel, that idea," interjected Nicholl.

"Good! Therefore I am a plagiarist!"

"Without doubt," Nicholl countered. "After the testimony of the Ancients, the Arcadians claimed that their ancestors had habituated the Earth before the Moon became its satellite. Starting from that fact, certain scientists have viewed the Moon as a comet; whose orbit had brought it one day so close to the Earth that it was retained by the attraction of terrestrial gravity."

"And is there any truth to that hypothesis?" demanded Michel.

"None whatsoever!" responded Barbicane. "And the proof is the Moon has not preserved any trace of that gaseous envelope which accompanies all the comets."

"But," replied Nicholl, "the Moon, before it became the satellite of the Earth, could it not have, in its perihelion, passed by so closely to the Sun as to cause the evaporation of all the gaseous substances?"

"It is potentially possible, Nicholl my friend, but it is not so probable."

"For why?"

"Because that... My faith, I know nothing."

"Ah! What hundreds of volumes," cried Michel, "we might produce regarding all that we do not know!"

"Ah, there you have said it! And what hour is it?" asked Barbicane.

"3 o'clock," responded Nicholl.

"How the time passes," said Michel, "in the conversation of scientific visionaries like us! Decidedly, I feel that I have been taught too much! I sense myself developing into a pit of knowledge!"

So speaking, Michel hauled himself to the projectile's vault, "for better observation of the Moon", as he put it. During that time, his companions considered their passage through space from their lowest window. Nothing new to signify.

When Michel descended, he approached one of the lateral portholes and suddenly a loud exclamation escaped his lips in surprise.

"What is you see?" asked Barbicane.

The president approached the thickened glass window and before his eyes a sort of flattened sack floated beside their exterior a few meters from the projectile. The object seemed as still as their cannon ball, and by consequence, it was being carried by the same ascending motion as they.

"What is that machine there?" repeated Michel Ardan. "Is it one of the corpuscles of space, some particle, which our projectile has retained with its rays of attraction, and which accompany us there all the way to the Moon?"

"That which astonishes me," said Nicholl, "is how the specific gravity of that body, which is very certainly inferior to that of our cannon ball, allows it to maintain that rigorous level with us!"

"Nicholl," responded Barbicane, after a moment's reflection, "I do not know what that object is, but I know perfectly why it maintains its travel with the projectile."

"And why?"

"Because we are floating in void, captain my friend; and in the void, the bodies fall or have movement- those are the same things- with an equal velocity, whatever their gravitational weight or shape. It is the air which, by its resistance, creates the differences in weight. When observing a pneumatically-created vacuum inside a tube, the objects which you project through it, grains of sand or grains of lead, they will fall with the same speed. Here, in space, it is the same cause and the same effect."

"Very correct," said Nicholl, "and all that we have launched outside the projectile will not cease to accompany us on our voyage to the Moon."

"Ah! We are such dense beasts!" cried Michel.

"Why make use of such a strong description?" demanded Barbicane.

"Because we could have filled our projectile with all kinds of useful objects; books, instruments, tools- the list goes on! We could have ejected all of them, and they would have followed in our train! But I am thinking. Why do we not promenade ourselves outside like that meteor? Why do we not launch ourselves out into space through this porthole? What joyousness could one feel suspended in the ether, even luckier than the birds who must flutter their wings to maintain their place in the air!"

"Very well, I will grant you that," said Barbicane, "but how will you breathe?"

"Damn that blasted air, it confounds my best intentions."

"But if your breath did not fail you, Michel, with a density that is lower than that of the projectile's you would soon be left behind."

Michel was feeling too confounded to inquire as to how the ejected bits of rubbish were expected to stay entrained, if they too had a lower density.

"Then, it is a vicious circle," he said.

"All that is, is most vicious."

"Then we must remain imprisoned in the carriage?"

"We must."

"Ah!" cried Michel in a formidable voice.

"What is wrong with you?" demanded Nicholl.

"I know, I guess what this pretend meteor is! It is no point from an asteroid which accompanies us! It is no tiny piece of a planet!"

"What is it then?" asked Barbicane.

"It is our unfortunate dog. It was the husband of Diane!"

In effect, that deformed object, unrecognizable, reduced to nothing; that was the corpse of Satellite, flattened like a set of deflated bagpipes- and it was rising, rising forever!

7. A Moment of Drunkenness

Hence a curious phenomenon- logical, bizarre, but explicable- was produced under these unusual circumstances. All objects launched outside of the projectile would continue on the same trajectory and ceaselessly move alongside them. It was an inexhaustible context of their conversation throughout that evening. The emotions of the three voyagers were elevated and besides, in measured progress they approached the journey's termination. Waiting for the unexpected, some new phenomenon, there was nothing that could have astonished their spirited disposition as they travelled. Their overexcited imagination moved faster than the projectile, whose velocity was gradually diminishing although imperceptibly to their senses.

However the Moon, as it grew before their eyes, aggrandized and it felt possible to extend one hand's outside the glass panes and touch it.

On the next day, 5th December, at 5 o'clock in the morning, all three were on their feet. This day was to be the last of their voyage, if the calculations proved correct. That same evening, at midnight, in 18 hours, at the precise moment of the full moon, they were due to attain that resplendent disk. Each impending minute drew them closer to the achievement of that grand experiment, which was the most extraordinary of times both ancient and modern. And so throughout that day, as silver rays passed through the portholes, they saluted that shining body of the night sky; shouting confident and joyous hurrahs.

The Moon advanced majestically upon a firmament of stars. A few degrees more and it would reach the precise point to intercede with the projectile. After his own observations, Barbicane calculated they would berth in the northern hemisphere, where immense plains extended and mountains were rare. Circumstances that were favorable; for if the lunar atmosphere, as they reckoned, might be found then it would be only be stored amongst the deepest places of its terrain.

"Besides," observed Michel Ardan, "a plain is rather an easier place to disembark than on a mountain. A Selenite who was deposited in Europe on the summit of Mount Blanc, or in Asia on a peak of the Himalayas, would not have arrived with precision!"

"Moreover," added Captain Nicholl, "on a flat terrain, the projectile would stay motionless where it has made contact. Upon a slope, in contrast, it would roll like an avalanche; and not being squirrels, we should not expect to emerge safe and sound. Hence, it is all for the best."

Indeed the success of their audacious attempt no longer appeared highly doubtful. However one reflection preoccupied Barbicane- but, not wishing to worry his two companions, he kept guardedly silent on the matter.

In effect the direction of the projectile towards the north hemisphere proved their course had become slightly modified. The shot, mathematically calculated, ought to have delivered the cannon ball into the exact center of the lunar disk. If it did not arrive there, then there was some cause for the deviation. But what had produced this? Barbicane could not imagine, nor determine, the purpose behind this deviation for landmarks were absent. His hopes were that there would be no other result than of being brought closer to the upper borders of the Moon, a region more propitious to landing.

Therefore Barbicane was content to frequently observe the Moon without communicating this inquietude to his friends, searching to determine by his gaze that the direction of the projectile was not further-altered. For the situation would be terrible if the cannon ball, its aim being defective, passed beyond the disk and their launch continued out onwards into interplanetary space.

At that moment the Moon, no longer appearing flat like a disk, now allowed them to view its convexity. If the Sun had struck there obliquely with its own rays, the shadow created would have shown the high mountains clearly detached from the surface. Their vision might have sunk into the abysmally-damaged gaping craters, and followed the capricious fissures which streaked over the immense plains. But all relief was leveled-out by the resplendently intense brilliance. With difficulty they could barely distinguish the large patches which gave the Moon that appearance of having the face of a human-like figurine.

"Face, so be it," said Michel Ardan disdainfully. "But I am sorry to say for the friendly sister of Apollo, it is also a pockmarked one!"

Meanwhile the voyagers, as they approached their target, did not cease taking their observations of the Moon. They imagined strolling across those unknown countries. Climbing with pickaxes over its graveled peaks. Descending into the depths of the largest of craters, and circular recesses formed by massive hills. Here and there, they imagined they saw vast seas scarcely contained beneath that rarified atmosphere and water coursing along slopes from mountain tributaries. At their portholes, leaning pensively against an empty void, they hoped to apprehend some kind of sound from that luminous orb; eternally mute in its vacuous solitude.

That final day left them with thrilling remembrances. They had noted the most minutest of details. And then, very gradually, as they approached journey's end a vague inexact sense of disquiet began to take ahold. This concern would more than have doubled if they had become aware of just how mediocre their velocity was. It would have seemed insufficient to conduct them towards their goal. This was because the projectile's 'gravity' was next to nothing. Their weight was incessantly decreasing and would be entirely annihilated along that line where the attractions between the Moon and the Earth are neutralized, provoking such surprising effects.

Despite these preoccupations, Michel Ardan did not forget to prepare the morning's meal with punctual habit. They ate with great appetite. Nothing could be excellent like that beef stock soup liquefied in the heat of the gas. Nothing could exceed the taste of their canned meat. Some glasses of good French wine crowned their refection. As he talked, Michel Ardan remarked that the lunar vines, undergoing their ardent solar recalescence, ought to distill wines which were more than generous- that is if they existed at all. In any case, the prescient Frenchman had taken care not to have forgotten the several packets of precious vine cuttings of *Medoc* and *Cote d'Or*, upon which he particularly counted.

The Reiset and Regnaut apparatus functioned consistently and with extreme precision. Their air had maintained a state of perfect purity. No molecule of carbon dioxide, the deadly carbonic acid, could resist the potash; and as to the oxygen, as Captain Nicholl had said, "it was certainly of the finest quality". The small amounts of water vapor which had condensed in the projectile meliorated that air tempered by a dry aridity; and many of the apartments of Paris, London, or New York, as well as many theatre halls were certainly not in such excellent hygienic conditions.

However to function at a perfect state the apparatus required regular maintenance. And so, each morning Michel attended to the exhaust conditioners, tested the faucets and regulated the pyrometer which was heated by their gas. Everything had worked well so far, and the voyagers, imitating the dignified J.T. Maston, commenced to affect a stout-heartedness that would have rendered them unrecognizable, if their imprisonment had been prolonged for a duration of several months. They comported themselves, in a word, like hens in a cage; they fattened.

As he regarded the progress of their travel through the portholes, Barbicane saw the specter of the dog and the many diverse objects they had thrown outside the projectile obstinately accompanying them still. Diane howled in melancholy as she perceived the remains of Satellite. Those refused things appeared as stationary as if they lay in repose on solid ground.

"Do you realize, my friends," said Michel Ardan, "that if one of us had succumbed to the repercussions of that initial shock on departure, it would have been a great deal of bother to inter their body? What I am saying is for that 'ether', because here the ether replaces earth! You would have seen that accusing corpse accompanying us through space like our remorse!"

"That would have been sad," said Nicholl.

"Ah!" replied Michel. "What I regret is that I have been unable to stroll outside our exterior. What a voluptuous sensation, to float in the midst of radiant ether; to bathe in it, to wrap oneself in pure solar rays! If Barbicane had only thought of furnishing us with diving apparatus and an air pump, I may have ventured beyond and affected the attitudes of a chimera or a hypogriffon at the summit of the projectile."

"Ah well, my dear old Michel," Barbicane responded, "you would not have been a hypogriffon for very long, for, in spite of your diving apparatus, swollen by the expansion of the air within you, you would have burst like an exploding artillery shell- or rather as a balloon that has risen too high into the sky. Therefore regret nothing, and do not forget this: as we float through the voids of interplanetary space, all sentimental promenading outside the projectile is forbidden!"

Michel Ardan allowed himself to be convinced to a certain measure. He conceded that the thing was quite difficult, but not exactly 'impossible'; which was a word he never pronounced.

The conversation from one subject passed to another, and never languished an instant. It occurred to the three friends that in those conditions ideas were emerging from their brains like the leaves spouting at the first warmth of springtime. It was dizzying.

In the midst of those demanding questions and answers which crossed between them throughout the afternoon, Nicholl posed a certain question to which an immediate solution could not be found.

"Well really!" said he. "It is all well and good that we make it to the Moon, but how shall we return?"

The two remaining interlocutors regarded him with an air of surprise. One might have said that eventuality had formulated itself for the first time.

"What do you mean by that?" demanded Barbicane gravely.

"To demand leaving a country," interrupted Michel, "when you are yet to have arrived strikes me as inopportune."

"I did not say that I wished for an immediate retreat," Nicholl defended himself, "but I reiterate my question: how shall we return?"

"In regards to that, I know nothing," responded Barbicane.

"And I," said Michel, "if I had known how to return, I should not have seen the point in going."

"There is a response!" cried Nicholl.

"I approve of Michel's words," said Barbicane. "And I add that the question is of no actual interest. But later, when we have judged it convenient to return, we shall share each other's advice. If there is no Columbiad cannon there, at least the projectile will always be."

"A wonderful advantage! A bullet without a gun!"

"The gun," responded Barbicane, "merely needs manufacturing. As for gunpowder, it is no trouble! Neither metals, nor the saltpeter, nor the coal will be absent from the deep entrails of the Moon's resources. Besides, for our return, we need only overcome the attraction of lunar gravity and it is sufficient to go 8,000 leagues out, then we re-tumble onto the terrestrial globe by virtue of the laws of gravitational weight."

"Enough," said Michel with a positive spirit. "Let there be no more question of our return! We have already spoken of it for too long. When we communicate with our former colleagues back on Earth, it shall not seem difficult."

"And how?"

"By means of meteors launched from the lunar volcanoes."

"Well done, Michel," responded Barbicane in a convincing tone. "Laplace has calculated that a force five times superior to that of our cannons would be sufficient to send a meteor from the Moon to the Earth. And there is no volcano which does not possess a greater power of propulsion than this."

"Hurrah!" exclaimed Michel. "There you have easy factors with these meteors, and they cost nothing! And how we must laugh at the administration of post offices! But, now I think of it..."

"What do you think of it?" encouraged Barbicane.

"A superb idea! Why did we not attach a wire to our projectile? We might have exchanged telegrams with the Earth!"

"A thousand devils!" cursed Nicholl. "And the weight of a wire 86,000 leagues long counts for nothing?"

"For nothing! They could have tripled the charge in the Columbiad! Or even quadrupled, quintupled!" cried Michel; and each verb he pronounced was with more and more violent intonation.

"I have just one small objection about your project," responded Barbicane, "and that is during the moving rotation of the globe our wire would have wrapped around the Earth like a chain being wound upon a winch, which would have inevitably rammed us into the ground."

"By the 39 stars of the Union!" said Michel. "I have nothing but impracticable ideas today! These are ideas dignified of J.T. Maston! But, I venture to say, if we do not return to Earth J.T. Maston is capable of coming to us!"

"Yes! He'll come," replied Barbicane. "He is my dignified and courageous comrade. Besides, what could be easier? Does not the Columbiad cannon remain buried in the Floridian soil? Is there any lack of the cotton and nitric acid necessary to manufacture the pyroxylin to detonate it? Won't the Moon once again pass through its zenith above Florida? In 18 years will it not occupy exactly the place it occupies above us today?"

"Yes," repeated Michel, "yes! Maston will make that rendezvous and come with his friends Elphiston, Bloomsberry, all the members of the Gun Club; and they shall be well-received! And then later, we will establish trains of projectiles between the Earth and the Moon! Hurrah for J.T. Maston!"

It is probable that, if the honorable J.T. Maston had overheard these powerful hurrahs uttered in his honor, at the least his ears should have tingled. What was he doing just then? Without doubt posted on the Rocky Mountains at the station of Long's Peak, and searching to discover their invisible cannon ball gravitating through space. If he had thought about his close companions then it must be acknowledged theirs rested with him; and that, under the influence of this unusual exaltation, they consecrated their finest thoughts towards him.

But what had brought about that animation which was so visibly sparkling upon the residents of the projectile? Their sobriety could not be placed in doubt. A strange euphoria of the mind, attributable to the exceptional circumstances where they found themselves, at a proximity from that shining body of the night sky which only a handful of hours separated- a certain influence secreted by the Moon which agitated their nervous system.

Their faces were rosy as if they had been exposed to the reverberating heat from a fiery oven, their breaths actively respired, their lungs pumped like bellows, their eyes brilliant with an extraordinary flame, their voices reverberated with formidable accents, their words escaping from their lips like corks of champagne popped from their own expanding pressure and their gestures becoming worrying because there was not enough space to develop them properly. And, a remarkable detail- none of them perceived that excessive tension contained within their spirits.

"Now," said Nicholl in a tone of brevity, "now I do not know if I shall ever return from the Moon, do you know what we are going to do there?"

"What we are going to so there?" Barbicane responded, stamping his feet as though he were in a fencing saloon. "I don't have the faintest idea!"

"You don't have the faintest idea!" laughed Michel and the words he provoked hurled and echoed throughout the vaulted interior of the projectile, resonating.

"No, and I don't even doubt it!" roared Barbicane, laughing, and his loud words bounced about in that small space in unison with his interlocutor's.

"Ah well, I know," said Michel.

"So speak, then," cried Nicholl, who could no longer contain the rumbling in his voice.

"I shall speak when it is convenient to me," cried Michel, violently taking hold of his companion's arms.

"It must be convenient to you," said Barbicane, his eyes fiery, his hand menacing. "It was you who brought us into this formidable voyage- and we wish to know why!"

"Yes!" said the captain. "Now I do not know where I am going, I want to know why I am going!"

"Why?!" exclaimed Michel, leaping a meter into the air. "Why? To take possession of the Moon in the name of the United States! To join it as the 40th State of the Union! To colonize the lunar regions; for their cultivation, for them to become populated, to transport all the prodigies of art, science and industry! To civilize the Moon's inhabitants, the Selenites, unless they are more civilized than us, and to constitute a republic there- if they do not already have one!"

"And if there are not any Selenites!" Nicholl contradicted him, who, under the influence of that inexplicable drunkenness was becoming quite argumentative.

"Who said there aren't any Selenites?" cried Michel in a menacing tone.

"Me!" hurled Nicholl.

"Captain," said Michel, "do not repeat that insolence, or I shall force your teeth down your throat!"

The two adversaries were about to fall upon one another as their incoherent conversation threatened to degenerate into battle, when Barbicane intervened with one formidable bound.

"Stop it, you wretched creatures," said he, moving his companions apart. "If there are no Selenites, we will do without them!"

"Yes," exclaimed Michel, who was not tenacious about his argument. "We shall do without them. We shall become the Selenites! Down with the Selenites!"

"The empire of the Moon shall be ours," said Nicholl.

"And the three of us constitute a republic!"

"I will be the congress," cried Michel.

"And I, the senate," replied Nicholl.

"And Barbicane the president," Michel shouted.

"But not a president nominated by the nation!" responded Barbicane.

"Ah well, a president nominated by the congress," said Michel, "and since I am the congress, it is a unanimous nomination!"

"Hurrah! Hurrah! Hurrah for the president Barbicane!" cried Nicholl.

"Hip! Hip! Hip!" supported the vociferous Michel Ardan.

Then, the president and the senate intoned in terrible voices the popular song 'Yankee Doodle' whilst the recently-appointed congress recited in a masculine accent the national anthem of the French, the 'Marseillaise'.

There commenced a disheveled round of dance with crazy gestures; stamping their feet like fools, somersaulting and tumbling like the clowns whose faces are painted as pale as bone. Diane, who joined in the dance, howling in her turn, jumped towards the vault of the projectile. An inexplicable fluttering of wings was heard, and an absurdly-sounding rooster's crow. Five or six hens emerged, striking against the walls like wild bats...

Then, the three companions of the voyage, whose lungs had become disorganized under an incomprehensible influence, more than drunkenness, burnt by the air which set their breathing apparatus on fire, fell without movement to the bottom of the projectile.

8. At 78,114 Leagues

What was it that had happened? What was the cause of that unusual intoxication whose consequences had proven so disastrous? A simple thoughtless blunder by Michel, which very fortunately Nicholl had remedied in time.

After a veritable fainting swoon of several minute's duration the captain, the first to revive, had recovered his intellectual faculties.

Having taken breakfast only 2 hours earlier, he experienced a terribly-famishing hunger gnawing him as though he hadn't eaten in several days. Everything in him, from stomach to brain, was overexcited to the highest degree.

He rose and then demanded of Michel a supplementary snack. Michel, overwhelmed, did not respond. Nicholl then went to prepare several cups of tea in order to facilitate the digestion of a dozen sandwiches. He occupied himself in procuring a flame from the gas, and struck a match.

What a surprise to see the sulfur shine with an extraordinary brilliance, which was almost unbearable to look at. The gas from stove burner that he ignited shot out a jet of flame that was comparable to an electrical light.

A revelation struck Nicholl. That intense luminosity, the physiological troubles which had come upon him and the overexcitement of all faculties of morality and passion he comprehended entirely.

"The oxygen!" he cried.

And leaning over the apparatus producing the air, he saw that the faucet was turned to full and allowing the colorless gas to escape- tasteless, odorless, eminently vital, but which, in a pure state, produced grave disorders within the organism. By mistake, Michel had opened the tap of the apparatus too far!

Nicholl hastily suspended the flow of oxygen which their atmosphere was saturated in, that would have brought about the death of the passengers, not by asphyxiation but by combustion.

An hour after, the air's charge had reduced and their lungs were rendered more normal. Bit by bit, the friends reanimated from their intoxication; but they were obliged to sleep it off, like a drunken man must sleep off his wine.

When Michel appraised his part of the responsibility in that incident, he was not overly disconcerted. That distracting insobriety had broken the monotony of the voyage. Many silly words had been spoken under its influence, but were also as quickly forgotten as they had been said.

"Plus," added the joyful Frenchman, "I am not sorry to have tasted a little of that capital gas. Do you know, my friends, what a curious establishment might be founded, with cabinets of oxygen where those gentlemen whose systems have weakened in health, for a few hours could live a more active life! Suppose having parties where the air has been saturated with that heroic fluid, or theatres where the administration has provided an ample dose; what passion in the souls of the actors and audience, what fire, what enthusiasm! And if, in lieu of a simple assembly, it was provided to saturate a whole population, what activity in their functions, what a supplement to their lives they would receive! From an exhausted nation would be delivered a nation grand and strong, and I can think of more than one state in our old Europe which could be remitted a regime of oxygen, in the interests of their health!"

Michel spoke with such animation that one may have imagined the faucet was still opened too far. However with one phrase Barbicane deflated his enthusiasm.

"That is all very good, Michel my friend," he said to him, "but would you explain to us where the chickens have come from, who made such a melee in our concert?"

"The chickens?"

"Yes."

In effect, a half dozen hens and one superb rooster were promenading about amongst them, fluttering about and cawing.

"Ah! The blasted things!" cried Michel. "The oxygen has created a revolution!"

"But what will you do with these chickens?" demanded Barbicane.

"To acclimatize them to the Moon, good heavens!"

"Then why did you hide them?"

"A joke, my dignified president, a simple joke which has proved a dismal failure! I wished to free them onto the lunar continent, without saying a thing! Hey! What would your confusion have been to see on those terrestrial birds pecking about on the fields of the Moon!"

"Ah! Mischief! Eternally mischievous!" responded Barbicane. "You do not need oxygen to elevate your head. You are always held under the influence of the gas! You are forever foolish!"

"Eh! And who is to say I am not always wise!" replied Michel Ardan.

After that philosophical reflection, the three friends repaired all the disorder which had been created inside the projectile. Hens and rooster were reinterred into their cage. But when proceeding through that operation, Barbicane and his companions experienced the feeling of a quite-markedly new phenomena.

Since that moment when they had left the Earth their own weight, that of the cannon ball and the objects it contained had all been subject to a progressive diminution. If they could not make an account of that sense of loss for the projectile, assuredly the moment would arrive when that effect would be perceived upon themselves and upon the utensils and instruments which served them.

It goes without saying that no balancing scales would indicate this depreciation, for the weight of gravity upon the object being measured would be exactly the same as the weights used by the balancing scales; but a steel spring coil, for example, whose tension is independent to gravitational attraction, could be used to precisely evaluate that rate of reduction.

We know that gravitic attraction, otherwise called an object's weight, is proportionate to their mass and reasoned to be the inverse squared of their distances. In that consequence: if the Earth was alone in space, and if the other celestial bodies had become suddenly annihilated, according to the law of Newton the projectile would also weigh less the further it was removed from the Earth- but without entirely losing its weight, for the terrestrial attraction would always be felt, no matter what distance.

However in the actual case the time would arrive when the projectile would no longer be subject to the laws of gravity, and the faint attraction of other celestial bodies would create a nullifying effect.

Indeed the trajectory of the projectile had traced between the Earth and the Moon supported this fact- as its distance from the Earth elongated, the terrestrial attraction diminished in an inverse proportion to the square of the distance; but also the lunar attraction augmented that by the same proportion. It would therefore arrive at a point where, the two attractions being neutralized, the cannon ball would be without specific gravity. If the masses of the Moon and the Earth were equal, the point where this would be encountered would be an equal distance between the two astral bodies. But in taking an account of the differences in mass, it was easy to calculate that the position of equilibrium was situated at the forty-seventh of fifty-two units of the total journey, which in figures is 78,114 leagues from the Earth.

At that point when the object's principle velocity was no longer displacing it, it would rest demurely immobile having attained an equal attraction by the two astral bodies; and nothing could solicit one from the other.

So, the projectile, if the initial implosive force had been calculated correctly, would have attained the point of equilibrium with a nil-velocity, having lost all indications of gravity, as would all the objects it carried.

What would occur then? Three hypotheses presented themselves.

Would the projectile still retain a certain velocity, and, passing through the point of the attraction's equilibrium, tumble towards the Moon by virtue of the lunar gravity now in excess of the Earth's influence?

Or would it lose the velocity which it managed to reach that point of equal attraction, and fall back onto the Earth in virtue of its excessive mass when compared to the Moon's?

Or, finally, animated by the velocity which was sufficient to attain that neutral point of equilibrium- but insufficient to pass beyond it- would it rest eternally suspended in that place, like the tomb of Mahommet, between the zenith and the nadir?

That was the extent of the situation, and Barbicane clearly explained these consequences to his companions of this voyage. And they were interested to a high degree. So, how would they determine when the projectile attained that point of neutrality situated 78,114 leagues away from the Earth?

Precisely when they and the objects encased within the projectile were no longer subjected to the laws of gravity.

Up until here, the travellers, whilst reporting that the action had diminished more and more, were yet to have experienced its total absence. But that day, towards 11 o'clock in the morning, Nicholl had let a glass slip from his hand; and the glass, instead of tumbling, rested suspended in the air.

"Aha!" exclaimed Michel Ardan. "That is a small piece of amusing physics!"

And then immediately diverse objects, their arms, bottles, abandoned to themselves, arose like portents of an enchanted miracle. Diane, also, placed by Michel in space, reproduced but without any trick a marvelous suspension performed by Caston and Robert Houdini. The dog, besides, did not seem to perceive that she was floating in the air.

They were equally surprised, stupefied, and despite their scientific reasoning, felt as though the three adventurous companions had been delivered into a marvelous domain as the weight of the bodies left them. Their arms, which they extended, did not seek to unbalance them. Their heads vacillated on their shoulders. Their feet were unable to take a foothold on the floor of the projectile. They were like drunken gentlemen who had lost their stability. The fantastic creations of men have produced stories of forms who have no reflection, others without their own shadows! But here in reality, by the neutrality of attractive forces, men were produced to whom nothing had any weight, and who weighed nothing themselves!

Suddenly Michel, displaying a certain hope, left the floor and rested suspended in the air like the monk of *Cuisine des Agnes* by Murillo.

His two friends launched themselves, joining him instantly, and all three in the center of the projectile performed miraculous figures of ascension.

"Is this creditable? Is this true? Is it possible?" screamed Michel with delight. "No. And yet this is! Ah! If Raphael had seen us thus, what an '*Assumption*' he might have thrown into his work painting!"

"This '*Assumption*' is only for a small duration," cautioned Barbicane. "If the projectile passes the point of neutrality, the lunar attraction will take us towards the Moon."

"Our feet will then rest on the vault of the projectile," reasoned Michel.

"No," said Barbicane, "because the projectile, whose center of gravity is very low, will turn about little by little."

"Then all our arrangements in the cannon ball will fall from the bottom and top, mark my words!"

"Reassure yourself, Michel," replied Nicholl. "There will be no upheaval to fear. Not an object will be scattered, for the evolution of the projectile will be imperceptible."

"Indeed," continued Barbicane, "and when we have continued past the point of equal attraction, the base, being relatively more-heavy, will be drawn perpendicularly towards the Moon. But for that phenomena to be produced, we must pass beyond that neutral line."

"Pass the neutral line!" cried Michel. "Then let us do as the mariners do when they pass the equator. A toast to our passage!"

A slight movement of his side brought Michel to the padded walls. There he took away a bottle and some glasses, placing them 'in space' before his companions, and, clinking glasses joyously, they saluted the line with a triple hurrah.

That influence of the attractions lasted scarcely an hour. The voyagers sensed themselves being insensibly drawn towards the floor, and Barbicane believed he noticed that the conical end of the projectile varied a little from its normal line towards the Moon. By an inverse movement, the base approached first. The lunar attraction was prevailing over the terrestrial attraction. The plunge towards the Moon commenced, however it was still imperceptible; it would deviate only a millimeter and one third in the first second, or five hundred and ninety thousandths of a line. But progressively the attractive force would accumulate, their fall become more accentuated; and the projectile, entrained by its base, would present its upper cone towards the Earth and tumble with a curving vector onto the Selenite continent. Their goal would then be attained. Now, nothing could prevent them achieving the success of their enterprise, and Nicholl and Michel Ardan shared in Barbicane's joy.

Then they chatted about all the phenomenon which had occurred so marvelously in successions. That neutralization of the laws of gravity especially, which their conversation never ceased to reflect upon. Michel Arden, forever enthusiastic, tirelessly discussed the consequences which were pure fantasy.

"Ah! My dignified friends," he cried, "what progress could be imaginable if we could throw-off, on Earth, all that gravity- that chain which rivets us onto the ground! It would be the prisoner awarded freedom! No more fatigues in the arms or legs! And, if it were possible to fly over the surface of the Earth, to move through the air with a simple contraction of the muscles; which needs a force one hundred and fifty times superior to that which we possess, but by a simple act of volition, we are transported into space by caprice, or if attraction no longer existed."

"In effect," said Nicholl in humor, "if we managed to suppress the gravity in the way they suppress pain and grief with anesthetics, then we would have changed the face of modern societies!"

"Yes!" agreed Michel, entirely taken by the subject. "Destroy the gravity, and no more burdens! We would not have to run cranes, jacks, capstans, winches and any of the other engines- there would be no reason for them!"

"Well said," replied Barbicane. "But if nothing weighed anything, nothing would maintain its place, not even the hat on your head, honorable Michel; or your house whose stones only adhere to one another by their weight! Not the boats whose stability on the water is in consequence of their weight. Not even the ocean, whose waves are at equilibrium by the terrestrial attraction. And finally not the atmosphere, whose molecules would no longer be retained and thereby disperse into space!"

"That is regrettable," Michel reflected. "Nothing like these factual gentlemen for brutally ramming reality back upon oneself."

"But console yourself, Michel," continued Barbicane, "for if there are no astral bodies where the laws of gravity have been banished, you are at least soon to visit a place where the laws of gravity are greatly-less than that of the Earth's."

"The Moon?"

"Yes, the Moon, on whose surface objects weigh six times less than on the surface of the Earth, a phenomenon that is easily certified."

"And will we perceive it?"

"Evidentially, since 200 kilograms in weight is but 30 on the surface of the Moon."

"And the strength of our muscles won't diminish?"

"None whatsoever. There you will jump a meter in the air, and will be elevated eighteen feet in height."

"But we will be like Hercules on the Moon!" cried Michel excitedly.

"And moreover," Nicholl responded, "if the Selinites are as tall as the proportionate mass of their globe, they will be barely one foot in length."

"Those Lilliputians!" Michel replied. "I should then play the role of Gulliver! We are going to realize the fables of giants! Here is the advantage of leaving your planet and being couriered throughout the solar system!"

"One moment, Michel," Barbicane countered. "If you prefer to play the part of Gulliver, only visit the inferior planets, which is to speak of Mercury,

Venus or Mars, whose masses are less than that of Earth's. But avoid the great planets of Jupiter, Saturn, Uranus, Neptune, for there the roles will be interchanged and you will become the Lilliputian."

"And in the Sun?"

"In the Sun, although its density is four times less than that of the Earth, its volume is one million, three hundred and twenty-four times more considerable and the attraction is seventy-four times greater than on the surface of our globe. Keeping in order all proportions, the inhabitants by those means should be 200 feet in height!"

"A thousand devils!" Michel exclaimed. "I would be nothing more than a pigmy, a shrimp!"

"Gulliver amongst the giants," mocked Nicholl good-naturedly.

"Correct," said Barbicane.

"And so it would be useless to carry a few pieces of artillery for self-defense." Michel reasoned.

"Good!" replied Barbicane. "Firing cannon balls would have no effect on the Sun, they would fall upon the surface after a few meters."

"That is quite a strong comment!" questioned Nicholl.

"It is quite certain," Barbicane assured them. "The attraction is so considerable on that enormous astral body, that an object weighing 70 kilograms on Earth would weigh 1,930 on the surface of the Sun. Your hat, 10 kilograms! Your cigar, half a pound. And finally, if you were to fall onto that solar continent, you would weigh... let me see- about twenty-five hundred kilos, and you would never be able to raise yourself!"

"The devil!" said Michel. "Then you would need a small portable crane. Ah well, my friends, we must content ourselves with the Moon for today. There, at least, we shall cut an impressive figure! Later on, we shall see about going to the Sun, where one cannot drink without a winch to lift the glass to their mouths!"

9. The Consequences of a Deviation

    Barbicane no longer had that inquietude, that restless worry; at least regarding the issue of their passage created by the initial implosive force upon the projectile. Their velocity had virtually passed them through the line of neutrality. Hence they would not be drawn backwards onto the Earth. And hence, they would not remain immobilized at the point of attraction. Only one single hypothesis remained to be realized, the arrival of the cannon ball under the influence of lunar gravitational attraction.

    In reality it would only be a plunge of 8,296 leagues onto the Moon's astral body, it is true, where the weight would be reckoned as a sixth of its terrestrial weight. A formidable fall nevertheless, and against which every possible precaution should be affected without delay.

    These precautions were of two sorts: the ones performed to reduce the shock at the moment where the projectile contacted with the lunar soil; and the others which were to be performed to retard their fall and which would, in consequence, render it less violent.

    To deaden the shock, it was unfortunate that Barbicane could not employ the means which had been utilized to attenuate the initial shock on departure, that is to say deploy the water which acted like a spring in the breakable partitions. The partitions still existed but the water was missing, for they could not make use of their reserves in that manner; which must preciously rationed in the case that, during their first days, that liquid element was absent from the lunar landscape.

    Besides their water reserves were too insufficient to be used in the hydraulic springs. The layers of water cloistered in the projectile at departure, and upon which rested the water-tight wooden disk above the projectile's base, occupied a height no less than 3 feet and a surface of over 54 square feet. It measured in volume the equivalent of 6 cubic meters and weighed more than 5,750 kilograms. The cistern did not currently hold a fifth of that part. It therefore followed they must renounce that effective means of amortizing the shock of their landing.

    Quite fortuitously Barbicane, not content in employing water, had equipped that mobile wooden disk with dampening steel springs designed to absorb the counter-shock against the base of the projectile after the horizontal partitions had crashed-through. The dampening springs still existed; it was sufficient to readjust them and put the mobile wooden disk back into place. All those pieces, easy to manage because their weight was barely felt, were quickly remounted.

That was that. The various pieces readjusted without pain. It was an affair of bolts and screws. Tools were not missing. Soon the wooden disk was restored to the position where it rested upon the steel springs. One inconvenience resulted from replacing the disk's position. The inferior glass porthole was obstructed. Hence, it was impossible to observe the Moon through that opening when they began to move perpendicular over it. But they needed to forgo that aspect. Besides, by the lateral portholes, they would be able to perceive the vast lunar regions as an aeronaught would view the surrounding Earth from a hot air balloon's gondolier basket.

The repositioning of the disk required an hour's work. It was past midday when all the preparations had been completed. Barbicane made new observations of the inclination of the projectile; but to his great annoyance, they had not turned sufficiently for the fall; they appeared to be holding a parallel curve with the lunar disk. That shining astral body of the night sky was brilliantly splendid in space, whilst opposing it, the solar astral body of daylight burned incendiously with fire.

The situation gave them a sense of uneasiness.

"Are we arriving?" asked Nicholl.

"We should conduct ourselves as through we will arrive," answered Nicholl.

"You are trembling," Michel Ardan told them. "We are arriving, and faster than you might have wished."

That response caused Barbicane to resume his preparatory work, and he occupied himself replacing the partition boards designed to retard their plunge.

We may recall the scene of that meeting held at Tampa Town, in Florida, when Captain Nicholl had posed as an enemy of Barbicane the adversary of Michel Ardan. To Captain Nicholl, who had maintained the projectile would shatter like glass, Michel had replied that he would retard its fall by means of rocket flares disposed appropriately.

In effect these powerful artifacts, placed at points about the base of the projectile and fused to the exterior, by producing movement through recoil could. to a certain proportion, disarray the cannon ball's momentum. These rockets were designed to burn in a vacuum, it is true, however oxygen would not be lacking- for they could furnish the incendiary devices with it themselves, like the lunar volcanoes, whose deflagration had never yet been prevented by the lack of atmosphere around the Moon.

Barbicane had therefore furnished their supplies with these rockets, which were encased in small steel guns and could be affixed to the bottom of the projectile. Inside, these miniature cannons were flush with the floor. At the exterior, they extended outwards by half a foot. There were twenty of them. An opening, emerging through the disk, permitted each to be lit by a match which had been provided for in its assembly. All of the effect produced would be outside. The mixture of combustible fuels had been forced into each barrel in advance. Hence it would be sufficient to lift out the metallic shutters that had been engaged into the base, and replace them with the small rocket cannons rigorously adjusted into position.

This new work was completed towards 3 o'clock, and all these precautions having been performed, they could do no more than wait.

Meanwhile the projectile was visibly approaching the Moon. They had evidently been subjected to its influence by a certain proportion; but their velocity had as well drawn them into an oblique line. From these two influences, the result was that a tangential line developed. However it was certain that the projectile would not fall in a normal manner onto the surface of the Moon; for its lowest part, by the distribution of weight, ought to have been turned towards there.

Those worrisome thoughts of Barbicane redoubled in their intensity when he saw the cannon ball resisting the influences of gravitation. The inconceivable opened before him, an inconceivable traverse of interstellar space. He, this man of science, had believed there were only three hypothetical possibilities: To be drawn back unto the Earth, to be drawn onto the Moon, or to stagnate at the neutral line! And now there was a fourth hypothesis, replete with all the terrors of infinity, that suddenly arose so inopportunely. To look upon this fate without faltering one must have been a resolute scientist like president Barbicane, a phlegmatic, argumentative man like Captain Nicholl or an audacious adventurer like Michel Ardan.

Their conversation dwelt upon this subject. Other men would have considered the question from a practical point of view. They would have demanded to know where their projectile-carriage was being drawn. These did not. They searched to understand the cause which had produced the effect.

"And so we have derailed?" asked Michel. "But why?"

"I fear greatly," said Nicholl, "that despite all the precautions taken, the Columbiad cannon was not correctly pointed. An error, howsoever small, would be sufficient to throw us beyond the lunar attraction."

"Then they must have had bad aim?" asked Michel.

"I do not believe so," Barbicane responded. "The perpendicularity of the cannon was rigorously established and the direction of the zenith from there was incontestable. So, as the Moon passes its zenith we should attain our target when it is full. It is for another reason, but that escapes me."

"Are we arriving too late?" asked Nicholl.

"Too late?" repeated Barbicane.

"Yes," said Nicholl. "The letter from the Cambridge Observatory contended that our transit had to have been accomplished in 96 hours, 13 minutes and 20 seconds. Which means to say, too soon and the Moon will not pass by the point indicated; and too late, we should soar past it."

"I agree,' Barbicane answered. "But we departed the 1st December at 11 hours, 13 minutes and 20 seconds to midnight; and we are due to arrive on the 5th at midnight, at the precise moment when the Moon is full. So, we are now at 5th December. It is now 3 and a half hours in the afternoon, and 8 and a half hours should be sufficient to conduct us to our target. Why shouldn't we arrive then?"

"Could it not be from an excess of speed?" suggested Nicholl. "For we have maintained an initial velocity that was greater than we had supposed."

"No! A hundred times no!" said Barbicane forcefully. "An excess velocity, if the direction of the projectile was good, would not have prevented us from reaching the Moon. No! There has been a deviation. We have deviated from our course."

"But why? But how?" questioned Nicholl.

"I am unable to say," Barbicane responded.

"Ah well," then Michel said. "Do you wish to know my opinion regarding the question of what had created this deviation?"

"Speak."

"I would not give half a dollar to know! We have deviated, this is a fact!

Where we are going is of little importance! We shall see well-enough! The devil! Since we are being drawn into space, we will finally tumble into some center of attraction!"

That indifference of Michel Ardan failed to content Barbicane. Not that he was worried about their future! But why had their projectile deviated? That he dearly wished to know at any price.

Meanwhile the cannon ball continued its lateral displacement along the Moon, and with it the procession of objects they had jettisoned outside. Barbicane could even state, by the points of the Moon's landmarks which were at a distance less than 2,000 leagues, that their velocity had developed uniformity. New proof that they would not fall onto the lunar surface. The force of their implosion had carried them beyond the Moon's gravitational attraction, however the trajectory of the projectile certainly approached the lunar disk and they might hope that as the distance neared the action of its gravity would form dominance and definitively provoke them into a downward plunge.

The three friends, having nothing better to do, continued their observations. However they could not yet determine the topographical position of the satellite. All reliefs were leveled beneath the projection of the solar rays.

And so they regarded the world outside beside the lateral glass portholes until 8 o'clock in the evening. The Moon had become so large before their eyes that it masked half of the celestial firmament. The Sun was on one side and the Moon, that shining astral body of the night sky, on the other. The projectile was inundated by their light.

At that moment Barbicane believed he could estimate that only 700 leagues distance separated them from their target. The velocity of the projectile appeared to be 200 meters a second, or roughly 170 leagues an hour. The base of the cannon ball tended to turn towards the Moon under the influence of a centrifugal force; but the centrifugal force continued to move them, and it was therefore probable that their rectilinear trajectory would change into a curve of some kind whose exact nature they could not determine.

Barbicane searched continuously for a solution to his irresolvable problem.

The hours moved by without any result. The projectile visibly approached the Moon, but it was also visible they would not attain it. Concerning the nearest distance which they would pass by was the result of two forces; attraction and repulsion, both of which solicited to their motion.

"I ask for but one thing," Michel told them. "That we pass closely enough to penetrate its secrets!"

"Blast the reason," cursed Nicholl, "which has caused the deviation on our projectile!"

"Blasted be the reason," said Barbicane, as though his spirit had suddenly been struck by lightning. "Blast that damn meteor which had crossed our route!"

"Hey!?" exclaimed Michel.

"What are you meaning to say?" cried Nicholl.

"I mean to say," said Barbicane in his most convincing tone, "I mean to say that our deviation is due only to the encounter with that errant body!"

"But we did not even brush against it," said Michel, baffled.

"Unimportant. That mass, comparatively enormous with that of our projectile, held sufficient gravitational attraction to influence our direction."

"So small!" Nicholl cried.

"Yes, Nicholl, however small it may have been," concluded Barbicane, "over a distance of 84,000 leagues, it wanted no more for us to miss the Moon!

10. The Observers of the Moon

Evidentially Barbicane had found the only plausible reason for their deviation. However small that influence might have been, it was sufficient to modify the trajectory of their projectile. An inevitable disaster. Their audacious attempt had failed by a circumstance of fortune and, unless an exceptional event developed, they would not attain the lunar disk.

Would they pass near enough to resolve certain questions of physics and geology heretofore unsolvable? That was the question, and now the sole preoccupation of these hardy travellers. As to what the future reserved for them, they did not even wish to consider.

However what would become of them in the midst of that infinite solitude, to whom air would soon be lacking? In a few more days they would collapse from asphyxiation inside the cannon ball and that would be the end of this adventure. But a few more days, these are like centuries for the intrepid. And so they devoted all their moments to the Moon which they no longer hoped to reach.

The distance which then separated the projectile and the satellite was estimated to be 200 leagues. In those conditions, from the point of view of the visibility of details on the disk, the voyagers were further from the Moon than were the Earth's inhabitants armed with powerful telescopes.

Indeed, that instrument mounted by John Rosse at Parsontown, which magnifies by 6,000 times, was superior when it brought the Moon to 6 leagues; and then even more-so with the powerful optical system established at Long's peak, which delivered that shining body of the night sky, magnified 48,000 times, to within 2 leagues and made objects of 10 meters diameter sufficiently distinct.

Hence at their distance the topographical details of the Moon, observed without powerful telescopes, could not sensibly be determined. The eye apprehended the vast contours and those immense depressions inappropriately named the 'seas', but they could not determine their nature. The vision dazzled their gaze as though they were leaning above a basin of molten silver, and involuntarily the voyagers turned away.

Meanwhile- the oblong form of that astral body was obvious. The apparition was like a gigantic egg with the smaller end-point turned towards the Earth. In effect, the Moon, liquid and malleable in the first days of its formation, was originally the figure of a perfect sphere; but, soon entrained by the Earth's center of attraction, its shape had elongated under the influence of that gravity. Changing into a satellite, it had lost the native purity of its form as the center gravity shifted away from the center of its figure, and, by that disposition several scientists formed an opinion that the air and the water had taken refuge upon the surface on the opposite side of the Moon; which is never seen from the Earth.

This alteration of the satellite's primitive form was only apprehensible for several moments' duration. The distance from the projectile to the Moon diminished quite rapidly under a velocity that was considerably inferior to their initial speed, but eight or nine times greater than that which animates the express steam-train. The oblique direction of the cannon ball, by the same reason of its obliquity, allowed Michel Ardan a certain hope of colliding into some point of the lunar disk. He could not imagine they wouldn't not arrive there. No! He refused to believe it, and he repeated that fact. However Barbicane, a better judge, never ceased to respond with implacable logic:

"No, Michel, no. We can only reach the Moon by a falling-plunge onto the surface, and we are not tumbling. The centripetal force maintains us within the lunar influence, but our centrifugal force is irresistibly drawing us onwards."

This was said in such a tone that it dashed the last of Michel Ardan's hopes.

That portion of the Moon which the projectile approached was in the northern hemisphere, which is where the selenographic charts place lowest, for the maps generally orient themselves after the image received by the telescopes, and we already know that telescopes reverse the objects in its image. Such was the *Mappa Selenographica* of Beer and Moedler which Barbicane consulted.

The northern hemisphere presented vast plains accentuated by isolated mountains.

At midnight the Moon was full. In that precise moment, the voyagers should have been placing their feet upon it; if only that untoward meteor-turned-satellite had not caused such a deviation to their direction. The astral body of the Moon arrived at the conditions which had been so rigorously determined by the Observatory of Cambridge. It had travelled with mathematical precision to its perigee and at the zenith of the 28th parallel. Any observer placed in the depths of the enormous Columbiad cannon would have their back perpendicular to the horizon, and the Moon would be framed in the mouth of the barrel. A straight line traced from the axis of the piece would have led to the exact center of that shining body of the night sky.

Needless to say that throughout that night of the 5th and 6th December the voyagers did not steal a moment's rest. Could they close their eyes when presented with that new world? No. All senses were concentrated upon that one unique thought: look! Representatives of the Earth, all of humanity past and present were summarized within them; and it was through their eyes that the human race regarded those lunar regions in order to penetrate the secrets of that satellite! A certain emotion took ahold of their hearts as they went silently from one glass portal to the other.

Their observations, recorded by Barbicane, were strictly determined. For their sight, they had binoculars and small telescopes. For verification, they referred to their maps.

The first observer of the Moon had been Galileo. His inadequate telescope only magnified thirty times. Nevertheless, in the dark patches which were scattered across the lunar disk, 'like the eyes arrayed in the peacock's tail', he was the first to recognize mountains and measured some of their heights to which he exaggeratedly attributed an elevation equivalent to a 20th of the disk's diameter, some 8,800 meters. Galileo did not draw any maps of his observations.

   A few years later, an astronomer of Danzig, Hevelius- by a procedure which could only be exact two times per month, during the first and second quarters- reduced those heights of Galileo to one 26th of the lunar diameter. An exaggeration in reverse. But it was this scientist who created the first map of the Moon. The light patches arranged there form circular mountains, and the shadowy patches indicate the vast seas which are in reality plains. To these mountains and expanses of water, he gave terrestrial names. He called the face *Sinai* in the middle of *Arabia*, *Etna* at the center of *Sicily*; the Alps, the *Apennines*; the *Carpathians* and then the Mediterranean, the *Palus Meotide*; the *Euxine*, the Caspian Sea. Names badly applied, moreover, for neither the mountains nor the seas resembled the configurations of their homonyms on the globe.

   It is difficult in that large white spot- attached onto the south to even vaster continents and terminating into a point- to recognize the reversed image of the Indian peninsula, the Bay of Bengal and the Cochin-China. And so these names were not retained. Another cartographer, who was better at recognizing the human nature, proposed a new nomenclature which the human vanity eagerly adopted.

   That observer was Father Riccioli, a contemporary of Hevelius. He drew a crude map that was largely in error. But to those lunar mountains he imposed the names of the great men from antiquity and the scientists of his epoch, a usage which has survived until today.

   A third map of the Moon was executed in the 17th century by Dominique Cassini; superior to that of Ricciolli in its execution, it is inexact in the measurements. Several smaller copies were published but the engraved plates of his copper originals, for a long time conserved at the Royal Imprimerie, were sold for their weight like scrap material.

   La Hire, celebrated mathematician and draftsman, drew a map of the Moon which was 4 meters high, but it was never engraved.

   After him, a German astronomer, Tobie Mayer, towards the middle of the 18th Century commenced the publication of a magnificent selenographic map, according to lunar measurements rigorously verified by himself; but his death, which happened in 1762, prevented the final execution of this beautiful work.

Next ensued Schroeter, of Lilienthal, who sketched numerous charts of the Moon; then a certain Lohrmann, from Dresden, who gave us illustrated plates divided into twenty-five sections, of which four were engraved.

It was in 1830 that MM. Beer and Moedler composed their celebrated *Mappa Selenographica*, according to an orthographic projection. This map reproduces the lunar disk exactly, as it appears; although the configurations of the mountains and the plains are only accurate from the central part; elsewhere, in the parts of the septentrional north and meridional south, the oriental east and occidental west, these configurations are cut short- which prevents their comparison to the center. That topographical map, 95 centimeters high and divided into four parts, is the masterpiece of lunar cartography.

After these scientists, we may cite the selenographic reliefs of the German astronomer Julius Schmidt, the topographical work of Father Secci, the magnificent prints of the English amateur Warren de la Rue, and finally a map from an orthographic projection by MM. Lecourtier and Chapuis; which is a beautiful model drawn in 1860, of very neat design and very clear arrangement.

Such is the nomenclature of the diverse maps depicting the lunar world. Barbicane possessed two, that of MM. Beer and Moedler and that of MM. Chapuis et Lecouturier. These both rendered his observational work much easier.

In regards to the optical instruments at his disposal; they had excellent nautical binoculars, specially constructed for their journey, and small collapsible hand-telescopes. These magnified objects a hundred times. These would have brought the Moon from the Earth a distance of less than a thousand leagues. But then, at an actual distance which towards 3 o'clock in the morning did not exceed 120 kilometers, and in a medium which had no atmosphere to trouble them, these instruments delivered the new Moon to less than 1,500 meters.

11. **Fantasy and Realism**

"Have you never seen the Moon?" once a professor asked ironically of his students.

"No, sir," answered one of the students, even more ironically. "But I must say that I have heard it spoken of."

In a sense, that joking response by the student might be offered by the immense majority of sublunary people. How many gentlemen have heard talk of the Moon, and have never seen it... at least through the lens of a set of binoculars or telescope? How many have never even examined a map of their satellite!

When regarding a selenographic world map, one peculiarity strikes us.

Contrary to the coherent disposition of Earth and Mars, continents particularly occupy the southern hemisphere on the lunar globe. These continents do not present the same finished lines, and are without the clear and regular definitions such as of South America, Africa and the Indian peninsula. Their angular coasts, capricious, deeply-torn, are rich in gulfs and peninsulas. They readily remind one of the confusion of the islands in a sound, where the lands are excessively divided. If navigation had ever existed on the Moon it would have been unusually difficult and dangerous, and we may feel sorry for the Selenite mariners and hydrographers; the former when sailing along those tormentingly high shores, the latter when performing their perilous surveys.

One might also remark that on the lunar sphere the south pole is much more continental than the north. For the latter, there exists but one slight piece of land separated by the other continents from its vast empty seas. Towards the south, the continents cover almost the whole of the hemisphere. Hence it is possible the Selenites have already planted their national flag upon at least one of the poles; whereas the explorers such as Franklin, Ross, Kane, Dumont-d'Urville and Lambert are yet to attain that unknown point on the terrestrial globe.

As to islands, these are numerous on the surface of the Moon. Nearly all of them are oblong or circular and as though traced by a compass, they seem to form one vast archipegelo, comparable to that charming group scattered between Greece and Asia Minor which mythology has brought to life with those graceful legends. Involuntarily the names of Naxos, Tenedos, Milo and Carpathos rise to one's mind and our eyes search in vain for the vessel Ulysses or the clipper of the Argonauts. This was, at least, demanded of Michel Ardan. To him they were Grecian archipelagos when he looked upon the map. To the eyes of his companions who were hardly drawn towards fantasy, the aspects of those coasts resembled more the partitions of New Brunswick and Nova Scotia. And where the Frenchman finds the traces of heroic fable, these Americans were picking out relevant places which were favorable for the establishment of trading posts; in the interests of lunary commerce and industry.

To complete the description of the continental parts of the Moon, several words must be said regarding its orthographical disposition. We can distinguish with great clarity the chains of mountains, isolated mountains, the circular depressions of craters and canyon-like chasms. The whole lunar relief is comprised of these divisions. It is extraordinarily tormented. The Moon is an immense Switzerland, a continual Norway where igneous activity has been everywhere. That surface, profoundly rugged, is the result of successive contractions of the crust in the era when that astral body was in the throes of its formation.

Hence the lunar disk is propitious to the grand study of geological phenomenon. According to the remarks of certain astronomers its surface, although more ancient that the surface of Earth, it has remained more new. Here, it is without water to deteriorate the primitive face whose erosive action produces a general leveling, and without an air whose influence erodes and modifies the orographical profiles. Here, the plutonic travail of tectonics, unaltered by neptunian oceanic forces, remain entirely in a state of pure nativity. The Moon is the Earth, but appearing as it was before the tides and the currents issued forth and covered it with layers of sediment.

After casting one's glance across the vast continents our attention is lured towards the seas which are still greater. Not only their formation; but their situated location, their aspects, recall those of the terrestrial oceans and yet still, as on Earth, these seas occupy the greatest portion of the globe. However in fact they are not liquid spaces, but plains which the voyagers hoped soon to determine the nature thereof.

The astronomers, we must admit, have decorated these imaginary seas with names of the most bizarre that science has respected to this day. It was reasonable for Michel Ardan to compare those lunar world maps to a valentine's *'card of tenderness'*, drafted by romantic poets in the traditions of Scudery and Cyrano de Bergerac.

"Only," he added, "this is not a map of sentimental ideas from the 17th Century! I can only imagine how anyone in the 21st Century must feel, when looking back at the modern ideals of our era in the 19th Century! This map here is a chart of life, very clearly sliced into two parts- one feminine, one masculine. For women, the hemisphere to the right. For men, the hemisphere to the left."

And when he had spoken thus, Michel elicited merely a shrug of the shoulders from his prosaic companions. Barbicane and Nicholl considered the lunar map from an entirely different point of view than their fantastical friend. Nevertheless the fantasy of their friend did possess some reason.

[see introductory comments*]

In the left hemisphere extends the '*Sea of Clouds*', where so often human reason drowns. Not so further afar lies the '*Sea of Rains*', into which feeds all the worries of existence. After this is the depression called the '*Sea of Tempests*', where man unceasingly struggles against his passions which too often prove victorious. Then, exhausted by the deceptions, the treasons, the infidelities and the total cortege of Earthly miseries, what does he discover at the termination of his career? That vast '*Sea of Humors*', scarcely softened by a few drops of water by the '*Gulf of Roses*'! Clouds, rains, tempestuous storms, humors, does the life of a man contain anything other than those things- are they not summarized by these four simple words?

The hemisphere to the right, dedicated "to the dames" as Michel had suggested, is formed by much smaller seas; whose significant names comport and compose the aspects of feminine existence. There is the '*Sea of Serenity*', above which the young girl leans; and '*The Lake of Dreams*', which reflects a cheerful, smiling future! There is '*The Sea of Nectar*' with its waves of tenderness and breezes of love! There is the '*Sea of Fertility*', there is the '*Sea of Crises*', then '*The Sea of Vapors*', whose dimensions are perhaps too constrained; and finally that vast '*Sea of Tranquility*', which absorbs entirely the false passions, all the useless dreams, all the restless desires, and whose waves then flow peacefully unto '*The Lake of Death*'!

What a succession of strange names! What an unusual division between the two hemispheres of the Moon, joined to one another like a man and a woman, and forming that sphere of life transported into space! And had not the fantastical Michel correctly interpreted the fantasies of the old astronomers?

But whilst his imagination circulated over these 'seas', his companions considered things more geographically. They were learning this new world by heart. They were measuring angles and diameters.

For Barbicane and Nicholl, the *Sea of Clouds* was an immense depression in the ground, sown with several craters, and covering a great proportion in the occidental part of the southern hemisphere- it occupied 184,000 square leagues, and its center was found at 15° latitude south and 20° longitude west. The ocean of tempests, *Oceanus Procellarum*, huge and vast plain on the lunar disk, superficially embraced 323,300 square leagues; whose center lay 10° latitude north and 45° longitude east. From its womb emerges emerge the admirable radiant mountains of *Kepler* and *Aristarchus*.

More northerly and separated from the *Sea of Clouds* by high mountain chains, extended the *Sea of Rains*, *Mare Imbrium*, at a central point of 35° latitude north and 20° longitude east; it forms an imprecise circular shape and covers a space of 193,000 square leagues. Not far in the distance, the *Sea of Humors*, *Mare Humorum*, is a little basin only 44,200 square leagues, and that is situated 25° latitude south and 40° longitude east. And finally, afterwards three gulfs are drawn onto the coast of that hemisphere: the *Torrid Gulf*, the *Gulf of Roses*, and the *Gulf of the Iris*, small plains narrowed by high chains of mountains.

The 'feminine' hemisphere as Michel had implied, naturally more capricious, was distinguished by seas smaller and more numerous. These were, towards the north, the *Sea of Cold*, *Mare Frigori*, at 55° latitude north and 0° of longitude, whose surface of 76,000 square leagues enclosed the *Lake of Death* and the *Lake of Dreams*; the *Sea of Serenity*, *Mare Serenitatis*, by 25° latitude north and 20° longitude west, comprised a surface area of 86,000 square leagues; the *Sea of Crises*, *Mare Crisium*, quite defined, very compact, encompassing at 17° latitude north and 55° longitude west a surface of 40,000 square leagues a veritable Caspian Sea enfolded by a ring of mountains.

Then at the equator, by 5° latitude north and 25° longitude west, appears the *Sea of Tranquility*, *Mare Tranquillitatis*, occupying 121,509 leagues squared; that sea connects to the south with the *Sea of Nectar*, *Mare Nectaris*, extending 28,800 square leagues, at 15° latitude south and 35° longitude west, and to the east with the *Sea of Fertility*, *Mare Fecunditatis*, and vastest plain in that hemisphere, occupying 219,300 square leagues, by 3° latitude south and 50° longitude west. And finally, entirely in the north and entirely in the south, two last seas are distinguished, The *Sea of Humboldt*, *Mare Humboldtianum*, which has a surface area of 6,500 square leagues, and the *Austral Sea*, *Mare Australe*, which superficially extends 26,000 miles.

At the center of the lunar disk, astride the equator and the zero meridian, extends a central gulf, *Sinus Medii*, a kind of hyphenated point joining the two hemispheres.

And so that was how to the eyes of Nicholl and Barbicane the lunar surface which always faces the Earth appeared. When they added all those different measurements together they proved that the superficial surface of the hemisphere was 4,738,160 square leagues, of which 3,317,600 leagues are volcanoes, chains of mountains, craters, islands, in a word all that seems to form the solid part of the globe; and 1,410,400 leagues for the seas, the lakes, the swamps, all which seem to form the liquid parts. And to this, accordingly, the dignified Michel Ardan was perfectly indifferent of.

That hemisphere, from our view, is thirteen and a half times smaller than the terrestrial hemisphere. However, the selenographers have counted there over 50,000 craters. Hence it is a surface that is bloated, crevassed; a veritably foaming, heaving barren ecology, dignified of the unpoetic qualification bestowed upon it by the English of being made of '*green cheese*'.

MIchel Ardan lept to his feet when Barbicane pronounced that unobliging name.

"That is there," he exclaimed, "how the peoples of the 19th Century treat their beautiful Diane, their blonde Phoebe, the amiable Isis, our charming Astarte, Queen of the Night, the daughter of Latonia and Jupiter, younger sister of radiant Apollo!"

12. **Orthographical Details**

The direction the projectile followed, as we have already observed, was taking it towards the northern hemisphere of the Moon. The voyagers were moving far beyond the central point they intended to strike, which they ought to have reached had not their trajectory been subject to an irredeemable deviation.

It was half-past midnight. Barbicane estimated then their distance at 1,400 kilometers- a distance slightly greater than the length of the lunar radius, which would then diminish by a measure as they advanced towards the north pole. Their projectile as it travelled was not yet at the height of the equator but by the line of the 10th parallel; and at that latitude, carefully determined from the map by the pole, Barbicane and his two companions observed a pure Moon under the best of conditions.

In effect, by their use of binoculars and small hand-telescopes, that distance of 1,400 kilometers was reduced to 14, a mere 3-and-a-half leagues. The telescope on the Rocky Mountains brought the Moon closer, however the terrestrial atmosphere reduced its optical power. And so Barbicane, posted within the projectile, glasses to his eyes, could perceive details unassailable to observers from Earth.

"My friends," the president of the Gun Club said in a grave voice, "I do not know where we are going, I do not know if we shall ever return to our terrestrial globe. Nevertheless, let us proceed as though one day our work shall serve a purpose. Let our minds remain free of all preoccupation. We are astronomers. This projectile is an office of the Cambridge Observatory, transported into space. Let us observe."

Saying that, their work commenced with an extreme precision; and they reproduced faithfully the diverse aspects of the Moon, at the variable distances which the projectile occupied throughout its rapport with that astral body.

At the same time that the cannon ball travelled along the 10th parallel north, it seemed to be strictly following the 20th degree of longitude east.

This is now the appropriate place to make one remark of importance on the subject of the map which served during their observations. In the selenographical maps of the moon where, due to the reversal of the objects by the lenses of the field glasses, the south is on high and the north is lowest- and it would seem natural by the same fashion that there is an inversion which places the east on the left and the west to the right.

However, this is not so.

If the chart was turned upside down and presented the Moon as it shows before our eyes, the east would be on the left and the west to the right, contrary to that which exists on terrestrial maps. This now is the reason for that anomaly. The observers situated in that boreal hemisphere, the northern, on their viewing perceive the Moon in the south in accordance with their position. When they are observing they turn their backs to the north, a reverse position to that which one would occupy when considering a terrestrial map. By turning their backs to the north, the east is found on their left and the west is on their right. For the observers situated in that austral hemisphere, the southern; in Patagonia, for example, the west of the Moon serves them perfectly to their left and the east is to their right, because the meridian is behind them.

Such is reason for the apparent reversal of the two cardinal points, and we must grasp that fact if we are to follow the observations of Barbicane.

Aided by the *Mappa Selenographica* of Beer and Moedler, without hesitation the voyagers could recognize any portion of the disk encased by the fields of their lenses in the glasses.

"What are we looking at in this moment?" asked Michel.

"The northern section of the *Sea of Clouds*," Barbicane answered. "We are too far away to determine its real nature. Are these plains composed of arid sand, as had been claimed by the first astronomers? Or are they immense forests, as according to the opinion of Warren de la Rue; who ascribed the Moon an atmosphere which was very low but very dense? It is something we will be aware of later. We shall affirm nothing unless we are able to affirm it directly."

That *Sea of Clouds* is rather doubtfully delineated on the charts. It is supposed the vast plain is strewn with blocks of lava vomited by the volcanoes located to its left; *Ptolemy*, *Purbach*, *Arzachel*. Meanwhile, as the projectile advanced, underneath their approach it became sensible and soon the summits appeared which enclose that sea by its northern limits. Before them towered a mountain radiant in all of its beauty, whose top seemed lost within an eruption of solar rays.

"That is?..." asked Michel.

"*Copernicus*," answered Barbicane.

"So we shall see *Copernicus*."

That mountain, situated by 9° latitude north and 20° longitude east, elevates to a height of 3,438 meters above the surface of the Moon. It is quite visible from the Earth, and the astronomers are able to study it to perfection throughout the durational phase that comprises the final quarter of the new Moon; because then shadows are projected lengthwise from east to west and this permits the measurement of such heights.

Copernicus Mountain forms the most important radiating system on the disk after *Tycho*, situated in the southern hemisphere. It's isolated elevation, like a gigantic lighthouse on that portion of the *Sea of Clouds* which is confined by the *Sea of Tempests*, illuminates beneath its splendid rays two oceans at the same time. It is an unequalled spectacle with its long luminous trains, so dazzling in the full moon that passes along the northern chains of bordering peaks, which extends from there onto the *Sea of Rains*. At 1 hour in the terrestrial morning, the projectile, like a balloon imported through space, surpassed that superb mountain.

Barbicane could recognize exactly its principle distinctions. *Copernicus* is comprised by a series of mountains ringed in a first order, in the division of the great cirques, which is what any circular rings of hills are called. The same as for *Kepler* and *Aristarchus*, who dominate that ocean known as the *Sea of Tempests*; it sometimes appeared like a brilliant point which penetrated through the ashen lunar light and was taken for an active volcano. But it is an extinct volcano, as they all are on that side of the Moon. Via the binoculars they discovered traces of stratifications produced by successive eruptions, and the environment thereabouts was strewn by volcanic debris some of which was still displayed on the insides of craters.

"There exists," said Barbicane, "several kinds of cirques on the surface of the Moon, and it is easy to see that *Copernicus* is part of that radiating genre. If we were to go closer, we would perceive the cones which ruffle their interior, that in other times were the mouths of igneous lava pits. There is one curious aspect there and without exception on the lunar disk, which is the interior surface of the cirques are notably lower than those on the exterior plain; contrary to the shapes of terrestrial craters. Hence it ensues that the general curvature at the bottom of these cirques gives a sphere that in diameter is less than that of the Moon."

"And why is that aspect special?" queried Nicholl.

"No one knows," said Barbicane.

"What splendid radiation," Michel commented. "It is difficult to imagine a more beautiful spectacle!"

"What would you say then," responded Barbicane, "if fate brought our journey towards the meridional hemisphere of the south?"

"Ah well, I would say that is even more beautiful!" replied Michel Ardan truthfully.

In that moment, the projectile was perpendicularly above the cirque. The circumference of *Copernicus* formed a perfectly exact circle and it's severely-steep escarpments stood out clearly. They could even distinguish a doubling-ring enclosed within. All around it spread a greyed plain, its disposition wild and desolate, on which every distinction of its landscape was etched in yellow.

At the depths of this cirque, as though enfolded by a jewelry case, for one scintillating moment two or three cones erupted, resembling enormous ebullient gems that sparkled and glistened.

Towards the north of the formation, the slopes reduced into a depression which quite probably would have given access to the interior of the crater.

In passing over the surrounding plains, Barbicane noticed a great number of mountains of lesser importance, and amongst others a little ring of mountains named *Gay Lussac*, whose size measured 23 kilometers. Towards the south, the plain displayed itself very-flatly, without one undulation, without one recess of soil. Towards the north, contrarily, where it's place was confined by the *Sea of Tempests*, there was a liquid surface agitated by a hurricane's anger, whose rocky outcrops and billowy flares created figures of sharp waves that had suddenly congealed. Across this ensemble in all directions ran currents of luminous streaks which converged at the summit of *Copernicus*. Several of these offerings were 30 kilometers in breadth and inestimably long.

The voyagers discussed the origin of these strange rays and could determine no more of their nature than terrestrial observers.

"But why," Nicholl asked, "are these rays nothing more than simple counterpoints of the mountains, that reflect the Sun's luminosity with more brightness ?"

"No," responded Barbicane, "if it were thus so, then when the Moon was in certain conditions those ridges would project shadows. Now, these project none."

Indeed, those rays appeared only at the height today on that astral body, when the Earth was in opposition to the Moon, and disappeared as soon as the shafts of cast sunlight became oblique.

"But what do they imagine could explain these luminous lines?" asked Michel, "For I have never known the scientists to resist offering a wealth of explanations!"

"Yes," agreed Barbicane. "Herschel formulated an opinion, but he did not offer to affirm it."

"That is unimportant. What was that opinion?"

"His thinking was that these rays must be formed by currents of cooled lava, shining when struck normally by the sun. That could be, but nothing is less certain. Otherwise, if we pass nearer to *Tycho*, we will find ourselves better-placed to reconnoiter the cause of these rays."

"Do you know, my friends, what that plain resembles to us from our view on high?" said Michel.

"No," Nicholl replied, succumbing to curiosity.

"Well, with all the pieces of lava elongated like spindles, it resembles an immense game of 'pick-up-sticks' thrown about in disarray. All that is lacking is the crochet hook to regather them one by one."

"Do be serious!" scoffed Barbicane.

"I am always serious," replied Michel tranquilly. "And in lieu of slender pickup sticks, scatter about bones. That plain of ours would then become an immense crypt on which the mortal remains of thousands of extinct generations repose! Do you better-like the effect of that grand comparison?"

"The one holds as the other," Barbicane said.

"The devil! You are difficult!" Michel told him.

"My dignified friend," replied the methodically factual Barbicane, "it is of little importance what you think they resemble, for at the moment we do not know what it is they are."

"Excellent response," cried Michel. "That will teach me to reason with scientists!"

Meanwhile, the projectile advanced with an almost uniform velocity as it extended over the lunar disk. The voyagers, as one can comfortably imagine, did not dream of taking a moment's rest. Each minute was displaced by their passage vanishing beneath their eyes. Towards an hour and a half in the morning, they began to glimpse the summits of another mountain. Barbicane, consulting his map, recognized *Eratosthenes*.

It was a ringed mountain rising to heights of 4,500 meters in one of those cirques so numerous on that satellite. And, in that regard, Barbicane reported to his friends the unusual opinion of Kepler on the formation of these cirques. According to that celebrated mathematician, these crater-shaped cavities were created by the hands of a man.

"For what intention?" questioned Nicholl interrogatively.

"For a rather natural intention," answered Barbicane. "The Selenites may have ventured upon an enterprise of such immense work hollowing out that enormous hole for a secure refuge from the solar rays which strike upon them for 15 consecutive days."

"Not stupid, those Selenites!" said Michel.

"A remarkable idea," responded Nicholl. "But it is probable that Kepler had not considered the actual dimensions of these cirques, for these holes are the works of giants, impracticable for the Selenites!"

"Why, if the gravity of the Moon is six times less than on the Earth?" said Michel.

"But if the Selenites are also six times smaller?" replied Nicholl.

"And if there are no Selenites!" was Barbicane's addendum. This served to terminate the conversation.

Soon *Eratosthenes* disappeared under the horizon without the projectile having approached sufficiently to permit a rigorous examination. This mountain separates the *Apennines* from the *Carpathians*.

In lunar orthography, several mountain chains have been distinguished which are principally distributed in the northern hemisphere. Some of these, nevertheless, occupy certain portions of the southern hemisphere.

Of the diverse chains the most important is the *Apennines*, which develops for 150 leagues- a lesser extent than the great orographical movements of the mountain chains on Earth. The *Apennines* lie along the southern border of the *Sea of Rains* and they are continued in the north by the *Carpathians*, whose profile measures approximately 100 leagues.

The voyagers could only catch diluted glimpses of the summit of the *Apennines* descending between 10° longitude west and 16° longitude east; however the chain of the *Carpathians* extended beneath their vision from 18° to 30° longitude east, whose distribution was clearly revealed.

One hypothesis looked very justifiable. Upon seeing that the chain of *Carpathians* was affected by those circular shapes and dominated by peaks they concluded it was formed in older, more ancient times by important cirques. The rings of mountains must have become disrupted by a vast cataclysm which had led to the formation of the *Sea of Rains*. These *Carpathians* then resembled, from their aspect, how the cirques of *Purbach*, *Arzachel* and *Ptolemy* would have looked if some natural disaster had destroyed the left-most lower slopes, transforming them into a continuous chain. They present an average height of 3,200 meters, a height comparable to that of the Pyrenees, such as the *Port of Pinede*. There, southern slopes fall brusquely towards the immense *Sea of Rains*.

Approaching two o'clock in the morning, Barbicane determined that their height was at the 20th lunar parallel, not far from that small mountain elevated but 1,559 meters high, which bears the name of *Pythias*. The distance of the projectile to the Moon was no more than 1,200 kilometers, brought to within 3 leagues by means of the binoculars.

Mare Imbrium extended before the eyes of the voyagers like an immense depression whose details were barely distinguishable.

Near them, on the left, stood *Mount Lambert*, whose altitude is estimated at 1,813 meters, and further along at the limits of the *Ocean of Tempests*, by the 23° latitude north and 29° longitude east, the splendidly radiant mountain called *Mount Euler*. That peak, elevated only 1,815 meters above the lunar surface, was the object of interesting work done by Schroeter. This scientist, seeking to understand the origination of mountains on the Moon, asked if the volume of the craters always showed an equal resemblance to the sloping rampart walls which formed them. Now, as this was discovered to generally exist in most cases, Schroeter concluded that a single eruption of volcanic materials had been enough to form the crater walls, for successive eruptions would have altered that relationship. Solely, *Mount Euler* refuted that general law and its formation by necessity must have been created from several successive eruptions, because the volume of that cavity is double that of its walls which enclose it.

All these hypotheses were permissible to the terrestrial observers, whose instruments served them in an incomplete manner. But Barbicane was not content to rely on them, and seeing that the projectile was still steadily approaching the lunar disk, did not despair- for if he failed to attain a surface landing, he would at least prize the secrets of the Moon's formulation.

13. Lunar Landscapes

At 2 and a half hours in the morning their cannon ball was over the 30th lunar parallel; at an effective distance of 1,000 kilometers, reduced to 10 by optical instruments. It seemed it would forever be impossible to reach a landing point somewhere on the disk. Their translation velocity, relatively mediocre, remained inexplicable for the president Barbicane. At that distance from the Moon, it must have been considerable enough to maintain an opposing force against the Moon's gravitational attraction. This was a phenomenon whose underlying cause escaped them still.

That lunar relief paraded before the eyes of the voyagers, and they would not allow a single detail to be lost.

The disk appeared through the lenses of their glasses at a distance of 2 and a half leagues. A hot-air balloon's aeronaught, transported to that distance above the Earth- what would they have distinguished on its surface? We cannot say with surety, because to this day the highest ascension accomplished has never exceeded 8,000 meters.

Here, however, is an exact description of what was seen at their height by Barbicane and their companions.

Various colorations in large patches were all over the lunar disk. Those who study the Moon, the selenographers, are not in agreement regarding the nature of these colorations. There are several diverse and lively branches of thought. Julius Schmidt claims that if the terrestrial oceans dried up, a Selenite observer on the Moon could not distinguish on the globe, between the oceans and the continental plains, a greater nuanced diversity of contrasting hues being shown than those which are displayed upon the Moon as seen by a terrestrial observer. According to him, the common colors on the vast plains known under the name of 'seas' are somber greys blended amongst greens and browns. Several of the grand craters also present that coloration.

Barbicane was aware of that German selenographer's opinion, an opinion shared by MM. Beer and Moedler. His contention by observation conformed with their good reasoning and was in contrast to certain astronomers, who were only willing to admit that the sole color of the Moon's surface was grey. In certain spaces, the color green was revealed vividly, such as the springs, according to Julius Schmidt, on the *Sea of Serenity* and the *Sea of Humors*.

Barbicane remarked that equally-so the large craters devoid of interior cones threw off a bluish color analogous to sheets of freshly-polished steel. These colorations really were part of the lunar disk; and not the result, as some astronomers say, from objective imperfections on their lenses interacting with the imposition of terrestrial atmosphere. For Barbicane, there was not any doubt in that regard. He observed it through a traverse of void which would not permit any optical error. He considered the establishment in fact of these colorations an acquisition of science.

Now were those shades of green evidence of a tropical vegetation, tended by a dense and low atmosphere? As yet he could not pronounce an opinion.

Further along, Barbicane noted a reddish taint which was quite-sufficiently defined. A parallel shade had been observed at the bottom of an isolated enclosure, recorded under the name of the *Cirque of Lichtenberg*, situated near *Mount Hercynian* at the borders of the Moon. However, no one was able understand the nature of these characteristics.

He was no more fortunate in discovering the reason for another peculiarity of the lunar disk, of which he could not exactly determine the cause. Here is that particular peculiarity:

Michel Ardan had been taking observations beside the president, when he remarked about some long white furrows; vividly clear like direct rays of the Sun. It was a succession of luminous grooves very different to the radiating lines which *Copernicus* had formerly presented. These were arranged parallel to one another.

Michel, with his habitual aplomb, did not hesitate to cry out:

"Take a look there! Cultivated fields!"

"Cultivated fields?" said Nicholl, heaving his shoulders.

"Ploughed, at least," replied Michel Ardan. "But what laborers are these Selenites, and what gigantic oxen they must harness to their harrows to create such furrows!"

"Those are not ploughed furrows," said Barbicane. "They are rifts."

"Those are rifts," responded Michel with docility. "Only what is meant by '*rifts*' in the scientific world?"

Barbicane immediately apprised his companion on what he knew of lunar rifts. He was aware they were deep furrows observed on all parts of the Moon that were without mountains; that these orderly furrows, more often isolated, measure from 4 to 50 leagues in length, that their width varied from 1,000 to 1,500 meters, and their borders were rigorously maintained in parallel lines; but he knew no further, not of their formation nor of their characteristic nature.

Armed with his binoculars, Barbicane observed these rifts with concentration; remarking that their borders were formed by extremely sharp and steep slopes. They were long parallel ramparts, and, with some imagination could have admitted the existence of those long lines might have been proof of fortifications created by the Selenite engineers.

Of these different rifts there were ones which were absolutely straight and as though etched with the use of a rope to guide their cut. Others presented a slight curvature, although maintaining the same parallelism at their borders. There were some which crossed one another; some which sliced through craters. Here they ploughed through ordinary cavities, such as *Posidonius* or *Petavius*; there, they made stripes within the seas, such as across the *Sea of Serenity*.

By necessity these natural accidents excited the imagination of terrestrial astronomers. The earliest observers had failed to discover these rifts. Neither Hevelius, Cassini, La Hire, nor Herschel managed to become aware of them. It was Schroeter who, in 1789, announced for the first time their scientific interest. Then other scientists studied their existence; such as Pastorff, Gruithuysen, Beer, and Moedler.

As of today the number of these rifts reaches to seventy. But if they have been counted, all are yet to have their nature determined. These are certainly not fortifications that have been struck, nor are they ancient dried riverbeds- for the one part, so slight and uniform upon the surface of the Moon they could not have been excavated like drains; and for the other reason, these furrows transverse through craters that in places rise to a grand elevation.

We must avow that Michel Ardan had an idea which, without his knowing, coincided with the suggestion of Julius Schmidt.

"Why," said he, "are not these inexplicable appearances simply due to the phenomena of vegetation?"

"How do you mean?" asked Barbicane vivaciously.

"There is no need to lose your temper, my dignified president," answered Michel. "Could it not be that those dark lines formed along the shoulders are rows of trees that have been planted regularly?"

"You are holding onto this idea of vegetation?" said Barbicane.

"I am holding," Michel replied, "onto an explanation about something which your other scientists cannot explain! At least, my hypothesis offers the advantage of indicating why these rifts disappear, or seem to disappear at regular periods."

"And by what reason?"

"By the reason that the trees become invisible when they have lost their leaves, and visible when they regrow."

"Your explanation is ingenious, my friendly companion," Barbicane responded accommodatingly, "but it is inadmissible."

"Why?"

"Because there are no, so to speak, seasons on the surface of the Moon, and which, by consequence, that phenomenon of vegetation that you speak of cannot be produced."

In effect, the small oblique lunar axis maintains the Sun at an almost constant height under every latitude. Outside the equatorial regions, that radiant astral body occupies a virtually invariable zenith and barely passes beyond the limits of the horizon into the polar regions. Hence according to every region there reigns a winter, a springtime, a summer or an autumn perpetually, as it is for the planet Jupiter whose axis is equally only-slightly inclined in its orbit.

And what is the origination ascribed to those rifts? It is a question difficult to resolve. They are certainly of a later date than the formation of the craters and the cirques, for several of them have been introduced into these formations and have broken their circular walls. Hence it may be that, contemporary with the later geological periods, their existence is due to the expansion of natural forces.

Meanwhile, at their height the projectile had attained the 40th degree of lunar latitude, at a distance above which did not exceed 800 kilometers. Objects appeared through the fields of their glasses at only 2 leagues away. At this point beneath their feet stood *Mount Helicon*, 505 meters high; and to their left lay a district of mediocre elevation that surrounded a small proportion of the *Sea of Rains* under the name of the *Gulf of Irises*.

Terrestrial atmosphere would need to be one hundred and seventy times more transparent than it is to permit the astronomers to make complete observations regarding the surface of the Moon. But in the void through which the projectile floated, no fluid interposed between the eyes of the observer and the object observed. Additionally, Barbicane was taken to a distance which had never been given by even the most powerful of telescopes, not even to that of Lord Ross, not even that of the observatory on the Rocky Mountains.

Hence it was those extreme conditions which were favorable for resolving the question of whether the Moon was inhabited. However that solution evaded him still. He could distinguish nothing but the immense plains of desert beds; and towards the north, arid mountains. No works betrayed the hands of any man. Not one ruin could be attested beneath their passage. Not one agglomeration of animals that life had developed even to an inferior degree. There was no part with any movement, no part with an appearance of vegetation. Of the three kingdoms which divide the terrestrial sphere, there was only one representative on the lunar globe: the reign of the minerals.

"Ah, that is that!" said Michel Ardan with a slight air of dejection. "Then there is not any person?"

"No," answered Nicholl. "Not one man, not one animal, not one tree. After all if the atmosphere has taken refuge at the depths of cavities, an in the interior of cirques, or vent on the opposite face of the Moon, it is nothing we can predetermine."

"Besides," Barbicane added, "even to the most pernicious vision, nothing lies visible to a man beyond 7 kilometers. So that if there are Selenites, they can see our projectile, but we cannot see them."

Towards 4 hours in the morning, at the height of the 50th parallel, their distance from the surface reduced to 600 kilometers. On their left developed a line of mountains capriciously contoured, patinated by full luminosity. Towards their right, in contrast, a black hole in the shape of a crescent like a vast well, unfathomable and dank, bored into the lunar soil.

This hole, a lake of blackness called *Pluto*, was a deep cirque that may be conveniently studied from Earth between the last quarter and new Moon, when the shadows jut from east to west.

That black coloration is rarely recognized on the surface of the satellite. So far it has been seen in the depths of the *Endymion Cirque*, which is east of the *Sea of Cold* in the northern hemisphere, and at the depths of the *Grimaldi Cirque* on the equator, towards the oriental border of that astral body.

Plato is a ringed mountain, situated by the 51° latitude north and 9° longitude east. Its cirque is 92 kilometers long and 61 kilometers wide. Barbicane regretted that they did not pass directly over that vast opening. It was an abyss to ponder, certainly containing within surprising mysterious phenomenon. But the projectile's march could not be modified. They must submit to its strict passage. If it is so with a balloon dirigible, even more so with a cannon ball, once you are entirely entombed inside its walls.

Approaching 5 o'clock in the morning, the northern limits of the *Sea of Rains* was finally passed by. The mountains of *Condamine* and *Fontenelle* remained; one on the right, the other on the left. That part of the lunar disk by the 60th degree developed into absolutely mountainous territory. Their field glasses brought them to within 1 league, a distance less than the separation between the summit of Mount Blanc and sea level on Earth. All of that region is ruffled by peaks and cirques. Towards the 70th degree *Philolaus* dominated, at a height of 3,700 meters, breeched by an elliptical crater 16 leagues long and 4 leagues wide.

They were nearing the dark side of the Moon.

And then the disk, viewed at that distance, offered an extremely bizarre aspect. In regards to the conditions, the landscape presented to their eyes was very different to that of the Earth's- but very inferior also.

For the Moon was without an atmosphere, and the consequences on a planet which arise from the absence of enveloping gasses has been demonstrated. There is no dusk on its surface, night follows the day and day follows the night, with the abruptness like a lamp illuminated in the midst of profound obscure depths. Without transition between coldness and heat, the temperature tumbles in an instant from the boiling point of water to the freezing chills of empty interplanetary space.

Another consequence of the absence of air is this: an absolute darkness reigns wherever the rays of the Sun are prevented from entering. That which is called light diffusion on Earth, which is the luminosity of matter held by the air in suspension, creates the twilight and dawn and produces the umbrae, the penumbrae and all the magic of *fata Morgana*, does not exist on the Moon. This brutality of contrasts admits only two colors, black and white. If a Selenite- those still-hypothetical inhabitants of the Moon- sheltered their eyes from the Sun's rays, the sky would appear absolutely black and the stars would shine brilliantly before their vision as though it were the darkest of nights.

You may judge the impression produced by that strange lunar aspect upon Barbicane and his two friends. Their eyes were deranged. They could no longer perceive the respective distances of the diverse plains. A lunar landscape whose points were unsoftened by shadows and light could not be rendered by a painter of Earthly natural scenes. Patches of black ink on a white page, and that is all.

This aspect remained unaltered, even when the projectile was at the height of 80° and separated from the Moon's surface by a distance of 100 kilometers. Not even when, at 5 hours in the morning, they passed to less than 50 kilometers from the *Gioja Mountain*, a distance reduced by the field glasses to an eighth of 1 league. It seemed as though one could touch the Moon with their hands, it appeared impossible for their cannon ball not to strike it before long; if only at the north pole, whose brilliant ridge outlined drastically against the deep blackness of the sky. Michel Ardan dearly wanted to open a porthole and hurl himself towards the lunar surface. A fall of a dozen leagues! He had no care. It would have been a useless attempt in any case, for if the projectile could not attain some point on the satellite, Michel, controlled by the same motion, would not have been able to attain it either.

In that moment, at 6 hours, the lunar pole appeared. The disk offered no more to their gaze than one luminously-emblazoned crescent-shaped half, whilst the other side had disappeared into darkness. Suddenly, the projectile passed the line of demarcation between the intensely-shining surface and an absolute funeral shadow, and they were immediately plunged into profound night.

14. The Night of Three Hundred and Fifty-Four and One Half Hours

At the moment when this abrupt phenomenon was produced, the projectile razed the north pole of the Moon at less than 50 kilometers. Several seconds were sufficient to drown them in the absolute darkness of interplanetary space. The transition had proceeded so rapidly, unnuanced, without any gradual degradation to the light, without any attenuation to the lunar undulations beneath, that the whole astral body seemed to have extinguished instantly; like a candle.

"My God! The Moon has melted and disappeared!" cried Michel Ardan, totally dumbfounded.

Indeed, there was not one reflection, not one shadow. Nothing more appeared of the disk, formerly so dazzlingly clear. The darkness was profound: more completely-still by the rays of the stars. It was 'that black' which impregnates the lunar nights for the duration of 354 and one half hours over every point of the disk- a long night resulting from the equal movements of translation and rotation of the Moon about itself, and the other around the Earth. The projectile, immersed within the shadow's cone of the satellite, no longer receiving the action of the solar rays, was just as invisible as that region of sojourn below.

In the interior, the obscurity which had ensued was complete. They could not see one another. So then, the necessity to dissipate that darkness. Whatever the desires of Barbicane to manage the gas reserves with restraint, they were obliged to make artificial light; an indispensible and yet lavish clarity which the Sun had refused them.

"The devil with that radiant star!" cursed Michel Ardan. "A Sun who induces us to dispense with our gas instead of gratifying us with its rays."

"Do not accuse the Sun," replied Nicholl, "whose fault it is not. Rather it is very-well the fault of the Moon, who had no grounds to place itself like a screen between the Sun and us."

"It is the Sun!" repeated Michel rebelliously.

"It is the Moon!" maintained Nicholl.

A pointless dispute, which Barbicane put an end to by saying:

"My friends, it is not the fault of the Sun, nor the fault of the Moon. It is the fault of the projectile which, instead of following the rules of our trajectory, has swerved clumsily. And, to be more correct, it is the malfeasance of that malevolent meteor which caused our deplorable deviation from the initial direction."

"Good!" concluded Michel Ardan. " And since this affair has been arranged, let us now take our breakfast. After an entire night of observations , it is convenient that we repair our appetites a little."

The proposal was met without contradiction. Michel, inside a few minutes, had prepared their repast. However, they ate without relish; deliberately, but without toasts, without offering any hurrahs. Those hardy and bold explorers, drawn into the somber recesses of interplanetary space, and now without their habitual cortege of the Sun's rays, sensed a vague uneasiness which had gathered upon their hearts. That shadowy, wild and fleeting '*farouche*' so cherished by Victor Hugo's pen encompassed them on all sides.

Meanwhile they talked about that interminable night of over 354 hours' duration, not quite 15 days, which the laws of physics have imposed upon the Moon's habitations. In order to fill that vast emptiness which lay before them, Barbicane provided his friends with some explanation as to the causes and the consequences of that curious phenomenon.

"A definite curiosity," said he, "for if each hemisphere is deprived of the Sun's light for 15 days, that which we are floating above in this moment does not even enjoy throughout its long night any view of Earth in splendid clarity. In a word, they do not have a moon- I am applying that qualification to our native sphere- for this side of the disk. If this was to occur on the Earth, for example imagine that Europe never saw the Moon because it was only visible from the antipodes, can you imagine for yourselves the astonishment of a European arriving in Australia?"

"Why, they would undertake the voyage for nothing more than to see the Moon!" Michel declared. "No one would even care to see their beaches!"

"Ah well," replied Barbicane, "that astonishment is reserved for Selenites who inhabit the face opposite the Earth, a face forever invisible to our compatriots on the ground of the globe beneath us."

"And which we would have seen," commented Nicholl, "if we had arrived here in the period when the Moon was new, that is to say 15 days later."

"I will add, on the other hand," continued Barbicane, "that the inhabitants on the face which is visible are uniquely favored by nature; to the detriment of their brothers on the invisible face. The latter, as you can see, have nights of darkness for 354 hours without the rupture of a single ray to break the obscurity. On the contrary the other face, when the Sun has given its light for 15 days and retires beneath the horizon, sees rising above their horizon a splendidly shining astral body. That is the Earth, which is thirteen times larger than the tiny Moon is to our perception; the Earth which develops a diameter of 2° and sheds a luminosity thirteen times more intense, without tempering from any layers of atmosphere; our Earth, who only disappears at the moment of the Sun's arrival when it returns from tour!"

"Beautiful phrases!" complimented Michel Ardan, "Although a little academic."

"In continuation of that," replied Barbicane, not batting an eyelid, "it follows that the visible face of the disk would be greatly more-agreeable to inhabit; since it looks forever upon either the Sun when the Moon is full, or the Earth when the Moon is new."

"But," said Nicholl, "that advantage is well mitigated by the untenable heat which the light brings with it."

"The inconvenience, in that regard, is the same for the two faces; for the luminosity from the Earth is evidentially deprived of its heat. However that invisible face is still more scorched by the heat than the visible face. I say this for you Nicholl, because Michel will probably not comprehend why."

"Thank you," Michel said.

"In effect," Barbicane explained, "when that invisible face receives at the same time the solar heat and light- which is when the Moon is new, that is to say it is in conjunction, it is situated between the Sun and the Moon. Hence it follows by respect to the situation which it occupies in opposition, when it is full, that it is much closer to the Sun by double the distance from the Earth. So that distance is estimated to be a 200th part of that which separates the Sun from the Earth, or in round figures, 200,000 leagues; and thereby the invisible face is nearer to the Sun by 200,000 leagues when it receives its rays."

"Quite correct," responded Nicholl.

"On the contrary...," said Barbicane, disagreeing with his own statement.

"One moment," said Michel, interrupting his serious companions.

"What do you want?"

"I ask that you continue your explanation."

"Why is that?"

"To prove that I understand."

"Give me leave," said Barbicane with a smile.

"On the contrary," said Michel, imitating the tone and gestures of president Barbicane, "on the contrary, when the visible face of the Moon is illuminated by the Sun, that is when the Moon is full; which is to say situated opposite the Sun in respect to the Earth. The distance that separates the radiant astral body is then accrued in round numbers to 200,000 leagues, and the heat it receives must be a little less."

"Well said!" cried Barbicane. "Do you know, Michel, that as an artist, you are quite intelligent?"

"Yes," responded Michel nonchalantly, "we are all like that in the bohemian quarter."

Barbicane grasped the hand of his companion seriously, and continued to enumerate the several advantages reserved for the inhabitants of the visible face.

Between other positives he cited the observation that eclipses of the Sun, which only take place on that side of the lunar disk- since, for them to be produced, it is necessary for the Moon to be in opposition. These eclipses, provoked by the interposition of the Earth between the Moon and the Sun, produced for a duration of 2 hours throughout which, by reason of the refraction solar rays by the atmosphere, the terrestrial globe appears like a small black point on the Sun.

"And so," said Nicholl, "there is a hemisphere, that invisible hemisphere, which is given a highly-evil portion, highly disgraced, by nature!"

"Yes," responded Barbicane. "But not entirely. In effect, by a certain movement of libration, by a certain balancing at its center, the Moon presents to the Earth a little more than half of its disk. It is like a pendulum whose center of gravity has been transferred towards the terrestrial globe and which oscillates regularly. From whence is that oscillation? It is due to the movement of rotation on its axis animated by a uniform velocity, whereas the movement of translation follows an elliptical orbit around the Earth. At the perigee is where velocity of translation is imparted, and the Moon mounts a certain portion of its western border. At the apogee the rotational velocity is imparted in a contrary manner, and small portions at the eastern border appear. Its spindle will at times shift approximately 8° on the orient side, and at times onto its occidental side. As a result, of a thousand parts, the Moon allows us to perceive 569 units.

"It is of no importance," said Michel. "If we ever do become Selenites, we shall inhabit the visible face. Me, I prefer the light!"

"Unless, however," Nicholl told him, "it is only condensed on the other side, as is the suggestion of certain astronomers."

"That is one consideration," Michel answered simply.

Meanwhile breakfast ended, and the observers returned to their post. They essayed to see through the darkened portholes by extinguishing all light from within the projectile. But not one atom of luminosity, not a single photon, could find them in that dense obscurity.

One inexplicable fact preoccupied Barbicane.

How had the projectile, after approaching so close of a distance to the Moon- roughly speaking, 50 kilometers- not plunged towards its surface? If their velocity had been relatively enormous, this would reduce the force acting on them to provoke such a fall. But with their relatively mediocre velocity, this resistance to the lunar attraction could not thus be explained. Was the projectile under some foreign influence? Did some kind of body maintain them in the ether?

It was dismally evident that they would not attain any point on the Moon. Where were they being taken? Were they approaching or was their trajectory elongating from the disk? Were they projecting through that deep profound night towards an infinite traverse? How could they understand, how could they calculate in the midst of such funeral darkness? All these questions made Barbicane uneasy, but to him they were without resolve.

In effect, that invisible astral body was there. Possibly only some leagues away, or several thousand, but neither he nor his companions could tell. If there was any noise being produced on the surface, they could not hear it. Air, the vehicle of sound, without which it would not allow the groans of the Moon to be transmitted- to that which the Arabic legends designate the label 'a man already half-granite and still breathing'!

We must acknowledge this would aggravate the most patient of observers. It was precisely caused by that unknown hemisphere which had been hidden from their eyes! That face which, 15 days sooner or 15 days later, would be displayed with splendid clarity in light by solar rays, had then perished in absolute obscurity. In 15 days, where would the projectile be? Would it be their fate to become entrained by the Moon's gravitational attraction? Who possessed the power to say?

After the observations of selenographers it is generally admitted that the invisible hemisphere of the Moon is, from its constitution, in absolute resemblance of the visible hemisphere. Indeed as we have discovered, in effect, about a seventh of this portion from the movements of libration which Barbicane had discussed.

   Now, on the visible zones they had met with, there had been nothing but plains and mountains, cirques and craters, substantive analogues to that which was depicted on their maps. One might thereby predict the same nature, the same world; arid and dead. And however, what if an atmosphere had taken refuge on this face? If, clothed by air, water had donated life to regenerated continents? If vegetation persisted there still? If animals populated continents of land and the seas? If man, in these habitable conditions, lived there already?

   Oh the interesting questions they might have resolved! What solutions might they have taken ahold-of in the contemplation of that hemisphere! What delight could they have felt, if they might have looked down upon a world which no human eye had ever before seen!

   Hence we can conceive of the displeasure experienced by the voyagers in the midst of that black night. All observation of the lunar disk was placed into an impossible interlude. Only the constellations solicited their presence; and we must acknowledge that never had the astronomers, not Faye, nor Charcornac, nor Secchi had ever entertained such favorable conditions for observation.

   Indeed, nothing could possess an equal splendor to that staggeringly ethereal world of stars; bathed in limpid quietude. Diamonds encrusted the celestial vault ejecting superbly cold fires. The voyager's vision embraced all from the Southern Cross to the Northern Star, those two constellations which, by reason of the processional equinox of the Earth's axis, will cede their roles as polar stars; unto Canopus in the austral hemisphere and unto Vega in the boreal hemisphere. Imagination was lost within such a sublime infinity, amidst which the projectile gravitated like a new star created from the hands of man.

   By a natural effect, the brilliancy of the constellations came from a soft luster. They were unscintillating; for the atmosphere was missing, which by the imposition of unequal layers of densities and diverse humidities produces that scintillation. These stars were gentle eyes, who gazed through that profound night in the midst of the complete and absolute silence of interstellar space.

For a long time, the adventurers, mute, in this manner observed the firmament of constellations; over which the Moon had like a vast screen formed an enormous black hole. But a painful sensation finally tore them away from these contemplations. It was a sharp intense coldness that soon covered the interior of the glass portholes in a thick layer of ice.

In effect the Sun no longer warmed the projectile with its direct rays, and little by little the stored heat emanated through their padded walls into the surrounding void. That warmth, by radiation, rapidly evaporated into space and produced a considerable abasement to the temperature. Hence the interior humidity changed to ice on contact with the glass, and prevented all observations.

Nicholl, consulting the thermometer, watched it tumble to 17° Celsius below zero. Therefore, despite all the reasons to maintain economy, after demanding luminosity from the gas they now also demanded warmth. The low temperature in that cannon ball was unsupportable. Its guests would soon freeze to death.

"We cannot complain," observed Michel Ardan, "about the monotony of our journey! What diversity, at least in the temperatures! Now we are blinded in light and saturated with warmth, like the Indians on the pampas! Now we are plunged into profound darkness, in the midst of boreal arctic cold, like the Inuit Eskimos of the pole! No, certainly! We don't have the right to complain, for nature has done excellent things in our honor."

"But," demanded Nicholl, "what is the temperature of our exterior?"

"Precisely that of interplanetary space," Barbicane told him.

"Then," replied Michel Ardan, "would this not be the occasion to perform that experiment which we could not attempt before, when we were drowned by the Sun's rays?"

"It is now or never," reasoned Barbicane. "For we have been usefully placed to verify the temperature of space, to see if the calculations of Fourier or Pouillet were exact."

"In any case, it is cold!" decreed Michel. "See how the humidity in here condenses onto the thick glass of the portholes. If the drop in temperature continued, the vapor of our breaths would start to precipitate like snow!"

"Prepare the thermometer," Barbicane instructed.

One might well think that an ordinary thermometer would not give any result in the circumstances to which that instrument would be exposed. The mercury would have frozen in its cuvette, as the liquidity is no longer maintained once exceeding 42° below zero. However Barbicane had furnished them with a spirit thermometer; designed according to Walferdin's system, which gives the indication of excessively-low temperatures.

Prior to commencing the experiment, the instrument's calibration was checked against an ordinary thermometer and then Barbicane was prepared to deploy it.

"How shall we go about this?" asked Nicholl.

"Nothing is easier," responded Michel Ardan, who was never thwarted. "We quickly open the porthole and launch the instrument; it will follow the projectile with exemplary docility; and after a quarter of an hour, we then retire it..."

"With the hand?" demanded Barbicane.

"Yes, with the hand," affirmed Michel.

"Well, my friend, do not expose yourself," warned Barbicane, "for the hand that you withdraw will be nothing more than a frozen stump deformed by an unimaginably awful cold!"

"Really?!"

"You will suffer the sensation of horrendous burns, which will feel like iron that is white hot; for whether heat brutally enters our flesh or leaves it, the effect is identically the same thing. Besides, I am not sure the objects we jettisoned out of the projectile earlier still follow us in procession."

"Why," asked Nicholl.

"It is that, if we are travelling through an atmosphere, of even the slightest density, these objects will become delayed in respect to our motion. Now the obscurity which has enclosed us prevents our verifying if they still float around us or not. Therefore in order not to expose ourselves or lose the thermometer, we can attach it to something and then it shall easily return."

Barbicane's council was followed. Through a rapidly-opened porthole Nicholl launched the instrument, which was retained by a very short cord so that it could be quickly drawn inside. The porthole window had not been opened for longer than one second, and yet that second had been enough to allow a vicious cold to penetrate within the projectile's interior.

"A thousand devils!" exclaimed Michel Ardan. "It's cold enough now to freeze a polar bear!"

Barbicane waited for a full half-hour to elapse, more than sufficient to permit the instrument to descend to the level of the temperature in space. Then, after that time, the thermometer was rapidly retired.

Barbicane calculated the quantity of wine-spirit which had overflowed into the small ampoule soldered to the lower part of the instrument, and said:

"142° centigrade below zero!!"

[Subsequent to those times, brave astronauts and unmanned satellites have determined the temperature of interplanetary space to be -270.15° centigrade below zero]

M. Pouillet was correct and Fourier had been contradicted. This was the undoubtable temperature of sidereal space! It was, perhaps, the temperature of the lunar continents; when that shining astral body of the night sky has lost to radiation all the heat which 15 days of the sun's libations gave!

15. Hyperbola or Parabola

Perhaps it may astonish one to see Barbicane and his companions with so little preoccupation for the future reserved for them, entombed in that prison of metal and being transported through that infinite ether. Instead of asking where they were going they passed their time immersed in experiments, as calmly as if installed in their private offices.

We may offer in response that these were men of strong temperament and above any anxiety that might be caused by their perilous state; that they did not worry about such inconsequential matters, and there were other things to preoccupy themselves with than their future.

The truth is they were not masters of the projectile, they could not halt its forward momentum nor modify their direction. A mariner can change as they please the direction of their ship, a aeronaut may impress upon the balloon vertical movements. They, on the contrary, could not affect any action upon their vehicle. All their maneuvers were prohibited. From this came their lassiez-faire dispositions, allowing things to '*run their course*' according to the maritime expression.

Where had they travelled to in that moment at 8 o'clock in the morning, termed the 6th December on the Earth? Very certainly they were in the vicinity of the Moon, and even close enough for it to appear to them like an immense black screen developed upon the firmament. As to the distance which separated them, it was impossible to evaluate. The projectile, maintained by inexplicable forces, had razed by the north pole at less than 50 kilometers. However, during the 2 hours from when they had entered the cone of shadow, that distance- had it accrued or diminished?

There was no point which could have served as a landmark to estimate the direction and speed of the projectile. Perhaps their distance from the disk rapidly lengthened, in a manner which would soon detach them from the pure shadow. Perhaps, on the contrary, they approached it so drastically they would hurtle into some elevated peak of that invisible hemisphere: this would have terminated their journey, without any doubt to the detriment of the voyagers.

A discussion emerged on that subject, and Michel Ardan, forever a wealth of explanations, emitted an opinion that the cannon ball, retained by lunar gravitational attraction, would eventually plunge downwards the way tumbling meteoric stones called aerolites fall onto our terrestrial surface.

"In any way, my comrade," answered Barbicane, "all of the aerolites do not fall upon the Earth; their number is small. Therefore, even if we entered into the state of an aerolite, it would not necessarily ensure that our trajectory would reach the surface of the Moon."

"However," responded Michel, "if we were to approach close enough..."

"You are in error," Barbicane interrupted Michel's suggestion. "Do you not see the filaments of shooting stars scratching the sky's surface by their thousands at certain seasons?"

"Yes."

"Ah well, these stars, or rather corpuscles, are made brilliant by the conditions of frictional heat as they slide against the atmospheric layer. So as they traverse the atmosphere, they must be at least 6 leagues above the globe, and yet they seldom fall. It is the same for our projectile. It could approach very close to the Moon, and yet at no point tumble into it."

"But then," asked Michel, "I should be very curious to understand how our errant vehicle will conduct itself in space."

"I see there are two hypotheses," answered Barbicane after several moments of reflection.

"Which are?"

"The projectile has the choice between two mathematical curves and it will follow one or the other according to the velocity which carries it, and that I cannot evaluate at this moment."

"Yes," said Nicholl, "it will either follow a parabola or a hyperbola."

"Indeed," agreed Barbicane. "With a certain velocity it takes the parabola, and the hyperbola with a more considerable velocity."

"I enjoy these grand words," cried Michel Ardan. "I find them coherent and direct. And what is this which you refer to as a parabola?"

"My friend," responded the captain, "a parabola is a curve of the second order which is the result of a section of cone intersected by a plane, parallel on both sides."

"Ah! Ah!" said Michel in a satisfied tone.

"It is very nearly," replied Nicholl, "the trajectory which a bomb launched by a mortar describes."

"Perfect. And the hyperbola?" demanded Michel.

"The hyperbola, Michel, is a curve of the second order, produced by the intersection of one conical surface and a plane perpendicular to its axis, and which constitutes two separate branches, the one and the other extending indefinitely in the two directions."

"Is it possible!" cried Michel in a tone even more serious, as though he had suddenly been informed of a grave event. "Then remember this well, Captain Nicholl. What I really like in your definition of the hyperbola- and I had almost said 'hyper*blague*'! [*blague* is a French word meaning 'to joke/tease']- is that it is even less clear than the word which you claim to define!"

Nicholl and Barbicane were hardly concerned about Michel Ardan's humorousness. They had been launched into a deep scientific discussion. What would be the curve followed by the projectile? Of this they were passionate. One held for the hyperbola, the other the parabola. They each gave their reasons with inundations of algebraic x's. Their arguments were presented in a language which caused Michel to leap about. The discussion was lively, and neither adversary would voluntarily sacrifice their favored curve to the other.

That scientific dispute was so prolonged that finally in impatience Michel said:

"So there! Distinguished sirs of the cosine, will you finally cease in throwing your parabolas and hyperbolas at one another's heads? I wish to understand, myself, the only interesting thing about this whole affair. We shall follow one or the other of those curves. Excellent. But where will they lead us?"

"Nowhere," grumbled Nicholl.

"How, nowhere?" asked Michel.

"Evidentially," said Barbicane. "As they are unconstrained curves, they are prolonged into infinity!"

"Ah! Scientists!" cried Michel. "I cradle you inside my heart! Eh! Why is it important to us, the hyperbola or the parabola, at the moment when one or the other caries us equally into the infinity of space!"

Barbicane and Nicholl could not prevent the smiles that came to their lips. It was the closest either would come to '*art for art's sake*'. Never had a question more obscure been entertained at such an inopportune moment. The sinister reality was that the projectile, apported hyperbolically or parabolically, would never reach the Moon or return to the Earth.

And so what would happen to these hardy adventurers in their very immediate future? If they were not dead from hunger, if they were not dead from thirst- it was that, in several days, when their gas failed them, they would die from the stale air if the cold did not murder them first!

Meanwhile, as important as it was to economize their gas, the excessive abatement of the ambient temperature obliged them to consume a certain quantity. Strictly speaking, they could forgo its light, but not its warmth. Quite fortunately, the heat of the calorific energy developed by the Reiset and Regnaut apparatus for breathing raised the temperature inside the projectile by a small amount, and, without a great expenditure, they were able to maintain a level that could support them.

Unfortunately observations had become very difficult through the portholes. The humidity inside their cannon ball condensed upon the glass and congealed immediately. They could only remove this opacity by repeated rubbing. In any case this would allow reporting certain phenomenon of very high interest.

Indeed, if the disk was invisible was provided with an atmosphere, would they not see rays of shooting stars striking through? If the projectile itself was passing through the same fluid layers, could they not detect some repercussive noise from the lunar echoes- the grumbling of a storm, perhaps, the fracas of an avalanche or the detonations of an active volcano? And if some electrically-charged mountain flashed with lightning would they not see its intense fulgurations? Such facts, carefully recorded, by themselves would have provided elucidation upon that obscure question as to the lunar constitution. And so Barbicane and Nicholl, posted beside the porthole like astronomers, observed with scrupulous patience.

Just now the disk remained demurely mute and somber. It would not respond to the multiple interrogations posed by their ardent spirits.

It provoked this reflection from Michel, which seemed justified in its appearance:

"If ever we recommence this voyage, we should fare well to choose the period when the Moon is new."

"Indeed," responded Nicholl. "That circumstance seems quite favorable. I agree that the Moon, submerged in the solar rays, whilst it would not be visible during the transit on the other hand we would perceive the Earth as full. And what is more, if we were drawn around the Moon, as we have arrived in this moment, we should have at least seen the invisible part of the lunar disk in magnificent clarity."

"Well said Nicholl," complimented Michel Ardan. "And what do you think, Barbicane?"

"I think this," answered the serious president. "If we ever recommence this voyage, we shall start from the same time and in the same conditions. Suppose we had attained our aim, would it not have been worth more to discover continents in full light instead of a country plunged into an obscure night? Would not our initial installations fared better in those circumstances? Yes, of course- it is evident. As to the invisible side, we could have visited it during our exploratory journeys of the lunar globe. Hence, that period of time when the full Moon occurred was fortunately chosen for us to have arrived where we aimed, and we would have arrived, if not for the deviation of our route."

"To that, I have nothing to respond," said Michel Ardan. "Here you have a lovely occasion with nothing preventing you from observing the far side of the Moon! Who can say if the inhabitants of other planets are not further advanced than the scientists of Earth on the subject of their satellites?"

One can see easily, to that remark from Michel Ardan, a fair response: Yes, the other satellites, by their great proximity, may be rendered more easily to study. The inhabitants of Saturn, Jupiter and Uranus, if they exist, may have established a connection with their moons more easily. The 4 satellites of

Jupiter gravitate at a distance of 108,260 leagues, 172,200 leagues, 274,700 leagues, and 480,130 leagues. However these distances are calculated from the center of the planet, and, deducting the length of the radius which is between 17,000 and 18,000 leagues, it may be seen the first satellite is less-further away from the surface of Jupiter than the Moon is from the surface of the Earth. Of the 8 moons of Saturn, in turn 4 are closer; Diane is 84,600 leagues distant, Thetys is 62,966 leagues, Enceldus 48,191 leagues and finally Mimas is at an average distance 34,500 leagues. Of the 8 natural satellites of Uranus, Ariel is 51,520 leagues from the planet.

Thereby, at the surface of these 3 astral bodies, an analogous experiment to that of president Barbicane would have presented fewer difficulties. If their inhabitants had attempted a similar adventure, they have perhaps recognized the constitution of that half of the disk, which the satellite eternally hides from their eyes. But if they had never left their planets, they will be no more advanced than the astronomers on Earth.

[Jules Verne note: Herschel established the movement of rotation on their axis for satellites always equals the movement of revolution about the planet, consequently they present the same face always. Only the system of Uranus offers a marked difference: whereby the movements of its moons are in a plane almost perpendicular to the plane of the orbit.][Since those times science has proven this to be mostly fallacy].

Meanwhile, the cannon ball was describing through the shadows an incalculable trajectory which no landmark permitted reckoning. Had their direction been modified, either under the lunar gravitational attraction, or under the actions of some unknown star or body? Barbicane could not say. But a change had taken place in the relative positioning of their vehicle, which he certified towards 4 o'clock in the morning.

The change consisted of this; the base of the projectile had turned towards the surface of the Moon, maintaining its perpendicular axis as it passed. The attraction, that is to say gravity, that is to say the distribution of weight, had brought about this modification. The heaviest part of the cannon ball inclined towards the invisible disk, exactly as though it was to fall upon it.

Did it fall? Were the voyagers going to reach their desired goal? No. And this observation was in fact facilitated by a sort of landmark, although moreover an inexplicable one, which demonstrated to Barbicane that the projectile was not approaching the Moon, rather it had been displaced from the curvature they followed little by little into a concentric one.

The landmark was a luminous brightness which Nicholl announced at once on the limit of the horizon formed by the black disk. That point of light could not be confused with a star. It was a red incandescence that grew progressively; providing incontestable proof the projectile's line had been displaced towards this direction and was not tumbling towards the surface, as would have been normally expected.

"A volcano! It is an active volcano!" exclaimed Nicholl. "An opening into the heart of the interior fires of the Moon! Therefore this world is still not entirely extinguished!"

"Yes! An eruption," said Barbicane, who carefully studied the phenomena through his night binoculars. "What else could it be, if not a volcano?"

"But then," said Michel Ardan, "to allow that combustion, it requires air. Hence, there is an atmosphere enveloping this part of the Moon."

"Perhaps," answered Barbicane, "but not necessarily. The volcano, by the decomposition of certain materials, can formulate its own oxygen and thereby eject flames out into void. It seems to me that deflagration has the intensity and clarity of a combustion produced with pure oxygen. We should not be hasty in affirming the existence of a lunar atmosphere."

The igneous mountain would have been situated somewhere about the 45° latitude south on the invisible region of the disk. But to the great displeasure of Barbicane, the curve they described in the projectile was drawing away from the point signaled by the eruption. Hence they could not exactly determine its nature. A half hour after they had seen that signal, the luminous point disappeared behind the shadow of the horizon.

Nevertheless the record of that phenomena had considerably aided the science of selenography. It proved that not all heat had disappeared from the entrails of this globe; and where heat exists, who could not affirm that a vegetal kingdom, even an animal kingdom, had not resisted up until then destructive influences? The existence of a volcano in eruption, inscrutably recognized by these scientists of Earth, would have facilitated well beyond doubt the favorable theories to that grave question about the habitability of the Moon.

Barbicane allowed himself to become lost in these reflections. It was a mute amnesia as he dreamed of the mysterious destinies of that lunar world. He sought to connect and relegate the entirety of facts that had observed until then, when a new incident brusquely struck him back into reality.

That incident was more of a cosmic phenomenon. It was a menacing danger whose consequences threatened to prove disastrous.

Suddenly, in the midst of the ether, in that profound darkness an enormous mass appeared. It was like a moon, but an incandescent moon; whose brilliance was all the more unbearable as the clarity of its form dismembered the outlines of that brutal obscurity of interplanetary darkness. The mass, of circular form, threw out a light which filled the projectile.

The faces of Barbicane, Nicholl and Michel Ardan, violently bathed in its white layers, affected spectral appearances, which the scientists of physics produce by an artificial light of alcohol impregnated with salt.

"A thousand devils!" cried Michel Ardan. "We look hideous. What is that malfeasant moon?"

"A meteor," responded Barbicane calmly.

"A meteor in flames, in the void?"

"Yes."

The globe of fire was a meteor, indeed. Barbicane had not been deceived. But if these cosmic meteors observed from the Earth generally present a luminance slightly inferior to that of the Moon, here in the shadowed ether they were resplendent. These errant bodies carry within themselves the principle of their incandescence. An ambient air is unnecessary to produce their own deflagration. And so, in effect, if certain of these meteors traverse the atmospheric layers at 2 or 3 leagues above the Earth, the others in contrast trace their trajectories at a distance where the atmosphere does not extend. Now these meteors, for example the one of 27th October 1844, appeared at a height of 128 leagues; another on 18th August 1841, disappeared at a distance of 182 leagues. Several of these bolides are 3 or 4 kilometers wide and possess a velocity which propels them at 75 kilometers per second, following a direction reverse to the Earth's movement.

This globe, a shooting star, appeared in the shadow at a distance of a hundred leagues at least and should have, according to the estimate of Barbicane, measured in diameter 2,000 meters. It advanced at a speed of roughly 2 kilometers a second, that is 30 leagues per minute. It sliced through the route of the projectile and would reach it in several minutes. As it approached, it grew to enormous proportions.

One can only imagine, if it is possible, how our voyagers in this situation must have felt. Their emotions were impossible to describe. Despite all their courage, their cold-blooded determination, their carelessness towards danger; they became silent, unmoving, their limbs as tense as steel, a prey to their savagely instinctual alarm. Their projectile, without the power to deviate from its course, unyieldingly moved straight towards that flaming mass which was more intense than the distorted mouth of a reverboratory furnace. They seemed precipitating towards that glowing abyss, a hell of fire.

Barbicane found himself holding the hands of his two companions, and the three regarded through semi-closed eyelids for the first time of their lives a white hot asteroid. If their thoughts had not become destroyed within their fear, if their minds still functioned within that dreadful appall, they must have thought themselves lost to perdition.

Two minutes after the abrupt apparition of the meteor- two centuries of anguish!- the projectile had closed to strike it, when the globe of fire exploded like a bomb, but without the sensation of sound in the midst of that void where any sound, which is but the agitation of layers of air, is unable to be produced.

Nicholl emitted a cry. He and his companions rushed to the glass of the porthole. What spectacle! What pen could render this vision, what palette was sufficiently rich in colors to render such magnificence!

It was like the blossoming of a crater; like the scattered dispersal of an immense incendiary conflagration. Thousands of luminous fragments ignited and radiated into space with their fires. All sizes, all colors, intermingling. There were irradiations of yellow, light yellow, red, green, greys, a corona of multicolored fireworks. Of that globe, enormous and imposing, there remained nothing as morsels of it were carried in all directions; transformed in turn to asteroids of their own, some flamboyant like swords, some wrapped in white clouds, others leaving the remnant of residue from bright cosmic dust.

The incandescent blocks interpolated, interposed, crisscrossed, struck one another and scattered in tiny fragments- some of which hurtled into the projectile. The glass porthole on the left was even cracked from the violent shock. It seemed they floated through a war ground of exploding shells, the least of which could annihilate them in an instant.

The light which saturated the ether developed with an incomparable intensity, for these asteroids dispersed in all directions. At a certain moment, it was so spectacularly vivid that Michel, entranced beside the glass window next to Barbicane and Nicholl, cried out:

"The invisible Moon, it is finally visible!"

And all three, in the travel of that luminous effluence of several seconds, caught a glimpse of the mysterious side of the disk which man's eye perceived for the very first time.

What could they distinguish at that distance which was not an approximation? Several bands lengthened across the disk, and veritable clouds formed in the midst of a restrained atmosphere; through which emerged not only all the mountains, but also the less-dramatic reliefs, the cirques, the capriciously strewn gaping craters- all these existed too on the visible surface. Then the immense spaces, now no longer arid plains but real seas, oceans widely distributed, which reflected on their liquid mirror all the magical explosions from the fires in space above, and vast dark masses which appeared to be forests in the quick illumination of light...

Was it an illusion, an error of the eyes, an optical deception? Could they provide a scientific affirmation at that observation so superficially obtained? Did they dare conclude their pronouncement on the question of its habitability, after such a feeble glimpse of the invisible disk?

Meanwhile the fulgent meteors falling from space diminished bit by bit, their accidental lights reduced to void, the asteroids that ran in diverse outward trajectories extinguished into the distance. After that culmination the ether returned to its habitual dark emptiness; the stars, momentarily eclipsed, sparkled again from their firmaments and the disk, scarcely shown, disappeared once more within its impenetrable night.

16. The Southern Hemisphere

The projectile had escaped a terrible danger, a danger well-unforeseen. Who could have imagined undergoing such an encounter with those bolides? These errant bodies could create serious perils for our travellers. To them they were hidden reefs strewn about that sea of ether which, being less fortunate than ocean navigators, they were unable to flee. But did they complain, these adventurers of space? No, because nature had donated to them a splendid cosmic spectacle of meteors brilliantly exploding formidably, because these were incomparable fireworks, which no Ruggieri could intimidate, which had given clarity for several seconds the invisible nimbus of the Moon. In that brief light, the continents, the seas, the forests had appeared. Had an atmosphere given to that incongruous face the necessary molecules to sustain life? Questions still unsolved, eternally posing themselves before human curiosity.

It was then 3 and a half hours in the afternoon. The cannon ball followed a curvilinear direction around the Moon. Had their trajectory once more been modified by meteoric forces? This was to be feared. The projectile's duty, however, was to describe a curve imperturbably determined by the scientific laws of physics. Barbicane was inclined to think this curve would rather be parabolic than hyperbolic. Moreover, that parabola admitted, their cannon ball must have moved quickly through the cone of shadow projecting into space opposite the Sun. This cone is, in effect, greatly-narrowed; as the angular diameter of the Moon is small when compared to that shining radiant body of daylight's sky. Up until now the projectile had floated in that profound shadow. Whatever their velocity was- and it could not have been mediocre- the period of occultation continued. That fact was evident, but perhaps this would not have been the case supposing their trajectory was rigidly parabolic. New problems which tormented the mind of Barbicane, who was truly imprisoned in a circle of unknowns from which he could not disengage.

None of the voyagers considered taking a moment's rest. Each watched for any unexpected facts which might throw a faint new glimmer of light onto the study of uranography, that science of distances between heavenly bodies. Towards 5 o'clock Michel Ardan distributed, under the name of supper, some pieces of bread and cold meat which were speedily consumed without any person abandoning their porthole, whose glass encrusted incessantly from the condensation of their breath.

At a quarter to 6 in the evening Nicholl, armed with a small telescope, took sight towards the southern meridional border of the Moon following in their direction. Several points of light stood out against the somber screen of the sky. They seemed to him a succession of sharp peaks, in profile like a trembling line. They were very bright and vivid. So appears the terminal line of the Moon when it is presented from one of the octants.

They could not be mistaken. It no longer held an appearance of simple meteors, possessing neither their decorations of sharp luminosity, color nor mobility. No longer could it have been a volcano in eruption. And so Barbicane did not hesitate to make the pronouncement:

"The Sun!" he cried.

"What- the Sun!?" responded Nicholl and Michel Ardan in unison.

"Yes my friends, it is that radiant orb- the very same- which is lighting the summits of those mountains situated on the southern meridional border of the Moon. We are evidentially approaching the south pole!"

"After seeing that we passed the north pole," Michel replied, "we have therefore made it around our satellite!"

"Yes, my brave Michel."

"Then, no more hyperbolas, no more parabolas, no more curves to terrify my brain!"

"None but a closed curve."

"Which is called?"

"An ellipse. Instead of becoming lost in interplanetary space, it is now probable that the projectile actually describes an elliptical orbit around the Moon."

"In truth!"

"It will develop into a satellite."

"Moon of the Moon!" cried Michel Ardan, simultaneously excited and aghast.

"Only, I wish you to observe, my dignified friend," replied Barbicane, "that we are no less perished for that."

"Yes, but in another manner, and well-more pleasantly," responded the carefree Frenchmen with a very amiable smile.

The president of the Gun Club was correct. They carved an elliptical course. The projectile was undoubtedly in an eternal gravitation around the Moon, its own satellite. It was a new star added to the solar world, a microcosm peopled by three inhabitants- which the lack of air would kill in a little while. Hence Barbicane could not rejoice at the now definitive situation, imposed upon the cannon ball from the double influence of the centripetal and centrifugal forces. However it may be, he and his companions would again see the lightened face of the lunar disk. Perhaps their existence would even prolong itself sufficiently for a general survey, one last time, of the full-Earth superbly lit by the rays of the Sun! Perhaps they might even declare one final adieu upon a globe they would never see thereafter!

Then their projectile would become no more than an extinct mass, dead, resembling one of those inert asteroids which circle in the ether. One sole consolation for them was they were finally leaving that unfathomable darkness; they were returning to the light, they were returning to the zone bathed by the Sun's radiance!

Meanwhile those mountains recognized by Barbicane detached themselves more and more from the black mass of the Moon's dark side. They were the *Doerfel* and *Leibnitz Mountains* which dominate the south circumpolar region of the Moon.

All the mountains of the visible lunar hemisphere have been measured to a perfect precision. A perfection that will perhaps be astonishing, and yet however, the methods of hypsography- that is to say, the scientific pursuit of measuring geographical heights- are rigorous. Studies have affirmed the altitude of the mountains on the Moon to no less exactness than the determination of mountains on Earth.

The method generally employed is to measure the shadow created by the mountains, and take account of the height of the Sun at the moment of observation. That measurement is obtained more easily by means of a portable telescope with a reticule of two parallel filaments upon the lens, as it is accepted the real diameter of the lunar disk is known exactly. This method equally permits one to calculate the depths of craters and cavities of the Moon. Galileo made use of it, and since that time, MM. Beer and Moedler have employed it to great success.

Another method, using the tangent rays, may also be applied to the measurement of the lunar landscape reliefs. This application can be performed at the moment when the mountains form distinct luminous points along the line of separation between night and day, which are shining from above the dark obscure sections of the disk. These luminous points are produced by the superior glancing solar rays and determine the limits of the phase. Hence, that measurement of the obscure interval which remains between the luminous point and the region which is lit by the lunar phase as it approaches provides the exact height of that point. But, as one will comprehend, this procedure may only be applied to the mountains on the verges of the line of separation between the hemispheres of shadow and light.

Exasperatingly-so, if Michel Ardan's opinion were required, there is yet a third method which exists; consisting in measuring the profile of lunar mountains outlined on their background by means of a micrometer. A micrometer is an optical instrument that is used to determine the length of both distances and objects. However, this is only applicable to heights along the border of the shining astral body of the night sky.

In any case, one must remark that the measurement of the shadows, the intervals or the profiles can only be executed when, in relation to the observer, the solar rays strike obliquely onto the surface of the Moon. When the rays are striking directly, in a word, the times when the Moon is full, and all shadow is imperiously chased from the disk then observation is not possible.

Galileo, the first, after discovering the existence of lunar mountains employed the method of using the shadows cast to calculate their heights. He attributed to them, as was stated earlier, an average of 4,500 toise- a unit of toise being almost 2 meters. Hevelius only reduced these figures, which Riccioli in contrast doubled. These measurements exaggerated one way or the other. Herschel, armed with better-perfected instruments, approached nearer to the hypsometric truth. However it was discovered, finally, in the reports of modern observers.

MM. Beer and Moedler, the most perfect selenographers in the entire world, have measured 1,095 lunar mountains. Their calculations resulted in six of these mountains being elevated above 5,800 meters, and twenty-two above 4,800 meters. The most highest summit of the Moon measures 7,603 meters; it is therefore inferior to those of the Earth, several of which exceed that altitude by 500 to 600 toise. But one remark regarding that fact. If we compare the respective volumes of the two globes, the lunar mountains are relatively more elevated than terrestrial mountains.

There are many further points of comparison excluded only for brevity's sake, which could further extend one's scientific appreciation about the heights of those lunar mountains.

Now, precisely, the trajectory followed by the projectile was drawn towards that mountainous region of the southern hemisphere where the most enchantingly-beautiful objects of lunar orography lie.

17. Tycho

At 6 o'clock in the evening the projectile passed over the south pole at an altitude of less than 60 kilometers. This was equal to the distance when they had approached the north pole. The elliptical curve maintained its obsequious pattern.

At that moment the voyagers re-entered the section of exalted benefaction from the Sun's rays. Once more they viewed the stars which slowly move across the sky from the orient to the occidental positions. They met that shining radiant astral body of daylight's sky, their Sun, with a triple salute of hurrahs. With the light, heat too was transferred and soon it transpired through the metal walls. The glass repaired to its accustomed appearance. Layers of ice dissipated as though wrought by an enchantment. Immediately, for the sake of economy, their gas was extinguished. Only the apparatus for air consumed its usual quantity.

"Ah," said Nicholl, "This is good, these rays of heat! With what impatience, after a night so long, must the Selenites dotingly wait for the reappearance of that magnificent orb of day!"

"Yes," responded Michel Ardan, directly imbibing upon that splendid ether. "Light and warmth, all of life comes from these!"

During this time the base of the projectile began to gradually tend towards the lunar surface, in a manner which followed an elliptical orb as it moved along. At this position, if the Earth had been in its full phase, Barbicane and his companions would have been able to gaze upon it. But, drowned by the Sun's irradiation, it was demurely invisible.

Another spectacle had attracted their attention; that which was presented by the southern region of the Moon, returned from their field glasses to within an eighth of a league. They did not leave their positions standing beside the porthole and noted all the details of that bizarre continent.

The *Doefel* and *Leibnitz Mountains* formed two groups separated by a small developed depression near the south pole. The first group extended between the pole and the 84th parallel, over that oriental area of the astral body; the second, drawn upon the oriental border, went from 65° latitude to the pole.

On their ridges, capriciously contoured, appeared dazzling sheets just as Father Secchi had first described when he had viewed them through his telescope. With more certitude than the illustrious Roman astronomer, Barbicane could identify their true nature.

"They are covered in snow!" he exclaimed.

"Snow, you say?" questioned Nicholl.

"Yes, Nicholl, the snow on that surface is heavily glazed in ice. Do you see how they reflect rays of light? Lava cooling would never provide a reflection so intense. Hence if water is there, then there is air on the Moon. It may only be a little, I would venture to say, but the fact may no longer be contested!"

No, it could not be contested. And if Barbicane ever returned to the Earth, his notes were a considerable testimony of fact regarding their selenographic observations.

The mountains of *Doefel* and *Leibnitz* rose in the middle of the plains to a modest extent, borne outwards in a succession of indefinite cirques and rings of steep hills. In this region predominated by cirques, those two chains were the only recognizable distinctions. Relatively only slightly-craggy, they project here and there several sharp peaks of which the highest summit measures 7,603 meters.

But the projectile rose above this ensemble and the relief disappeared in that intense dazzling light of the disk. The eyes of the voyagers accustomed to the light and returned to the breathtaking gaze of the lunar landscape's archaic aspects; crude in tone, without degradations of color, without the nuances of shadows, brutal blacks and whites since the light was without diffusion.

Yet the view of this desolate world did not fail to captivate them by its very strangeness. They were promenaded above this chaotic region as though carried along by the wake of breath of some outrageous thunderous storm; watching the summits stream below their feet, excavating the cavities with their eyes, hurtling down rifts, climbing steep ramparts, sounding the mysterious holes, leveling all the crevices. Not a trace of vegetation, no appearance of cities; nothing but these stratifications, these hardened flows of lava, these arid depths polished like immense mirrors which reflected the solar rays with an untenable, unbearable clarity. Nothing in this world grew; it was a world of death, where avalanches, rolling from the summits of mountains, perished soundlessly at the bottom of abysses. They purported movement, but noise of the fracas was utterly absent.

Barbicane established through repeated observations that the reliefs at the border of the disk, although they had been formed by different geological forces to that of the central region, presented uniform conformance. The same circular aggregations, the same resemblances of soil. However, it could be considered that their disposition was not entirely analogous. At the center, in effect, the crust of the Moon was still malleable; subject to the double attraction of the Moon's and the Earth's gravities, agitated towards inverse directions by a radius that prolonged from one to the other. In contrast, at the bordering edges of the disk the lunar attraction is, so to speak, perpendicular to the terrestrial attraction.

It seems that the reliefs upon these soils produced by two different conditions ought to have affected different forms. Yet this had not happened. Nothing had developed from foreign forces. Which justified that remarkable proposition of Arago's: '*No exterior action upon the Moon has contributed to the production of its reliefs*'.

Howsoever in its actual state that world below them, a pure image of death; it was impossible to say that any form of life had ever existed there.

Michel Ardan thought he recognized an agglomeration of ruins, which he announced to Barbicane. It was very near to the 80th parallel at 30° longitude. That piled array of stones, arranged with regularity, had the figure of a vast fortress dominating above the long rifts which had once served as riverbeds in the prehistoric times. Not far away, at a height of 5,646 meters, the mountain rings of *Short*, equal in majesty to the Asiatic Caucasus mountains. Michel Ardan, with his accustomed ardor, submitted this as "evidence" for his fortress.

Beneath this, they perceived the dismantled ramparts of a town; here, the still-intact arch of a portico; there, two or three columns lying about their bases; further along, a succession of cylinders that must have supported the conduits of an aqueduct; besides these, the collapsed pillars of a gigantic bridge, engaged against the walls of the rift. He distinguished all of this, but with an imagination that took such little regard, through the fantasy of his binoculars, that we may distrust his observations. And yet, who could not affirm, who would dare to say that the amicable bachelor had not really seen what his two companions could not see?

Moments were too precious for sacrificing to trivial discussion. The abandoned city of the Selenites, pretending or not, had already disappeared a long way off. The distance of the projectile to the lunar disk tended to increase, and the details of the soil started to become lost in confusing muddles. Only the reliefs, the craters and the plains resisted and stood out clearly against the terminal lines.

To their left drew one of the most beautiful cirques of lunar orography, one of the curiosities of the continent. It was *Newton*, which Barbicane recognized without difficulty by consulting his *Mappa Selenographica*.

Newton is exactly situated by the 77° latitude south and 16° longitude east. It forms a ringed crater, whose ramparts, elevated to 7,264 meters, seem insurmountable.

Barbicane had his companions observe that the height of this mountain above the surrounding plain was far from equaling the profound depths of its crater. The enormous hole evaded all measurement, formed in a dark abyss where the rays of the Sun could never attain their bottom. Here, following the remarks of Humboldt, reigns an absolute obscurity where the light of the Sun and the Earth are prevented from their play. The mythologists could have made it, with good reason, the mouth of hell.

A quiet, indefinable fear crept into their minds as their imaginations encompassed that unfathomable darkness. Yet Barbicane's cold-blooded scientific reasoning prevented any extrapolation of their thoughts.

"*Newton*," said Barbicane, "is the type of perfect ringed mountain which the Earth does not possess any examples. These prove that the formation of the Moon, by way of cooling, is due to violent causes; for, while the reliefs, under the power of its fiery interior, were projected to considerable heights, it's base retired and abated substantially below the level of the surrounding lunar surface."

"I cannot speak," was Michel Ardan's response.

Several minutes after watching *Newton* pass by, the projectile directly carried them over the annular ringed mountains of *Moret*. It was not far from the summits of *Blancanus*, and towards 7 o'clock in the evening they attained the cirque of *Clavius*.

That cirque, one of the most remarkable on the disk, is situated by 58° latitude south and 15° longitude east. Its height is estimated to be 7,091 meters. The voyagers, 400 kilometers distant, reduced to 4 by their binoculars and small collapsible telescopes, could admire the complete form of that vast crater.

"Terrestrial craters," Barbicane told them, "are but molehills compared to the volcanoes on the Moon. In measuring those ancient craters formed by the first eruptions of Vesuvius and Etna on Earth, they were found to be no wider than 6,000 meters. In France, the cirque of Cantal is counted at 10 kilometers; at Ceyland, the island cirque, 70 kilometers and is considered the largest on the globe. But what of those diameters when considering that of *Clavius*, which our line of trajectory travels above at this moment?"

"What is the width?" demanded Nicholl.

"It is 227 kilometers," answered Barbicane. "The cirque, it is true, is the most significant on the Moon; but there are many others who well-measure 200, 150 or 100 kilometers!"

"Ah, my friends," cried Michel, "can you picture to yourselves what this peaceful, shining astral body of the night sky must have resembled? When the craters, reverberating with thunders, vomited all at the same time torrents of lava, deluges of stones, fuming clouds and the layers of flames! What a prodigious spectacle then, and now what degeneration! This Moon is no more than a putridly-sick carcass of fireworks whose bangers, rockets, streamers and catherine wheels, after a superb bang and flash, have left behind nothing more than their sad and wretchedly-empty fissured pyrotechnic cartons. Who can say the cause, the reason, the justification for these cataclysms?"

Barbicane did not hear Michel Ardan. He contemplated the ramparts of *Clavius*, formed by large mountains over several leagues thickness. At the depths of that immense cavity were the hollows of hundreds of small extinct craters which riddled the soil like foam, and which were dominated by a peak of 5,000 meters.

All around the plain took on a desolate aspect. Nothing was arid like those reliefs, nothing was as melancholy like the ruins of those mountains, and, if one may express themselves so, these fragments of peaks and mounts which jutted out of the soil! The satellite appeared to have experienced an explosive burst at this location.

The projectile always advanced, and the chaos did not alter. The cirques, the craters, the collapsed mountains succeeded one another incessantly. No more plains, no more seas. An interminable Switzerland and Norway. And finally, at the center of that region of crevices, at the culminating point, a supremely splendid mountain of that lunar disk; the ebullient *Tycho*, whose posterity will forever preserve the name of that illustrious astronomer of Denmark.

In observing the full Moon in a cloudless sky, there is no one who has not remarked about that brilliant point of the southern hemisphere. Michel Ardan, to qualify his words, employed all the metaphors which could furnish his imagination. For him, that *Tycho*, ardent focus of light, a center of irradiation, a crater of expurgatorial rays! It was the central hub of a spoked wheel, a star which serrated the disk with its silver tentacles, an immense eye replete with flames, a wreathed nimbus cut for the head of Pluto! It was a star launched by the hands of our Creator, which had been crashed against the lunar face!

Tycho forms such a concentration of light that the inhabitants of Earth may perceive it without telescope, although it is at a distance of 100,000 leagues! One can imagine then what intensity it developed in the eyes of observers placed only 150 leagues away! And through the pure ether it shone with unbearable glittering sparkle, so that Barbicane and his friends blackened the lenses of their binoculars with the fumes arising from the gas flame in order to reduce the glare's intensity. Then, mutely, with difficulty emitting a few interjections of admiration, they contemplated that massive place. All their sentiments, all their impressions were concentrated upon that vision, which, under violent emotions, one entirely concentrates into their heart.

Tycho is part of that system of radiating mountains, like *Aristarchus* and

Copernicus. But of them all it is the most complete, the most accentuated and irrefutable proof of that terrifying volcanic activity to which the formation of the Moon is due.

Tycho is situated by the 43° meridional latitude and by 12° longitude east. Its center is occupied by a crater 87 kilometers wide. The feature affects a slightly elliptical shape, surrounded by an enclosing ring of annular ramparts, which, to the east and the west overlook the exterior plains by a height of 5,000 meters. It is an aggregation of many Mount Blancs, arranged around a communal center and crowned by reflective radiating beams.

It is that incomparable mountain, which collects the surrounding reliefs into a convergent point, drawn unto the extensive interior of its crater, that photography could never adequately render such magnificence. It is, indeed, when there is a full Moon that *Tycho* reveals all of its splendor. There, when the shadows have been banished, the shortening of one's perspective disappears and the whole ordeal becomes bleached white. It is a sorrowful circumstance, for that strange region would be a curiosity to all others were it possible to reproduce with perfect accuracy. A vast accumulation of holes, craters, cirques and vertiginous networks of crests; and then, endlessly unraveling before the eye, a whole system of volcanoes jutting from the soil as though they were formed from pustules. One may comprehend how the bubbles of the central eruption have retained their initial forms. Crystalized in their cooling, they are stereotypes of that initial aspect in times past when the Moon was under the influence of plutonic forces.

The distance which separated the voyagers from those ringed mountain peaks of *Tycho* was not to such a considerable extent that they could not recover its principle details. Even on the embankment forming the circumvallation of *Tycho*, hanging from the flanks of steep interior and exterior slopes, the mountains rose like gigantic terraces. They appeared more elevated towards the west than the east by 300 or 400 feet. There was not any system of terrestrial castrametation comparable to that natural formation. A town built at the bottom of that circular cavity would have been absolutely inaccessible.

Inaccessible and marvelously played over the soil so accidentally, the results were picturesque! Nature had indeed not left an empty plate at the bottom of the crater. It possessed a special orography, a system of mountains which made it like a world of its own. The voyagers distinguished clearly the cones, the central hills, the remarkable movements of the terrain, naturally disposed to receive the masterpieces of that selenographical architecture. There was a place to design a temple, here an emplacement for a forum, and then straight ahead, the foundations for a palace, and over that, a plateau for a citadel. Over all this stood a central mountain of 1,500 feet. A vast circuit, which could have held the Rome of antiquity ten times over!

"Ah," exclaimed Michel Ardan in enthusiasm at the view. "What a grandiose town might be constructed within the ring of these mountains! Tranquil city, peaceful refuge, a place beyond all the miseries of humans! How well they could live there, calm and isolated, all the misanthropes, all the haters of humanity, all those disgusted by social life!"

"All! It would be too small for all of them!" Barbicane responded simply.

18. Grave Questions

Meanwhile, the projectile had passed the encircling walls of *Tycho*. Barbicane and his two companions then observed with the most-scrupulous attention the brilliant rays of that curious mountain dispersed so curiously across all the horizons.

What is that radiant aureole? What geological phenomenon had designed those ardent beams? Rightly-so, the question preoccupied Barbicane.

Underneath his eyes, indeed, elongated in all directions luminous furrows rolled. High at their edges and concave in their middle, some as wide as 20 kilometers, the others as wide as 50. These brilliant trains in certain places extended as far as 300 leagues to *Tycho* and seemed to cover- especially towards the east, the north-east and north- half of the meridional hemisphere. One of these jets extended until the *Cirque of Neander*, situated on the 40th meridian. One other followed in that district and furrowed into the *Sea of Nectar*, breaking against the *Pyrenees* after it ran 400 leagues. There were others, towards the west, covering the luminous network of the *Sea of Clouds* and the *Sea of Humors*.

What was the origin of those sparkling rays which appeared on the plains as they did upon the reliefs, from what great heights they had fused? All shared a common center, the crater of *Tycho*. They all emanated from here.

Herschel attributed their brilliant aspect to the ancient currents of lava hardened by the cold, an opinion that has not been adopted by many. The other astronomers have seen in these inexplicable rays a kind of moraines, strewn rocks collected below glaciers, a range of erratic blocks, credited to have been ejected during the period time when *Tycho* formed.

"And why not?" asked Nicholl of Barbicane, who had related the diverse opinions on this repulsion.

"Because the regularity of those luminous lines, and the violence necessary to send volcanic matter to such distances, is inexplicable."

"Good heavens!" Michel Ardan responded. "It strikes me there is quite a simple explanation of the origin of these rays."

"Really?" said Barbicane.

"Really," replied Michel. "It would be sufficient to say a vast starburst, resembling to that which is produced by the shock of a ball or stone against a pane of glass!"

"Good!" replied Barbicane humorously. "And what hand could possess sufficient power to launch a rock to create such a shock?"

"The hand is not necessary," answered Michel, who was not riled. "And, as to a stone- allow for it to be a comet."

"Ah! Those comets!" exclaimed Barbicane. "And abuse heaped upon them! My brave Michel, your explanation is not bad, but your comet is useless. The shock which produced that crack could only have originated from the inside of the planetoid. A violent contraction of the lunar crust, under the inward-pressure of cooling, could have been sufficient to print that gigantic star shape."

"Away with your contraction, something more like lunar colic!" chided Michel Ardan.

"Besides," added Barbicane, "this opinion is that of the English scientist, Nasmyth; and to me seems to adequately explain the radiant lines of the mountains."

"'That Nasymth was not a complete fool!" Michel replied.

For a long time the voyagers, who could not be blasé towards such a spectacle, admired the splendors of *Tycho*. Their projectile, soaked in waves of light, in that double irradiation of the Sun and the Moon, must have appeared like an incandescent globe. They had suddenly passed from a considerable cold to an intense heat. Nature was preparing them to become Selenites.

Become Selenites! That idea once again posed the question of the habitability of the Moon. After all they had seen, could the voyagers resolve it? Would they conclude for or against? Michel Ardan incited his two friends to formulate their opinions, asking them squarely if they thought both humans and animals were represented on the lunar world.

"I believe that we can provide a response," said Barbicane: "but, in accordance with my thinking, the question should not put in that form. I request you pose it in another way."

"Pose it your way," responded Michel.

"This is it," replied Barbicane. "The problem is two-fold, and demands a double solution. Is the Moon habitable? And, was the Moon ever inhabited?"

"Excellent," responded Nicholl. "First let us discover if the Moon is habitable."

"To speak truthfully, I know nothing," declared Michel.

"And for me, I respond negatively," replied Barbicane. "In its actual state, which with certainty the envelope of atmosphere is very reduced, it's seas for the most part parched dry, the water insufficient, the vegetation restrained, the sudden alternation between cold and hot, the nights and days of 354 hours; overall the Moon does not strike me as habitable, nor does it seem propitious to the development of an animal kingdom, nor is it sufficient for the needs of existence- in the way we comprehend it."

"I agree," Nicholl said. "But is not the Moon habitable for those organized with different constitutions to ourselves?"

"For that question," replied Barbicane, "it is more difficult to respond. I shall attempt to however, but I ask you Nicholl if you believe that movement is a necessary result of life, whatever the sort of its internal organization?"

"Without any doubt," answered Nicholl.

"Ah well, my dignified companion, my response to you is that we have observed the lunar continents at a distance of 500 meters and we saw nothing moving on the surface of the Moon. The presence of any sort of humanity would have been betrayed by evidence of their appropriations, by diverse constructions, even by their ruins. So, what have we seen? Everywhere and always the geological works of nature, never the works of man. Hence, if the representatives of the animal kingdom exist on the Moon, they must have hidden in those unfathomable cavities which we saw but could not penetrate with our eyes. I cannot admit this, for they would have left traces of their passage on the plains which are without the cover of atmospheric layers, however slight their elevation is. So, traces are not visible in any part. Hence only one hypothesis remains, which is for a race that lives entirely without movement- and if that is life, it is very strange!"

"It is as much to say living creatures which do not live," Michel considered philosophically.

"Precisely," responded Barbicane. "Which for us does not make any sense."

"Then, we may form our opinion," said Michel.

"Yes," agreed Nicholl.

"Ah well," replied Michel Ardan, "The scientific commission formed in the projectile of the Gun Club, after seeing their arguments based upon the facts of new observation, decide in a unanimous voice about the question of the actual habitability of the Moon: No, the Moon is not habitable."

This decision was consigned by the president Barbicane into his journal of records noting the verbal process of their meeting on the 6th December.

"Now," said Nicholl, "attacking the second question, an indispensable compliment of the first. I therefore ask the honorable commission: If the Moon is not habitable, was it ever inhabited?"

"The citizen Barbicane is to speak," said Michel Ardan.

"My friends, responded Barbicane, "I did not attend this voyage in order to form an opinion on the past habitability of our satellite. Despite this, I will add that my personal observations still allow me to confirm an opinion. I believe, I even affirm that the Moon was inhabited by a human race with an organic constitution like ours and which produced animals that anatomically conformed to our terrestrial animals; but I must declare that these races of humans and animals have had their time and they are now forever extinct!"

"Then," asked Michel, "the Moon must be older than the Earth?"

"No," answered Barbicane with conviction, "although it is a world that has aged more-quickly, and whose formation and deformation have been more rapid. Relatively, the organizational forces of matter were abundantly more violent inside the interior of the Moon than the interior of the terrestrial globe. The actual state of the disk- crevassed, tormented, and exploded proves this prescription. The Moon and the Earth were no more than masses of gas in their originality. These gasses have passed into a liquid state under many diverse influences, and the solid mass is then formed later. But very certainly, our own planet existed in a state of gas or liquid still whilst the Moon had solidified by cooling, and developed habitability."

"I believe it," supported Nicholl.

"Then," Barbicane continued, "an atmosphere surrounded it. The water, contained by that gaseous envelope, was prevented from evaporating. Under the influence of air and water, the light, the solar warmth, the geological warmth from within, the vegetation seized continents who prepared to receive them and with certainty life manifested there in that epoch; for nature does not dispense her actions in vain, and a world if it is marvelously habitable is by necessity inhabited."

"However," replied Nicholl, "many of those phenomena inherent to the motion of our satellite might have hampered the development of the vegetable and animal kingdoms. These days and nights of 354 hours, for example?"

"At our terrestrial poles," argued Michel, "they endure 6 months!"

"An argument of little value, because here the poles are not inhabited."

"It should be noted, my friends," maintained Barbicane, "that if, in the actual state of the Moon, the long nights and the long days create differences in temperature insupportable for organisms, it would not have been so during those epochs of prehistoric times. The atmosphere enveloped the disk in a mantle of fluid. The vapors which were disposed about underneath formed the clouds. That natural screen tempered the ardor of solar rays and contained the radiated heat during the nocturnal cycle. Light, just as heat, can diffuse in the air. And that forms an equilibrium between those influences which no longer exists, now that the atmosphere has almost disappeared entirely. Furthermore, I shall now astonish you..."

"Astonish us," encouraged Michel Ardan.

"I am willing to imagine that in the epoch when the Moon was inhabited, the nights and days did not extend for the duration of 354 hours!"

"And why?" Nicholl vehemently demanded.

"Because, very probably then, the movement of the rotation of the Moon on its axis did not equal it movement of revolution, an equality which now presents to each point on the disk a period of 15 days of solar rays activity."

"Be that as it may," questioned Nicholl, "why shouldn't these two movements have been equal, as they are now?"

"Because that equality has been decided by the attraction of terrestrial gravity. And who is it that can say this attraction possessed sufficient power to modify the movements of the Moon, during an epoch when the Earth was no more than fluids?"

"A fact," conceded Nicholl. "And who can say that the Moon was always a satellite of Earth?"

"And who can say," cried Michel Ardan, "that the Moon had not existed well before the Earth?"

Their imaginations exported them into fields of infinite hypothesis. Barbicane wished they would refrain.

"These are hereby," said he, "speculations too high, the problems are really unsolvable. Do not engage in them. Let us only admit the insufficiency of primordial attraction; and then, by the inequality of the twin motions of rotation and revolution, the days and the nights could have succeeded one another on the Moon as they succeed each other on the Earth. Besides, even without these conditions, life would have been possible."

"And so afterwards," asked Michel Ardan, "humanity had disappeared from the Moon?"

"Yes," concluded Barbicane, "after, no doubt, persisting for thousands of centuries' duration. But little by little, their atmosphere rarified, the disk gradually became uninhabitable, as the terrestrial globe will one day develop by its own cooling."

"By its own cooling?"

"Undoubtedly," Barbicane answered with nonchalance. "By measures, as the interior fires extinguished, the incandescent matters concentrated and after a time the lunar crust cooled. Bit by bit the consequences of this phenomenon are produced: this disappearance of all the organisms, the disappearance of all the vegetation. Soon the air becomes rarified, very probably drawn-off by the terrestrial attraction; and the air responsible for respiration disappears, so too the water disappears by way of evaporation. At that epoch the Moon, becoming uninhabitable, could never be inhabitable again. It is a dead world: such as it appears today."

"And this same sort of peril has been reserved for the Earth?"

"Quite probably."

"But when?"

"When the planetary cooling of the crust renders it uninhabitable."

"And have they calculated the time which our unfortunate planet will take to cool?"

"There is no doubt."

"And you understand these calculations?"

"Perfectly."

"Then speak them, you sullen scientist!" cried Michel Ardan. "You make me to boil with impatience."

"Very well, my brave Michel," responded the tranquil Barbicane. "As we know what the diminution in temperature the Earth is subject to in the lapse of one century, so, after certain calculations, the mean temperature will approach zero after a period of 400,000 years!"

"400,000 years!" cried Michel. "Ah! I can breathe! Really, you terrify me! I had entertained, in my imagination, that we had not more than 50,000 years to live!"

Barbicane and Nicholl could not prevent themselves from laughing at the sincere worries of their companion. Then Nicholl, who wished to draw their final conclusion, posed the second question again, which they had been discussing.

"The Moon- has is it been inhabited?"

The response was for the affirmative, unanimously.

But during that discussion- fruitful in theories which were slightly hazardous and excellently summarizing the general ideas acquired by science until that point- the projectile raced rapidly towards the lunar equator, regularly lengthening its height above the disk. They had passed the cirque of *Wilhelm* and the 40th parallel at a distance of 800 kilometers. Then, leaving to their right *Pitatus* on the 30th degree, that prolonged southwards towards that *Sea of Clouds*, which they had previously approached from the north. Many diverse cirques appeared in confusion upon that white bleached clarity of the full Moon: *Bouillaud*, *Purbach*, the shape of which was almost square with a central crater; then *Arzachel* whose interior mountain was brilliant with an indefinable shine.

And finally, with the projectile forever lengthening away from the Moon, the lineaments grew indistinct to the eyes of the voyagers, the Mountains merged confusedly into the distance- and of all that marvelously bizarre and alien ensemble belonging to the satellite of Earth, there soon remained nothing more than an imperishable memory.

19. Struggle against the Impossible

For a length of time's duration Barbicane and his companions, mute and pensive, regarded that world which they had only viewed from afar- just as Moses had seen the land of Canaan- and which they were exceeding away from, without return. The position of the projectile relative to the Moon had modified and now its base turned towards the Earth.

That change, recorded by Barbicane, left them all surprised. If the cannon ball had gravitated around the satellite following an elliptical orbit, why was their heaviest part not presenting itself to the Moon, just as the Moon endlessly shows its face towards the Earth? An obscure point which they sought to avail themselves upon.

Through observing the path of their projectile, they recognized as they slipped away from the Moon they were following an analogous course to that which they had traced on approach. Within that vehicle they were describing a very-elongated ellipse, which in probability would extend onto the point of equal attraction; where the influences of the Earth and its satellite were neutralized.

Such was the conclusion Barbicane justifiably drew from the observed facts.

Questions fell suddenly, like rain.

"And when we have returned to the dead point, what will happen to us?" Michel Ardan demanded to know.

"It is unknown!" answered Barbicane, somewhat sharply.

"But one might offer one of those hypotheses, I suppose?" beseeched Ardan.

"Two," said Barbicane. "Either the velocity of the velocity is insufficient, and then we will eternally rest motionless inside that line of double attraction..."

"I feel better about the second hypothesis, whatever that may be," Michel said quickly.

"Or otherwise our velocity remains sufficient," continued Barbicane, "and we will repair to our elliptical route- to gravitate eternally around that ancient shining body of our night sky."

"An evolvement of small consolidation," said Michel. "Moving to a state of humble servitude towards the Moon, of which we have taken the habit of considering our servant. And so there we have it- our futures to await!"

Neither Barbicane nor Nicholl responded.

"You are quiet?" Michel stated impatiently.

"There is nothing to respond," said Nicholl.

"There is nothing we can attempt?"

"No," said Barbicane evenly. "You portend to struggle against the impossible?"

"Why not? Should one Frenchman and two Americans recoil from such a word?"

"But what would you have us do?"

"Master the motion which moves us!"

"Master it?"

"Yes," replied Michel animatedly. "Stop or modify it, finally employ it to the accomplishment of our plans."

"And how?"

"It is for you to decide in that regard. If the artillery men are not the masters of their cannon balls, then they are not real artillerists. If the projectile commands the cannoneer, we would fare better to place the cannoneer inside of the cannon! The beautiful scientists, my foot! There you have it, who do not know what will become of me, after I was induced..."

"Induced!" Barbicane and Nicholl incredulously exclaimed simultaneously.

"There are no recriminations!" said Michel. "Do not pity me! Our promenade through space has given me pleasure! The cannon ball is agreeable to me! But let us venture to do all that is humanely possible for us to plunge and fall somewhere, even if that is not on the Moon."

"We do not ask for anything else, my brave Michel," Barbicane told him kindly. "But the means to do so escapes us."

"We do not possess the power to modify the movement of the projectile?"

"No."

"Nor diminish its velocity?"

"Not even by alleviating some of our weight- throwing things overboard, as does a ship that has been over-burdened by her cargo?"

"What would you eject?" questioned Nicholl. "We do not have any ballast on board. And besides; it seems to me that if lightened in weight, the projectile would move much faster."

"Slower," said Michel.

"Quicker," Nicholl contradicted.

"Neither slower nor quicker," interceded Barbicane, in order to bring his two friends to accordance. "For we are floating through void, and we must not take account of the specific gravity of objects."

"Very well," cried Michel Ardan in a determined tone, "then there is only one more thing for us to do."

"Which is?" asked Nicholl sternly.

"Breakfast!" responded the imperturbably audacious Frenchman, who somehow always managed to apport that magnificent solution onto the most difficult of conjectures.

Indeed, if this operation had no apparent influence on the direction of their projectile, it could at least be tended to without inconvenience; and even with success from the point of view of the stomach. Decidedly, that Michel had nothing but good ideas.

They breakfasted at 2 o'clock in the morning, but the hour held little importance. Michel served his regular menu, crowned with a pleasant bottle drawn from his secret wine cellar. If any ideas did not heap themselves upon their brains, it was the despair of the *Chambertin* of 1863 vintage.

When their repast terminated, the observations commenced.

Around the projectile, maintaining the same invariable distance, the objects they had jettisoned still followed outside. Evidentially the cannon ball in its movement of translation around the Moon had not traversed any atmosphere, for the specific weights of these diverse objects with their lower momentum would have modified their relative march.

On the side of the terrestrial globe, nothing to be seen. The Earth had counted but one more day, having turned anew at midnight; and two days were still needed to pass before its crescent, disengaged from the solar rays, would serve as a clock for the Selenites- because in its movement of translation, each point of the planet returns and endlessly passes by every 24 hours over the same lunar meridian.

On the side of the Moon, the spectacle was entirely different. That brilliant heavenly body was in all of its splendor in the midst of innumerable constellations whose rays, in the stillness of their purity, did not tremble or agitate. On the disk, the plains once again had the resemblance of that same dark taint as when they are viewed from Earth. The rest of its nimbus demurely tinkled and sparkled; and in the midst of that general dazzling reflection, Tycho stood detached once more, like its own sun.

Barbicane had not any facility to apprise the velocity of the projectile, but reasoned accordingly that their velocity must begin to diminish with uniformity in conformance to the laws of physics.

Indeed, having admitted that the cannon ball described an orbit around the Moon, that orbit would necessarily be elliptical. Science proves that this must be so. There is not any object moving in a circular path around a planetary body which can fail this fundamental law. All the objects who orbit in space are described as elliptical- those satellites around the planets, those planets around the Sun, and the Sun around that mysterious astral body which serves as the central pivot of the galaxy. Why should the projectile of the Gun Club evade that natural arrangement?

So, in the elliptical orbits, the attracting body always occupies the focus of the ellipse. The satellite finds itself then at one moment closer and in another moment further away from around the astral orb which it gravitates. When the Earth is its most-nearest to the Sun it is in the perihelion, and in the aphelion at the most elongated point. Regarding the Moon- it is the most-closest to the Earth at its perigee, and at the longest point in its apogee. To employ the analogous expressions which enriches the language of astronomers, if our projectile remains demurely in its state as a satellite around the Moon we must say that it travels through its 'aposelene' at the furthermost point, and its 'periselene' at the nearest.

In the latter case, the projectile attains its maximum velocity and in the former case, it reaches its minimum. Here, they were evidently progressing towards the aposelenitical position and Barbicane had good reason to expect their velocity would decrease up until that point; then restore its speed little by little in measures until they re-approached the Moon. That velocity might even become annulled, if their orbit intersected with the point of neutrality; where the Earth's gravitational force was equivalent to the Moon's.

Barbicane quietly studied the consequences of the two different situations to himself, racking his mind searchingly in order to grasp some course of action, and was on the verge of their final conclusions when his thoughts were jarringly interrupted by a cry from Michel Ardan.

"Good heavens!" he exclaimed. "I declare that frankly we are imbeciles!"

"I do not say we are not," responded Barbicane. "But why?"

"Because we have a very simple means to retard that velocity which is moving us towards the Moon, and we do not make use of it!"

"And what are the means?"

"To utilize the force of recoil that lies enclosed in those rocket flares."

"As a fact!" said Nicholl enthusiastically, immediately comprehending Michel Ardan's wonderful idea.

"We are yet to utilize that force," said Barbicane in his typical measured tones, "it is true. But we shall make use of it." And then he laughed to himself delightedly.

"When?" demanded Michel.

"When the moment is upon us. Notice, my friends, that in the position our projectile currently affects- a position more oblique in respect to the lunar disk- those rocket flares, in modifying our direction, might adversely send us further from the Moon? So then, it is good for us to watch the Moon and wait."

"Why, it is essential for us to do so," concurred Michel.

"Wait then. By an inexplicable influence, the projectile is tending to bring its base back towards the Earth. It is probable that at the point of equal attraction the conical cap will be rigorously redirected towards the Moon. At that moment, we can only hope that our velocity will be annulled. This will be the instant to act, and under the effort of those flare rockets we can, perhaps, provoke a fall directly onto the surface of the lunar disk."

"Bravo!" cheered Michel.

"It is what we could not do in our first passage through the dead point, because the projectile had already attained a powerful velocity that was too considerable."

"Excellently reasoned," approved Nicholl.

"Let us wait," replied Barbicane, "and gather together all the chances to our side; and after so much seeming so desperate, I do declare that I dare to believe we may attain our target!"

That conclusion emitted the hips and the hurrahs from Michel Ardan. And not one of those audacious fools remembered the question they had had resolved in the negative: No! The Moon is not inhabited. No! The Moon is probably not habitable. And yet, however, they were going to attempt a landing there!

Only one question remained for solving: At what precise moment would the projectile attain that point of equal attraction where the voyagers will gamble it all?

For calculating that moment to within a few seconds of precision, Barbicane needed only to refer to his notes of the voyage and take down the different heights he had evaluated at the lunar parallels. And so, the time required to run the distance situated between the dead point and the south pole would be equal to the distance which had separated the north pole and that point of death. These hours representing the time they had journeyed had been carefully noted, making the calculation easy.

Barbicane found that the position would be attained at 1 o'clock in the morning on the night of the 7th to the 8th December. Now it was 3 o'clock in the morning, on the night of the 6th and 7th December. Hence, if nothing troubled their forward progress, they and the projectile would reach that intended destination in 22 hours.

The flare rockets had been originally positioned as a relent against the fall of the cannon ball onto the Moon, and now these audacious fellows were going to make use of its effects for the absolute opposite purpose. In any way or so, they were prepared and all they must do now was wait for the moment to set them to afire.

"Since there is nothing to be done," said Nicholl, "I have a proposition."

"What is it?" asked Barbicane.

"I propose we sleep."

"What a proposition!"

"It is now 40 hours since we have closed our eyes," said Nicholl. "Several hours of sleep will return all our strength."

"Never," defied Michel.

"Good then," replied Nicholl. "Each must act as they wish. I shall sleep!"

And extending on the divan, Nicholl commenced without delay in snoring as loudly as 48 pound artillery shell.

"Nicholl is full of sense," said Barbicane soon afterwards. "I will imitate him."

Several moments later, he accompanied with his bass notes to the continued baritone sounds of the captain.

"Decidedly," said Michel Ardan to no one else, "these sharply intelligent souls, gentlemen of practicality, oftentimes have opportune ideas."

And, his long legs stretched out, his great arms folded replete under his head, Michel in turn slept.

But this slumber could be neither extensive, nor peaceful. Too many preoccupations rolled in the minds of the three men and a few hours afterwards, towards 7 o'clock in the morning, all three rose to their feet at the same instant.

The projectile always distanced itself from the Moon, inclining more and more their conical part towards its surface. An inexplicable phenomenon just now, but which served as good fortunate for the designs of Barbicane.

17 hours more, and the moment of action would be upon them.

This day appeared long. However bold they might be, the voyagers were vividly aware of the approach of that moment which would decide all- whether they would fall onto the Moon, or sustain an eternal enthrallment within an immutable orbit. Hence they counted out the hours, too slow for their liking; Barbicane and Nicholl obstinately plunged into their calculations, Michel pacing to and fro between those narrow walls and contemplating with those avid eyes the impassive Moon.

Sometimes memories of Earth flashed insights rapidly through their minds. They recalled all their friends at the Gun Club, and especially the dearest of all- J.T. Maston. In that moment, the honorable secretary was occupying his post on the Rocky Mountains. If he could view the projectile upon the mirror of the gigantic telescope, what would he think? After seeing them disappear behind the south pole of the Moon, he would have seen them reappear by the north pole! They had hence become a satellite of a satellite! Had J.T. Maston released to the world that unexpected news? Was this to be the final outcome of that grand enterprise?

Meanwhile their day passed without incident. The terrestrial midnight arrived. The 8th of December proceeded to commence. An hour more and they reached point of equal attraction. What velocity animated the projectile? They could not arrive at an estimation. But no error could distort the calculations of Barbicane. At 1 hour in the morning, their speed ought to have become nothing.

Besides, another phenomenon would develop marking the intersection of the projectile's path with the line of neutrality. In that place the two attractions of terrestrial and lunar gravity annulled one another. The object would have 'weight' no more. This singular fact, whose curious nature had surprised Barbicane and his companions, would be reproduced as they returned to those identical conditions. It was at that precise moment they were required to act.

Already the conical cap of the projectile had noticeably turned towards the lunar disk. The cannon ball presented itself in the manner which would enable them to utilize the total recoil produced by the apparatus of those flare rockets. Hence chances were pronounced in the voyagers' favor. If the velocity of the projectile reached an absolute annulment at the point of neutrality; one determined movement towards the Moon would be sufficient, however slight upon their entombed craft, to propel them into a downward plunge upon the lunar surface.

"5 minutes to 1 o'clock," rang Nicholl, a clock unto himself.

"All is prepared," Michel Ardan diligently reported, and as supervisor moved the preparatory match towards the flame of gas which would be used to ignite the rockets.

"Wait," instructed Barbicane, tending to the pocket watch in his hand.

At that moment, the gravity no longer produced its usual effect. The voyagers sensed their insides become completely disparate. If they had not precisely attained that point of neutrality, they were touching upon it!...

"1 hour!" barked Barbicane.

Michel Ardan put the flaming match to the detonation apparatus, whose function was to bring the fuses of the rockets together into one wick. They communicated the combustion instantly down into the gun barrels which directed the rocket flares. However, through the portholes, Barbicane perceived that the fuses uselessly prolonged in their deflagration; and then extinguished immediately.

The projectile experienced a certain shock which was quite noticeably felt within.

The three friends regarded one another, listening without speaking, scarcely breathing. One might have heard the beating of their hearts in the midst of that absolute silence.

"Are we falling?" Michel Ardan asked finally.

"No," responded Nicholl. "Because the base of the projectile is not turning towards the lunar disk!"

At that moment, Barbicane, leaving the glass of the porthole window, faced his two companions. He had become dreadfully pale, his forehead creased, his lips contracted.

"We are plunging!" said he.

"Ah!" cried Michel Ardan with satisfaction. "Towards the Moon?"

"Towards the Earth!" replied Barbicane.

"The devil!" Michel exclaimed, and then added philosophically: "Good! When entering the projectile, we did not well-doubt that it would be easy to leave!"

In effect, their appalling downward plunge had commenced. The velocity inertially-conserved by the projectile had moved them out past the dead point. The explosions of the flare rockets could not mitigate such force. The projectile, entangled by velocity, drew them beyond the line of neutrality and had caused them to return. The laws of physics required, in their elliptical orbit, for the voyagers to go by every point they had earlier passed through.

It was to be a terrible fall, from a height of 78,000 leagues, and no springs to soften their impact. According to the laws of ballistics, the projectile would strike the Earth with a velocity equal to the force which had propelled them out of the Columbiad cannon- a speed of 16,000 meters in the last second!

And, for delivering some figures of comparison, we calculate that an object launched from the high towers of the Notre Dame cathedral, which is at an altitude of 200 feet, will arrive on the pavement at a velocity of 120 leagues an hour. Here the projectile would strike the Earth with a velocity of 57,600 leagues an hour- four hundred and eighty times that speed!

"We are lost," said Nicholl rigidly.

"Very well! If we are to die," responded Barbicane with a sort of religious fervor on his face, "the results of our voyage will be magnificently and widely spread. It is the secrets of his own which God will tell us! In the other life, the soul has no further needs, not for knowledge, nor any machines or engines! It identifies with eternal wisdom!"

"In fact," replied Michel Ardan, "the other world shall give us little consolation for not having attained that damned astral body they call the Moon!"

Barbicane crossed his arms over his chest in a gesture of sublime resignation.

"So is the will of heaven!"

20. The Soundings of the *Susquehanna*

"And well, lieutenant, what are our soundings?"

"I believe, sir, that our operation is reaching its final touch," replied Lieutenant Bronsfield. "But who would have considered finding such a depth so close to land, and only 100 leagues from the American coast?"

"Indeed, Bronsfield, it is a powerful depression," said Captain Bloomsberry. "There exists in this place a submarine valley created by Humboldt's current which runs along the American coast as far as the straits of Magellan."

"Those are great depths captain," replied the lieutenant. "Unfavorable for laying telegraphic cables. Better upon a smooth and level plateau, such as that which supports the American cable between Valentia and Newfoundland."

"I agree, Bronsfield. And, with your permission lieutenant, where are we now?"

"Sir," replied Bronsfield, "at this moment we have 21,500 feet of line put out and the sounding ball has not yet touched the bottom, for then it would wind itself back on its own."

"An ingenious invention is that apparatus by Brooke," said Captain Bloomsberry. "It permits us to obtain soundings to a fine exactness."

"Touch!" at that moment cried one of the men at the fore-wheel, who was supervising the operation.

The captain and lieutenant returned to the quarterdeck.

"What depth do we have then?" demanded the captain.

"21,762 feet," responded the lieutenant and he inscribed those numbers into his notebook.

"Excellent, Bronsfield," said the captain. "I shall enter this result into my charts. Now, haul that sounder onboard. It will be several hours work. During that time the engineer can light the furnaces, and we shall be prepared to depart as soon as you have finished. It is 10 o'clock in the evening, and if you will excuse me, I shall retire for the day."

"Please do, sir, please do!" obligingly responded Lieutenant Bronsfield.

The captain of the *Susquehanna*, as brave as a man should be, very humble servant to his officers, returned to his cabin. Taking a glass of brandy with interminable terminology he gave his satisfaction to the head steward, then lay down- and not before complimenting his domestic servant for the neatness of his bedding- slept a peaceful sleep.

It was then 10 o'clock in the evening. The 11th day of the month of December was nearing its close in a magnificent night.

The *Susquehanna* of the United States Navy, a corvette of 500 horsepower, occupied with the operation of taking soundings of the depths of the Pacific Ocean, was approximately 100 leagues off the American coast; along the traverse of that long peninsula which stretches down to the coast of Mexico.

The wind had little by little turned sluggish. There was no agitation disturbing the layers of air. The pennant of the corvette, motionless, inert, hung from the mast as though that colorful parrot- a parrakeet- had swung itself upside down.

The Captain Jonathon Bloomsbury, close cousin of Colonel Bloomsbury- one of the most-ardent members of the Gun Club- who had married a Horschbidden, an aunt of the captain and daughter of an honorable Kentuckian merchant... Captain Bloomsbury could not have wished for finer weather to bring about a successful close to the delicate operations of soundage. This corvette had felt nothing of that vast tempest which, having sweeping away the clouds accumulated over the Rocky Mountains, permitted the observation of the famous projectile's path. Everything had gone agreeably-well, and he had not forgotten to stop and thank the sky with the fervor of a presbyterian.

Their series of soundings had been executed by the *Susquehanna* with the goal of reconnoitering the most favorable depths for the establishment of an submarine cable, which would relay between the Hawaiian Islands with the coast of America.

That vast project had been the initiative of a powerful company. Its director, the intelligent Cyrus Field, intended to even cover all the isles of Oceania in an extensive electrical network- an immense enterprise to the dignity of American genius.

To that end the corvette *Susquehanna* had been confined for its initial operations of sounding. During the night between 11th and 12th of December, she travelled exactly 27° 7' latitude north and 41° 37' longitude west of the meridian of Washington.

The Moon, then in its last quarter, commenced to rise above the horizon.

After the departure of Captain Bloomsbury, Lieutenant Bronsfield had met with several of his officers on the foredeck. At the Moon's apparition, their thoughts hovered towards that shining astral body of the night sky which all eyes of the hemisphere then contemplated. The best nautical binoculars could not have discovered the projectile passing errantly around the globe; and yet, however, all were turned towards the very same disk that glinted brilliantly into the eyes of the millions whose own gaze, at the same moment, rested upon it.

"They have been departed for 10 days," then said the Lieutenant Bronsfield. "What has become of them?"

"They will have arrived, my lieutenant," declared a young midshipman. "And they will be doing what all travellers do when they have arrived in a new country- taking a stroll!"

"I am certain, because you tell me, my young friend," Lieutenant Bronsfield responded humorously.

"However," replied another officer, "I would not set their arrival in doubt. The projectile was due to reach the Moon at the moment it was full, on the 5th at midnight. We are now on the 11th December, which is 6 days. So, in six times 24 hours, without the obscurity of night, they would have had time to install themselves comfortably. I can just imagine them, our brave compatriots, encamped at the base of some valley beside the banks of a gurgling Moon-stream that glints in their daylight; nearby the projectile is half-buried from the fall of their landing amidst stones of volcanic debris. That Captain Nicholl is commencing his surveying operations, the president Barbicane attending to his journal records of their passage and Michel Ardan embalming the solitude of that lunar landscape with the perfume of his cigars that are making it smell like London..."

"Yes! It certainly is so, it is so!" exclaimed the young midshipman, enthused with this idealistic description supplied by his superior.

"I should like to believe it," responded the Lieutenant Bronsfield, whose sentimentality had hardly been swayed. "Unfortunately, direct news from the lunar world has been recalcitrant."

"Pardon, my lieutenant," said the midshipman innocently, "but cannot the president Barbicane write?"

A burst of laughter was the response he received.

"Not with post-stamped letters," replied the lively young man. "The Postal Office has nothing to see there."

"Hence it is the lines belonging to the Telegraphic Administration that are at fault?" demanded one of the officer ironically.

"Not at all," responded the midshipman without losing countenance. "But it is very easy to establish graphic communication with Earth."

"And how?"

"By means of the telescope built at Long's Peak. You will know that it brings the Moon to two leagues' distance, and it permits the astronomers to even see on the surface objects that are only 9 feet in diameter. And well, so our industrious friends can construct a gigantic alphabet! They can write their words one hundred toises long, and their sentences as long as 1 league, and this empowers them to send us their news!"

They applauded the young midshipman loudly to whom it must be allowed had demonstrated a certain imagination. Even Lieutenant Bronsfield acknowledged that the idea was executable. He added that rays of light concentrated by means of concave mirrors could also establish direct communications; in effect, these rays would also be visible from the surface of Venus or Mars, as the planet Neptune is on Earth. He finished his discourse by stating that the brilliant points observed on the nearest planets could very well be in fact signals to the Earth. But he then observed that if, by those means, they were able to see the news from that lunar world; they would not be able to send news from the terrestrial world unless the Selenites also had at their disposal those instruments of their own, which allowed for making distant observations.

"Evidentially," responded one of the officers. "But what has become of those voyagers, what have they done, what have they seen? Above all that is what interest us. Besides, if the experiment has succeeded, and there is no doubt it has, they will recommence another. The Columbiad cannon is forever encased in the Florida soil. It is then only the question of the cannon ball and powder, and each time the Moon passes through zenith, they will send another cargo of visitors."

"It is evident," responded Lieutenant Bronsfield, "that J.T. Maston will one day go to join his friends."

"If he will have me," exclaimed the young midshipman, "I am prepared to accompany him."

"Oh! There will be no lack of amateurs," replied Bronsfield, "and if they were allowed, half the inhabitants of Earth would soon emigrate to the Moon!"

That conversation between the officers of the *Susquehanna* prolonged until nearly 1 o'clock in the morning. We cannot say what dizzying systems, what backwards theories were emitted by these boldly-spirited men. Since the attempt of Barbicane there seemed nothing that was impossible for the Americans. They had already projected an expedition, not just a commission of scientists, but an entire colony towards the Selenitic shores; a whole army with infantry, artillery and cavalry dispatched for lunar conquest.

At 1 hour in the morning, still the complete haulage of the sounding equipment in was yet to be achieved. 10,000 feet remained below, which necessitated more work for several hours. Following the orders of their commander, the fires below had been stoked and their steam pressure mounted. The *Susquehanna* was ready to depart at that instant even.

In that moment- it was 1 hour and 17 minutes past midnight- Lieutenant Bronsfield had been feeling inclined to quit the quarterdecks and return to his cabin; when his attention was caught by a distant ringing, a humming sound that was entirely unexpected.

He and his comrades initially thought that ringing hum came from above decks, and was being produced by the smoke funnel connected to the steam engines underneath their feet; but, reclining their heads to locate the source of the sound, their ears reported the noise was emanating from the highest and remotest atmospheric layers of air above.

There was no time to interrogate one another when the ringing hum took upon a terrifying intensity, and suddenly before their eyes there bloomed a cloud of fire with the appearance of an enormous meteor, enflamed into a conflagration by the rapidity of its course through the sky's abrasive layers of atmosphere.

The vision of that mass ignited grandly before their gaze, and, plunging with the sound of a tornedo's thunder upon the bowsprit, smashed it closely to its stem, and was destroyed by the waves with deafening rumbles!

Several feet closer and the *Susquehanna* would have sunk with all on board!

At that instant, Captain Bloomsbury appeared half-clothed, and dashed onto the foredeck towards where all the officers had gathered:

"Permit me to interrupt, gentlemen, but what has just occurred?" he demanded politely.

And the midshipman, speaking as though he were the echo for all of them, cried out:

"Commander, it is 'they'- who have returned!"

21. The Recall of J.T. Maston

There was a grand emotion onboard the *Susquehanna*. Officers and seamen forgot that terrible danger which they had just encountered, the possibility of being crushed and sunk to the depths. They could not think but for the catastrophe which had terminated the space voyage. And if so hence the most audacious enterprise of both ancient and modern times had cost the lives of those three hardy adventurers who dared attempt it.

"It is 'they'- who have returned," the young midshipman had cried, and all comprehended who he was referring to. No one had any doubt that the fiery meteoric bolide was anything other than the projectile of the Gun Club. As to the voyagers which it contained, there were divided opinions regarding their lot.

"They are dead!" said one.

"They live," responded another. "The layer of water here is deep, and their plunge was softened."

"But their air would be gone," pronounced a third, "and they will be dead from asphyxiation!"

"Burnt!" a fourth contended. "That projectile was no more than an incandescent mass as it travelled through the atmosphere."

"No importance!" they all declared unanimously. "Dead or alive, we must get to them!"

Meanwhile the Captain Bloomsbury had united his officers, and, "with their permission" held a council. It was a matter where they must take an immediate course of action. The more hasty were for fishing the projectile out. Given a difficult operation, though not impossible; but the corvette lacked the necessary engine, which needed to be both powerful and precise simultaneously. Therefore it was resolved to conduct their vessel to the nearest port, and advise the Gun Club where the projectile had plunged.

This determination was taken unanimously. The choice of port was discussed. The neighboring coast presented no anchorage at the 27° latitude. More higher, above Monterey Peninsula, there lies the important town to which was given the same name. However, founded on the borders of a veritable desert, there was no relay point to the interior by telegraphic network, and electricity alone could spread their important news sufficiently fast enough.

Several degrees above this opened the bay of San Francisco. Through the capital of the country of gold communications could easily be facilitated with the center of the Union. In less than two days, the *Susquehanna*, forging ahead at full steam, could arrive at the Port of San Francisco. Hence she must depart without delay!

The steam-engine fires were fully-powered. They could set their course immediately. Two thousand fathoms of sounding line were still by the depths. Captain Bloomsbury, not wishing to lose precious time hauling them in, resolved to cut the line.

"We will fix a buoy to the end of the sounding ball," said he. "That buoy will indicate the precise point where the projectile fell and those hardy adventurers lie entombed."

"Besides," added Lieutenant Bronsfield, "we have our exact position: 27° 7' latitude north and 41° 37' longitude west."

"Excellent, Mr. Bronsfield," responded the captain. "And now, with your approval, cut and decouple that line!"

A strong, resilient buoy, further reinforced by a couple of spars, was launched onto the surface of the ocean there. The sounding ball and line had been solidly lashed over it, and, abandoned solely upon the to-and-fro of the swell, that buoy would not sensibly drift.

At that moment the engineer informed the captain they had reached steam pressure and that they could depart. The captain gave his thanks for the excellent communication. Then they set upon a course of north-north-west. The corvette, developing speed, steered at full steam towards the bay of San Francisco. It was 3 o'clock in the morning.

200 leagues to encompass, that is a small thing for an excellent steamer like the *Susquehanna*. In 36 hours, an interval which had been devoured, on 14th December at 27 minutes past 1 in the afternoon, she entered the bay of San Francisco.

At the sight of a ship of the United States Navy arriving with great speed, its bowsprit razed its main-mast propped up, the curious public was markedly aroused. A dense crowd had soon assembled by the quay, waiting for their debarkation.

After seeing the anchor lowered, Captain Bloomsbury and Lieutenant Bronsfield descended into a rowboat armed with eight oars, which transported them rapidly onto land.

They jumped onto the quay.

"The telegraph!" they demanded, without responding any of the thousand questions addressed to them.

The officer of the port conducted them himself to the telegraphic bureau, in the midst of an immense concourse of the curious who had gathered about them and now followed.

Bloomsbury and Bronsfield entered into the office while the crowd crushed against the front door.

A few minutes later a dispatch was sent quadruply across the electrical wires: the first to the Naval Secretary, Washington; the second to the vice-president of the Gun Club, Baltimore; the third to J.T. Maston, Long's Peak, Rocky Mountains; the fourth to the sub-director of the Cambridge Observatory, Massachusetts.

It composed these terms:

By 20° 7' latitude north and 41° 37' west longitude the 12th December, at 17 minutes past 1 in the morning the projectile of the Columbiad was plunged into the Pacific Ocean. Send instructions- Bloomsbury, Commander Susquehanna.

5 minutes after, all the city of San Francisco knew of the news. Before 6 o'clock in the evening, the diverse States of Union had been informed of the

supreme catastrophe. After midnight, by cable the entirety of Europe knew the result of that grand American attempt.

One must renounce the responsibility of painting the effect produced upon the whole world by that unexpected outcome. It was so much despair and disappointment

On receipt of the dispatch, the Naval Secretary telegraphed the *Susquehanna* ordering them to wait at anchor in the bay of San Francisco without extinguishing their fires. Day and night, they needed to be ready to take to the sea.

The Cambridge Observatory called together an extraordinary meeting, and, with that serenity which distinguishes the body of scientists, peacefully discussed the scientific aspects of the question.

At the Gun Club it was an explosion. All the artillerists had reunited. Precisely, the honorable vice-president, the honorable Wilcome, was in the act of reading that premature dispatch by which J.T. Maston and Belfast announced that the projectile had been sighted by the gigantic reflector telescope of Long's Peak. That communication portended, in exaggeration, that the cannon ball, retained by the gravitational attraction of the Moon, played the part of a sub-satellite in the solar world.

One will know the verity of that point.

Meanwhile the dispatch of Bloomsbury had arrived, which so positively contradicted J.T. Maston's telegram that two parties immediately fragmented within the Gun Club. On the one side was the division of gentlemen who admitted the plunge of the projectile into the Pacific Ocean, and by consequence the return of the voyagers. The other, the party of those who, holding to the observations of Long's Peak, concluded that the Commander of the *Susquehanna* had been in error. For the latter group, the portrayal of the projectile had been no more than a meteor, nothing but a bolide, the globe of a shooting star which in its tumble downwards had struck against the corvette. They did not quite know how to respond to this argument for the velocity which had propelled the object would have made its motion very difficult to observe. The commander of the *Susquehanna* and her officers had avowed with certainty but they might have been, in good faith, mistaken.

Nevertheless, one argument fought in their favor: which was that, if the projectile had tumbled back onto the Earth it's re-encounter with the terrestrial sphere would have occurred on the 27° northern latitude, and- taking account of the time passed by the rotational movement of the Earth- between 41° and 42° longitude west.

In any case it was unanimously decided by the Gun Club that Colonel

Bloomsbury- for not only had he been so intimately involved with the initial preparations of their endeavor, but was cousin to the commander- and the dashing Bilsby along with Major Elphiston engage without delay transportation for San Francisco; and once there to seek immediate advice for the means to recover the projectile from where it lay submerged by the profound depths of the Pacific Ocean.

Those devoted men departed without losing an instant and were soon to travel straight across all of Central North America; powerful steam-engines carried them all the way to St. Louis, where swift mail coaches awaited them.

Almost at the same moment when the Secretary of the Navy, the vice-president of the Gun Club and the sub-director of the Observatory received the dispatch from San Francisco, the honorable J.T. Maston was experiencing the most highly-violent emotions in all of his existence; an excitement which had not even been procured by the explosion of his celebrated burst cannon, and which nearly, for one more time, cost him his life.

One may recall that the secretary of the Gun Club had departed within several moments after the projectile, and travelled almost as quickly as it had, for the post at Long's Peak in the Rocky Mountains. The scientist J. Belfast, director at the Observatory of Cambridge, accompanied him. Arriving at their new station, the two friends had summarily installed themselves and nevermore left the summit where that enormous telescope had been installed.

As discussed previously, in effect, that gigantic instrument had been established according to the conditions of the reflector system named as a 'front view' by the English. That system subjected objects to but one reflection, and rendered in consequence, a very clear vision. The result was that J.T. Maston and Belfast, when making observations, were placed by the upper part of the instrument and not beneath it. They reached that point of the telescope by clambering up a tightly-winding staircase, in itself a masterpiece of light-weight construction, whilst below them opened a pit of silver terminated by a metallic mirrored disk measuring 280 feet in depth.

So, it was on a narrow platform placed above the telescope that the two scientists whiled away their existence; confounded by the daylight which hid the Moon from their eyes, and by the clouds which so obstinately veiled it during the night.

Hence what was their joy, when, after several days of waiting, on that night of the 5th December they perceived the vehicle which carried their friends through interplanetary space! To that joy there ceded a profound deception, when, relying on incomplete observations they sent, with their first telegram that travelled the world, that erroneous affirmation which was that the projectile had become a satellite of the Moon gravitating in an immutable orbit.

Since that moment, the cannon ball had had not shown itself to their eyes; a disappearance all the more explicable, as it was then passing behind the invisible part of the Moon. But when it was due to reappear on the visible hemisphere of the disk, one may then judge the impatience of the brimming J.T. Maston and his companion, who was no less impatient than he! At every minute of the night they believed that they had spotted the projectile, only to realize each time they had not! And so there, upon their rickety-seeming platform, as they incessantly argued and violently disputed amongst one another Belfast affirmed that the projectile was not visibly apparent, whilst J.T. Maston maintained that the magnification had "punctured his eyes"!

"There it is, the cannon ball!" repeated J.T. Maston.

"No!" replied Belfast. "It is an avalanche that has loosened from the lunar mountain!"

"Oh well, we will see in the morning."

"No! We shall no longer see it! It has been drawn into space!"

"Yes!"

"No!"

At these moments, when their interjections precipitated like hail, the growing irritability experienced by the irascible and honorable secretary of the Gun Club constituted a permanent danger towards the esteemed astronomer Belfast.

The existence between those two would have soon developed into the impossible, but for an unexpected event which cut short their eternal discussions.

During that night of the 14th and 15th December, the two irreconcilable friends were occupied in observing the lunar disk. J.T. Maston abusing, according to his usual custom, the scientist Belfast who was mounted beside him. The secretary of the Gun Club had been maintaining for the thousandth time he had located the projectile, even adding he had seen the face of Michel Ardan gazing through one of the portholes. And he augmented his argument with a series of provocative gestures with that redoubtable hook of his that strongly rendered an unsettling level of support.

At that moment, Belfast's domestic servant appeared on the platform- it was 10 hours in the evening then- and remitted them a dispatch. The telegram from the Commander of the *Susquehanna*.

Belfast tore open the envelope, and, reading it uttered a loud cry of exclamation.

"Hey!?" said J.T. Maston, disturbed from the oracle.

"The cannon ball!"

"And well?"

"It has fallen back upon the Earth!"

Another cry, this time a howl, answered his proclamation.

Belfast turned towards J.T. Maston. But he was not there- he had disappeared! Unfortunately, by imprudently leaning behind Belfast and over the telescope to gain a perspective view of the paper which Belfast read from, J.T. Maston had disappeared into the immense telescope- a plunge of 280 feet! Belfast, exasperated and fearing the worst, rushed to the orifice of the gigantic reflector telescope.

But that wily fellow breathed yet! J.T. Maston, held only by his hook of metal, was grasping one of the extrusions of rail that ran through the gap, which supported the body of the instrument.

Belfast, who was a slightly-framed man, appealed for help. His aides ran up. A hoist was miraculously found and quickly installed; and they hauled-in, although not without some pain, the brazen secretary of the Gun Club.

He was restored without accident to the platform that stood above the great hole of the reflector telescope.

"Hey!" said he. "And if I had broken that mirror!"

"You would have assuredly paid," responded Belfast severely; who had forgotten in his sense of professional propriety that the telescope was originally placed there only as the result of the Gun Club's efforts- and this technically being provided at the disposal of the Gun Club for their endeavor, would have absolved Maston of his sins.

"And that damn cannon ball has fallen back?" demanded J.T. Maston.

"Into the Pacific!"

"Let us depart!"

A quarter of an hour after, the two scientists descended the slope of the Rocky Mountain; and after a further 2 hours, at the same time as their friends from the Gun Club, they arrived at San Francisco having broken five horses on their route.

Major Elphiston, Colonel Bloomsbury and the dashing Bilsby rushed towards them on their arrival.

"What shall we do?" they cried.

"Fish out the cannon ball," responded J.T. Maston practically. "As soon as possible!"

22 The Rescue Attempt

Even the place where the projectile had sunk beneath the waves was known exactly. The instruments to take ahold of the aluminum cannon ball and restore it to the surface of the Pacific Ocean, however, were still lacking. They needed to be invented and then made. This had not hampered the American engineers at all, not even slightly. Grapples of iron were established, aided by the power steam engines, that were assured of retrieving the projectile, despite its weight, which besides was diminished by the density of the liquid in the midst of which they had plunged.

But fishing out the cannon ball was not sufficient. They needed to act promptly in the interests of the hardy voyagers. No one doubted they were still alive.

"Yes!" J.T. Maston repeated incessantly, whose confidence won over all the world. "They are adroit gentlemen, our friends, and they could not have perished like simpletons. They are alive, quite alive, but we must hurry to rescue them. Their provisions, their water- that does not cause me any worry! There is enough for a long time! But their air, their air! That is what they will soon be lacking. Hence quickly! Quickly!"

The went quickly. They appropriated the *Susquehanna* for her new destination. The powerful machines were provided onboard courtesy of heavy hauling chains. The projectile was aluminum and so then only weighed

19,250 pounds, a burden of weight quiet inferior to that of the transatlantic cable which they had relieved under parallel conditions. Therefore the sole difficulty was in fishing out the cylindro-conical cannon ball whose smooth walls would render themselves difficult to hook.

To that aim, the engineer Murchison rushed to San Francisco, in order to fix the enormous grappling irons with an automatic system, which would prevent its escaping once seized by the powerful pincers. They had also prepared deep sea diving apparatus which, in their impermeable resistant envelope, allowed divers to reconnoiter the mightiest depths of the sea. He simultaneously embarked onboard the *Susquehanna* a compressed air apparatus, very ingeniously imagined. It was a veritable chamber, pierced by portholes of thickened glass, and which the water, introduced into certain compartments, could draw it downwards unto grand depths. These apparatus had existed in San Francisco, where they had served in the construction of a submarine breakwater. And this was extremely fortunate, for time was lacking to enable such an instrument's construction.

However, despite the perfection of their apparel, despite the ingenuity of the scientists charged with their deployment, there was nothing less-assured than the success of that operation. How the chances were uncertain, since they must retrieve the projectile beneath 20,000 feet of heaving water! Then, even if the cannon ball could be seized and drawn to the surface, how would the adventurous explorers have managed to support themselves against that terrible shock which the 20,000 feet of water had perhaps only insufficiently amortized?

And finally, they needed to act with exceptional haste. J.T. Maston pressed the dockworkers day and night. He was prepared close by, instantly, to don the diving suit, to test the air apparatus, to safely restore the situation of his courageous friends.

But, in spite of all the diligence employed for the construction of the diverse machinery and engines, in spite of the considerable sums of money placed at the disposal of the Gun Club by the Government of the Union, five long days- five centuries!- had elapsed before their preparations were ended. During this time, the opinions of an overexcited public had reached an impossibly frenetic pitch. The telegrams were incessantly exchanged along the wires of the electrical cables. The rescue of President Barbicane, Captain Nicholl and that audacious Frenchman, Michel Ardan, constituted an international affair. All of the peoples of the world who had subscribed to the endeavor of the Gun Club, and all others besides, maintained a direct interest in the salvation of the voyagers.

And finally, the haulage chains, the air chambers, the automatic grapples were embarked onboard the *Susquehanna*. J.T. Maston, the engineer

Murchison and the delegates of the Gun Club already occupied their cabins. There was nothing which remained but to depart.

The 21st December, at 8 o'clock in the night, the corvette steamed onto a beautiful sea, a north-east breeze and an excessively sharp cold. All the population of San Francisco had presented by the quays, excited, however quiet, reserving their hurrahs for the return.

The steam engines powered under their maximum tension, and the propeller of the *Susquehanna* clawed them rapidly beyond the bay.

It is unnecessary to relate the conversations onboard between the officers, the sailors, the passengers. All those men had only one pensive thought. All those hearts palpitated under the same emotion. Whilst they coursed towards the rescue, how fared Barbicane and his companions? What had happened to them? Had they tendered some audacious maneuver to reconquer their liberty? There was no one who could say. The truth was any of the means they might consider would have failed! Immersed by the pressure of 20,000 feet of ocean, that prison of metal defied all the efforts of its prisoners.

The 23rd December, at 8 hours in the morning, after rapid traverse, the *Susquehanna* was due to arrive at the place of the disaster. They needed to wait until midday to obtain an exact reckoning by the sextant. The buoy onto which the sounding line had been lashed was still to have been located.

At noon, Captain Bloomsbury, aided by his officers who controlled the observation, took point in the presence of the Gun Club delegates. It was then a moment of anxiety. Their position determined, the *Susquehanna* was found to be west by several minutes from the same place the projectile had disappeared beneath the waves.

The order for the corvette was duly given to enable them to reach the precise point.

At 27 minutes past midday, they came across the buoy. It was in a perfect state and appeared to have hardly drifted.

"And finally!" exclaimed J.T. Maston.

"Shall we then commence?" asked Captain Bloomsbury.

"Without losing a second," answered J.T. Maston.

Every precaution was taken to hold the corvette completely immobile where she lay.

Before the search to seize the projectile, the engineer Murchison wished to reconnoiter the position of the ocean's floor. The submarine apparatus, destined to undertake that search, received its provisions of air. The management of these engines was not without danger, for, at 20,000 feet underneath the water's surface and subject to an immense pressure, both men and machine were exposed to the threat of fracture- whose consequences were exceedingly terrible.

J.T. Maston, Colonel Bloomsbury- Captain Bloomsbury's cousin- and the engineer Murchison, without batting an eye towards their own danger, assumed their places in the air chamber. The commander was by his place on the bridge, presiding over the operation, prepared to stop the haulage chains at the slightest signal. The propeller had been disengaged, and all the force from the *Susquehanna*'s machines had been transferred to the capstan, so that they might rapidly bring the submarine apparatus back onboard if required.

The descent commenced at 25 minutes past 1 in the afternoon, and the chamber, drawn downwards by the ballast chambers filled with water, disappeared under the surface of the ocean.

The emotion of the officers and the seamen on board was now divided between the prisoners of the projectile and the prisoners of the submarine apparatus. As for J.T. Maston's crew, they forgot themselves, and, glued to the portholes of glass, observed attentively the masses of liquid through which they traversed.

The descent was rapid. At 17 minutes past 2 o'clock they reached the bottom of the Pacific. But they could see nothing, it was just an arid desert which neither marine flora nor fauna animated. By the light of their lamps, equipped with powerful reflectors, they could observe those dark layers of water as far as the rays extended, however the projectile remained invisible to their eyes.

The impatience of those hardy divers cannot be described. Their technological apparel included a device for electrical communication with the corvette. They fired an agreed signal, and the *Susquehanna* walked over the space of a mile with their chamber suspended a few meters above the seafloor.

And so they explored all of the submarine plain, trumped at every instant by the optical illusions which then broke their hearts. Here it was a rock, there an extrusion of seabed, things that appeared like the projectile for which they searched; then, they would soon recognize their error, and each time grew more desperate.

"But where are they? Where are they?" exclaimed J.T. Maston, anguishing.

And the poor man appealed with great cries for Nicholl, Barbicane and

Michel Ardan as if those unfortunate friends could hear or provide him with a response through the traverse of that impenetrable medium!

The search continued in those conditions, right until the moment when the air in their submarine chamber became so tainted the divers were obliged to ascend.

The hauling began towards 6 hours of the evening, and had not finished until midnight.

"In the morning," said J.T. Maston, and placed his foot on the bridge of the corvette.

"Yes," agreed Captain Bloomsbury.

"And in another place."

"Yes."

J.T. Maston did not doubt their eventual success, but already his companions, no longer intoxicated by the animation of the previous hours, comprehended all the difficulty in their enterprise. What had seemed so easy in San Francisco, appeared here, in full ocean, almost unrealizable. Their chances of success diminished in great proportion to the time that had been used; and it was solely through fate they might ask to encounter the projectile.

The next day, 24th December, despite the fatigues of the day before, the operation renewed. The corvette displaced itself by several minutes to the west, and the submarine apparatus, provided with fresh air, anew drew the same explorers downwards into the depths of the ocean.

That total day was passed in fruitless searching. The seabed was a desert. Then the day of the 25th turned by without result. And then, that of the 26th.

It became desperate. They thought of those unfortunates, trapped in that cannon ball since 26 days earlier! Perhaps at that very moment they were sensing the first attenuations of asphyxia, if howsoever they had escaped the dangers of their interplanetary plunge! Their air had exhausted, and, no doubt along with that air, their courage, their morale!

"The air, it is possible," J.T. Maston responded invariably. "But their morale, never!"

The 28th, after two other days of searching, all hope was lost. The cannon ball, as diminutive as an atom within the immensity of the sea! They needed to renounce the retrieval.

However, J.T. Maston would not entertain any talk of departure. He would not abandon this place without seeing at least the recovery of the tomb of his friends. But the Commandant Bloomsbury could not persist any longer, and, despite the reclamations of the dignified secretary, he delivered the order to set their steam underway.

On the 29th December, at 9 'o'clock in the morning, the *Susquehanna*, her head to the north-east, retraced the route towards the bay of San Francisco.

It turned to 10 hours in the morning. The corvette spread into the distance under half-steam as though it regretted to leave the catastrophe, when a sailor, mounted on the bars of the top-gallant, who was in observation of the sea, cried out as though delivering a blow:

"There is a buoy by the lee-bow!"

The officers looked in the direction indicated. With their marine glasses, they reconnoitered the object which had been signaled and which, in effect, held the appearance of those buoys which serve as marker beacons along the passes of bays and rivers. But, a single detail, a flag, floated in the wind, atop a cone which emerged 5 or 6 feet. That buoy glittered and shone resplendently as though its walls were covered by plated silver.

The commander Captain Bloomsbury, J.T. Maston, the delegates of the Gun Club, were stationed in the bridge, and they examined that errant object venturing above the waves.

They regarded it with a feverish anxiety, but in silence. None dared to formulate the thoughts which hovered upon the minds of all of them.

The corvette approached tow within two cable-lengths of the object.

A trembling, shuddering current coursed through the whole crew.

That flag was an American flag!

In that moment, a veritable roaring was heard. It was the brave J.T. Maston, who had fallen down like a dead mass. Forgetful of that part of his arm which had been replaced by an iron hook, and as well, the simple protective plate which covered part of his skull, in his excitement he had delivered himself a formidable blow.

They rushed towards him. They lifted him up. He was revived to life. And what were the first words he spoke?

"Ah. Dagnabit. Triple brutes! Quadruple idiots! Quintuple fools that we are!"

"What is it?" they all exclaimed around him.

"What is it?..."

"But speak then."

"It is that, imbeciles," yelled the terribly-tempered secretary, "it is that the cannon ball weight is 19,250 pounds!"

"And well?!"

"And that in tarnation displaces 28 tons, otherwise said as 56,000, and by which consequence it floats!"

Ah! How that dignified man emphasized the verb 'floats'! And it was true! All of it, yes! All of the scientists had forgotten that fundamental law: and that is by the effects of the lightness of its specific density, the projectile, after being sighted as it was drawn just there into the deepest part of the Pacific Ocean's most profound depths, it would naturally return to the surface! And now, it floated tranquilly as it liked upon the waves...

The rescue boats were prepared for the sea. J.T. Maston and his friends ran to them. Emotions were transported to unimaginable heights! All their hearts palpitated and trembled, whilst the dinghies advanced towards the projectile. What did it contain? The living or the dead? The living, yes! The living, unless death had struck Barbicane and his two friends since they had displayed their flag.

A profound silence reigned upon the boats. All hearts panted. The eyes saw nothing else. One of the portholes of the projectile had been opened. Several shards of glass, resting in their encasement, proved that it had shattered. The porthole held its actual place at a height of 5 feet above the waves.

One rescue boat accosted the floating cannon ball, that of J.T. Maston's. The honorable secretary moved to the edge of the broken glass...

In that moment, there extended a voice, joyous and clear, the voice of Michel Ardan and he cried out, oh how he exclaimed with the greatest accent of victory- and that is, love-:

"White all, Barbicane, white all!"

Barbicane, Michel Ardan and Nicholl were playing dominos.

23 For the End

One may recall the immense sympathy which had accompanied the three travellers on their departure.

If at the debut of their enterprise they had excited such emotion in the ancient and the new world, what enthusiasm would accrue upon their return? The millions of spectators who had invaded that Floridian peninsula, would they not rush upon those sublime adventurers? Those legions of strangers, hurrying from all points of the globe towards the American shores; would they leave the territory of the Union without saying goodbye to Barbicane, Nicholl and Michel Ardan? No, and the ardent passion of the public would be a dignified response to the grandeur of their enterprise. These human creatures who quit their terrestrial sphere, who had returned after that strange voyage in celestial space, could not fail to be received as though the prophet Elijah had descended back upon the Earth. To see them once more, and afterwards to hear them speak, such was the general wish of everyone.

This wish was to be realized very promptly, almost unanimously by the inhabitants of the Union.

Barbicane, Michel Ardan, Nicholl and the delegates of the Gun Club returned without delay for Baltimore. They were welcomed with an indescribable enthusiasm.

The journal records of the voyage by president Barbicane were lent and collated into a volume for the public. The New York Herald purchased the manuscript for a price not yet known, but the consideration was excessive. In effect, during the publication of *Voyage to the Moon* the circulation of the newspaper amounted to 5,000,000 copies. Three days after the return of the voyagers upon the Earth, the slightest details of their expedition was known. There remained nothing more than to see these amazing heroes of that superhuman enterprise.

The exploration by Barbicane and his friends around the Moon had permitted a check to the diverse theories admitted by the subject of the terrestrial satellite. These scientists had observed visually, and under totally particular conditions. One now knew what systems should thereby be rejected and which were to be accepted; regarding the formulation of that shining astral body of the night sky, regarding its origin and regarding its habitability. Its past, its present, its future even, they all had surrendered their final secrets.

Who could object to those conscientious observers who found themselves at an elevation of less than 40 kilometers above that curious mountain Tycho, that extremely strange system of lunar orography? Who could answer against these pioneering scientists whose gaze had plunged into the abyss of Plato's Cirque? How to contradict audacious explorers whose fate had tentatively drawn them over the face of the invisible hemisphere of the disk, where not any human eye had ever seen before then? It was now their duty to impose the limits upon that science of selenography who had reconstructed the lunar world like Cuvier had done to the skeleton of a fossil, and to say: the Moon was this, a habitable world and inhabited previously to the Earth! The Moon is that, an uninhabitable world and now uninhabited!

To celebrate the return of their most-illustrious members and their two companions, the Gun Club conceived to give a banquet; but a banquet worthy of these triumphant ones, worthy of the American people, and under such conditions that all the inhabitants of the Union could directly take part.

The heads of all the lines of the railroads in the States were brought together by their rail wheels. Then, on all the station platforms, strewn with flags of the same drapery, decorated by the same ornaments, tables were dressed with uniform service. At certain hours, successively calculated, marked by electrical clocks which beat to the second and even instant, the populations were cordially invited to take their places at the tables of the banquet.

Throughout 4 days, between the 5th and 9th January, the trains were suspended as though it were a Sunday on all the railways of the Union, and all the lines were left free.

Only one locomotive at a grand speed, drawing a wagon of honor, held the right of circulation on those wondrous paths of iron intersecting the whole of that diverse United States.

The locomotive, mounted by driver and engineer, carried in distinguished thanks the honorable J.T. Maston, secretary of the Gun Club.

The carriage was reserved for president Barbicane, Colonel Nicholl and the brave Michel Ardan.

At the blow of the engineer's whistle, after the hurrahs, the hips and all the onomatopoeias of admiration in the American language, the train left Baltimore station. It marched onwards with a speed of 80 leagues per hour. However- what was that velocity, compared with that which had drawn those three heroes from the expulsion of the Columbiad?

And so they went from one town to another, coming upon whole populations at their tables along their passage, saluting them with the same acclamations, the same prodigious bravos.

They ran to the east of the Union, traversing Pennsylvania, Connecticut, Massachusetts, Vermont, Maine, and New-Hampshire; they travelled the north and the west by New York, Ohio, Michigan, and Wisconsin; they re-descended to the south by Illinois, Missouri, Arkansas, Texas, and Louisiana; they were couriered south-east by Alabama and Florida; they returned up by Georgia and the Carolinas; they visited the center by Tennessee, Kentucky, Virginia, and Indiana; and then, after the station at Washington, they returned to Baltimore and during those four days, they purely believed the entire United States of America had attended that unique and immense banquet, saluting them simultaneously with the same hurrahs!

The apotheosis was worthy to the dignity of those three heroes whom fable would have placed in the ranks of demigods.

And now, that attempt without precedence in the annals of the world's voyages- would it result in anything practical? Would direct communications with the Moon ever be established? Will they ever lay the foundations for a service which navigates the traverse of interplanetary space, to bring our attendance upon the entire solar system? Will they travel from planet to planet, to Jupiter and Mercury, and much later to one star and then another, perhaps that of Polaris and Sirius? Would this mode of locomotion permit humanity one day to be the visitor of the billions of suns which swarm throughout the firmament- both the visible and the hidden?

To these questions there is no valid response. However, knowing the audacious ingenuity of the human race, no person could be astonished at what might be sought after that tentative attempt performed by president Barbicane and his friends.

And then, sometime after the return of the voyagers, the public received with remarkable favor the announcement of a company (ltd), with a starting capital of $100,000,000; partitioned into 100,000 shares worth $1,000 each, under the name of the *National Company of Interstellar Communications*. Company President, Barbicane; Vice-President, The Captain Nicholl; Secretary of Administration, J.T. Maston; General Manager Michel Ardan.

And as it is the American custom to foresee all possible eventualities in business affairs, even a bankruptcy, the Honorable Harry Troloppe, Judge Commissioner, and Francis Dayton, Magistrate, were nominated in advance!

The wise reader will understand this was yet but the beginning of a vast and grand enterprise, of a scale which only the limits of one's imagination may portend.

Printed in Great Britain
by Amazon